Overcoming Barriers to Student Understanding

Overcoming Barriers to Student Learning explores why certain students 'get stuck' at particular points in the curriculum whilst others grasp concepts with comparative ease. It proposes a 'threshold concepts' approach to the curriculum, arguing that in certain disciplines there are 'conceptual gateways' or 'portals' that lead to previously inaccessible, and initially perhaps 'troublesome', ways of thinking about something. A new way of understanding, interpreting, or viewing a topic may thus emerge – having a transformative effect on internal views of subject matter, subject landscape, or even world view.

While maintaining that knowledge should indeed be 'troubling' in order for it to be transformative, this book provides new perspectives on helping students through such conceptual difficulty in order to enhance learning and teaching environments in higher education, and in other educational sectors. It discusses:

- ways of dealing with the kinds of anxiety, self-doubt and frustration that learning can evoke in students;
- how we might help our students not to avoid the troublesomeness, but to feel more confident in coping with it, resolving it and moving on with confidence;
- what might account for variation in student performance when dealing with concepts;
- what teachers might do in relation to the design and teaching of their courses that could help students overcome such barriers to their learning;
- what makes particular areas of knowledge more troublesome than others.

The illustrative case studies presented here will help teachers analyse their own practice. *Overcoming Barriers to Student Learning* will serve the needs of educational researchers and developers, and academics within various disciplines who wish to learn more about threshold concepts and troublesome knowledge.

Jan H. F. Meyer is a Professor of Education and the Director of the Centre for Learning, Teaching, and Research in Higher Education at Durham University. He is also an Adjunct Professor in the Division of Business at the University of South Australia.

Ray Land is Professor of Higher Education and Director of the Centre for Academic Practice and Learning Enhancement at the University of Strathclyde in Glasgow.

Overcoming Barriers to Student Understanding

Threshold concepts and troublesome knowledge

Edited by Jan H. F. Meyer
and Ray Land

Routledge
Taylor & Francis Group

LONDON AND NEW YORK

First published 2006 by Routledge
2 Park Square, Milton Park, Abingdon, Oxon OX14 4RN

Simultaneously published in the USA and Canada
by Routledge
270 Madison Ave, New York, NY 10016

*Routledge is an imprint of the Taylor & Francis Group, an informa
business*

© 2006 Selection and editorial matter, Jan H. F. Meyer and Ray Land;
individual chapters, the contributors

Typeset in Times New Roman by RefineCatch Limited, Bungay,
Suffolk
Printed and bound in Great Britain by
TJI Digital, Padstow, Cornwall

All rights reserved. No part of this book may be reprinted or
reproduced or utilised in any form or by any electronic,
mechanical, or other means, now known or hereafter
invented, including photocopying and recording, or in any
information storage or retrieval system, without permission in
writing from the publishers.

British Library Cataloguing in Publication Data
A catalogue record for this book is available from the British Library

Library of Congress Cataloging in Publication Data
Overcoming barriers to student understanding : threshold concepts
and troublesome knowledge / edited by Jan Meyer and Ray Land.
p. cm.
Includes bibliographical references and index.
1. Concept learning. 2. Knowledge, Theory of. I. Meyer, Jan, 1946– II.
Land, Ray. III. Title.
LB1062.O94 2006
370.15'23 – dc22
2005034793

ISBN10: 0–415–37430–8
ISBN13: 978–0–415–37430–9

Contents

Contributors

Simon Bishop is Senior Lecturer, Centre for Equine and Animal Science, Writtle College, University of Essex in Chelmsford, UK.

Jennifer Booth is currently studying for her doctorate at the University of Warwick, UK in the philosophy of mind and action. Her research interests focus on the relationship between the concept of agency and elusiveness claims about the self, in particular the roles of spatial representation, perceptual experience and attention. She has a background in both psychology and philosophy, and has teaching experience in a wide range of contemporary and historical epistemology, philosophy of mind and philosophy of science.

Glynis Cousin has a background in the sociology of education and has worked in teacher training across the school, adult, community and higher education sectors. Her publications are on issues of diversity, e-learning and higher education research and evaluation methods. Glynis is senior adviser at the Higher Education Academy in York, UK.

Peter Davies is Professor of Education Policy and Director of the Institute for Educational Policy Research (IEPR) at Staffordshire University, Stoke-on-Trent, UK. His current research focuses on economic and access issues in education policy and disciplinary contexts for assessment for learning. He is co-editor of the *International Review of Economics Education* and is currently directing a project on 'Embedding threshold concepts in undergraduate Economics' supported by the Higher Education Funding Council.

Anastasia Efklides is Professor of Cognitive Psychology at the Aristotle University of Thessaloniki, Greece. She was President of the Hellenic Psychological Society, currently of the Psychological Society of Northern Greece, and vice-president of the European Association of Psychological Assessment. She was editor of *Psychology: The Journal of the Hellenic Psychological Society*, currently editor of *The Hellenic Journal of Psychology*, associate editor of *Learning and Instruction* and *European Psychologist*, and she will be the editor of *Learning and Instruction* for the period of 2006–9. She is the author or (co-)editor of nine books and four monographs in Greek and English and author or co-author of over 140 articles/ chapters and of five special issues in international and Greek journals/ books. Her research interests include motivation, metacognition, and particularly the relation of metacognition with affect.

Ian Jackson is a Senior Lecturer in Economics in the Faculty of Business and Law at Staffordshire University, Stoke-on-Trent, UK. Ian teaches on a wide number of business and economics courses in the UK and China. He has published research in various academic journals such as *Applied Economics* and *Defence and Peace Economics*. Ian has also written many articles in newspapers on topics ranging from the local economy to an economic analysis of defence and security. His main research interest in economics education is module design and pedagogy.

Ray Land is Professor of Higher Education and Director of the Centre for Academic Practice and Learning Enhancement at the University of Strathclyde in Glasgow. In addition to threshold concepts and troublesome knowledge his current research interests include the practice of educational development, and theoretical aspects of digital learning. Recent books have included *Educational Development: Discourse, Identity and Practice* (Open University Press) and, as joint editor, *Education in Cyberspace* (RoutledgeFalmer).

Ursula Lucas is Professor of Accounting Education at the Bristol Business School, University of the West of England. Her main research area is in Accounting Education and current interests include the student and lecturer experience of learning and teaching introductory accounting, students' perceptions of key skills development and the introduction of reflective practice within the accounting curriculum. Ursula currently serves as an Associate Editor for *Accounting Education: An International Journal*. In 2001 she was awarded a HEFCE National Teaching Fellowship for excellence in teaching.

Jan H. F. Meyer is a Professor of Education and the Director of the Centre for Learning, Teaching, and Research in Higher Education at Durham University, UK. His main research interest is in student learning in higher education and, in particular, the modelling of individual differences and the construction of discipline-centred models of student learning. He is the originator of the notion of Threshold Concepts in the context of a discussion that occurred within the Enhancing Teaching–Learning Environments in undergraduate courses (ETL) project in 2000. Since that date he has, with Ray Land, been developing a theoretical framework around the notion of Threshold Concepts, the seminal paper by Meyer and Land appearing in 2003.

Rosina Mladenovic is the Senior Academic Advisor in the Faculty of Economics and Business, University of Sydney, Australia. Her current research interests include investigating assessment methods, student's perceptions and approaches to learning as ways to improve accounting education practice. In 2001, Rosina was recognised as a highly accomplished teacher of large groups and participated in a project sponsored by the Australian Universities Teaching Committee (AUTC). In 2004, she received the American Accounting Association 'Outstanding Research in Accounting Education' award. Rosina currently serves as an Associate Editor for *Accounting Education: An International Journal* and is on the editorial board of several international accounting education journals.

David Perkins is a Senior Professor of Education as well as founding member and senior co-director of Project Zero, Harvard Graduate School of Education, Cambridge, MA.

Nicola Reimann is CPD Academic Practice Programme Leader in the School of Health, Community and Education Studies at Northumbria University in Newcastle upon Tyne, UK.

Maggi Savin-Baden is Professor of Higher Education Research, Coventry University, UK. Her early research focused on the pedagogy of problem-based learning and her current research is exploring troublesome knowledge in face-to-face and online problem-based learning. To date she has published four books on problem-based learning, and, as joint editor, *Problem-based Learning Online* (McGraw-Hill Education).

Martin Shanahan is Associate Professor in Economics at the University of South Australia. He researches in a variety of fields including economic education, economic history, wealth and income distribution, and applied cost-benefit analysis. He is currently co-editor of the *Australian Economic History Review*. He has worked for a number of years with Professor Jan H. F. Meyer modelling variation in undergraduate students' approaches to learning and postgraduate students' conceptions of research. The practical applications of their research recently received a University of South Australia Vice-Chancellor's award for Innovation – 'Learning to Learn in Economics'. Much of their research has been published in the *Journal of Economic Education; Higher Education Research and Development; Studies in Higher Education; International Review of Economics Education*; and the *Scandinavian Journal of Educational Research*.

Charlotte Taylor is a Senior Lecturer in the School of Biological Sciences, and Associate Dean for Learning and Teaching in the Faculty of Science, at the University of Sydney, Australia. As deputy director in the First Year Biology Unit, Charlotte had fifteen years' experience in course design, assessment and online learning for large classes of over 1,500 students, and received a University of Sydney Teaching Excellence Award in 2000 for this work. She is the Chair of the Science Faculty Education Research Group (SciFER) and has published collaborative papers in areas of learning through writing, teaching large classes, giving feedback and the use of online discussions in development of academic writing skills. Her research on threshold concepts in Biology encompasses investigations into teachers' and students' conceptions of troublesome knowledge.

Foreword

It's always interesting to observe, amid the great volume of educational research and development that is now taking place in higher education around the world, how every so often one particular idea or perspective will emerge that, for whatever reason, seems to fire the imagination of teachers and researchers and which is seen as having immediate relevance to issues within their own practice.

This quality – David Perkins of Harvard has characterised it nicely as 'action poetry' – seems to arise from conceptual ideas that are essentially both simple and memorable and yet which are also highly generative, in that they contain richly layered implications for all kinds of educational contexts. It seems to me that the theoretical framework of threshold concepts that Jan Meyer, Ray Land with Glynis Cousin and others have been developing in recent years has just this quality of action poetry. Their innovative model presents refreshingly different insights into the way that certain conceptual understandings can have a powerfully transformative effect. As we now find ourselves, across the globe, working within the new environments of mass higher education systems, and with greatly widened student participation, this helpful approach allows us to think anew why certain students 'get stuck' and find difficulty in negotiating particular conceptual transitions. How might we explain the variation in student experience and performance in encountering threshold concepts and how might we better help them through difficult conceptual and affective transitions? What is it in the nature of the knowledge they are encountering that might give rise to this difficulty? How are shifts in understanding caught up inextricably with affective factors and with shifts in the learner's identity? The threshold concepts approach offers a valuable approach to addressing these matters.

The approach had its origins in the ETL project, Enhancing Teaching–Learning Environments in Undergraduate Courses, funded by the Teaching and Learning Research Programme of the UK Economic and Social Research Council. Threshold concepts might be seen as a conceptual gateway to the 'ways of thinking and practising' within disciplines that the ETL project explored. The thresholds approach subsequently became a project in its own right, Embedding Threshold Concepts, funded by the Higher Education Funding Council for England (HEFCE) as part of its Fund for the Development of Teaching and Learning (FDTL5). It has since then also been adopted as the pedagogical framework for at least two of the new Centres for Excellence in Teaching and Learning that HEFCE has established. And it is well established as an informing perspective across the national Subject Centres co-ordinated by the UK Higher Education Academy. It provides a means of thinking and talking about learning within the disciplines which practitioners in those disciplines can use and develop themselves in relation to their own subject. From philosophy to automotive design, from economics to engineering, academics are using the idea of threshold concepts to inform their pedagogy in ways that make sense within their own communities of practice, and for their own students.

The broad international scope of this book is testimony to the speed with which the notion of threshold concepts has taken hold through many disciplines in universities around the world. Threshold concepts is thus now moving from a position of being a leading edge new perspective to one which is catching the interests of academics and educational researchers in a growing number of countries. The approach is already being cited in Australia, Hong Kong, Sweden, Greece, Scandinavia, South Africa, Canada, New Zealand and the USA. This seems a timely juncture to provide a scholarly but accessible foundational text to serve the needs of educational researchers and developers, and academic colleagues within various disciplines, who have expressed a wish to learn more about threshold concepts and troublesome knowledge. The book combines chapters which open up the theoretical aspects of these new perspectives with practical instances of how academics in specific disciplinary contexts have sought to design their courses around notions of threshold concepts.

This book reports on early beginnings to scope out the power of this concept to understand the difficulties in interactions between learners and their teachers. In my previous life as an educational researcher I was involved in exploring the concept of *deep and surface approaches to study* first coined by Ference Marton and his colleagues in Sweden in the late 1970s (Marton *et al.* 1997). I witnessed the power of this concept to help teachers understand how their students learn. That example of *action poetry* has enhanced the development of learning and teaching for the past 25 years and is still influential. Recently our focus of attention has become more sensitive to differences between individual learners and in the different pedagogies within disciplines. Thus threshold concepts is action poetry for our time and I will enjoy observing its influence over the next 25 years as its power is explored in more contexts.

I am delighted that this volume is now available for academics in all disciplines to encounter this intriguing field of enquiry. I heartily commend the book also to teachers and researchers in other educational sectors. I hope they will use it to enhance their own approaches to teaching and course design, and to support the learning and development of their students.

Liz Beaty
Director of Learning and Teaching
Higher Education Funding Council for England
Bristol, November 2005

Reference

Marton, F., Hounsell, D. and Entwistle, N. (eds) (1997) *The Experience of Learning: Implications for Teaching and Studying in Higher Education*, second edition, Edinburgh: Scottish Academic Press.

Editors' preface

In the Brothers Limbourg's depiction of *The Fall and Expulsion from Paradise* (1415), a serpent with a human face passes the fruit of the tree of knowledge to a curious Eve. The consequences of this acceptance of a knowledge which proves to be troublesome are arrayed sequentially in the tableau that this painting presents. What appears is that as Eve, and then Adam, gain access to this troubling knowledge, their world changes around them. They can no longer stay where they are, in a comfortable and familiar place, much as they might wish to. They are unceremoniously moved on by a rather forbidding scarlet angel and ushered firmly through an imposing gateway, a threshold, into a different kind of space. The expressions on these medieval faces suggests that this new space, this transformed landscape, no longer feels like home. They wish to return. The new space feels, to use Freud's famous phrase, *unheimlich* – unhomely or strange. However the scarlet angel covers their means of retreat. This new state is irreversible. Adam and Eve have in fact learned. They see the landscape now very differently. They have gained a new understanding and their identity has shifted, as signified by the fig leaves with which they are adorned in the final section of the tableau. They have grown up. They have become adult and have left a world of innocence. However, their gain feels like loss. Their new knowledge is troublesome.

As all teachers know, teaching is a complex and often challenging process, because learning is a complex and challenging process. Nor, we wish to say at the outset, would we really wish for it to be otherwise. When knowledge ceases to be troublesome, when students sail through the years of a degree programme without encountering challenge or experiencing conceptual difficulty, then it is likely that something valuable will have been lost. If knowledge is to have a transformative effect it probably *should* be troublesome, or at least troubling, but that does not mean it should be stressful or should provoke the kinds of anxiety, self-doubt and frustration that can lead students to give up.

It has long been a matter of concern to teachers in higher education why certain students 'get stuck' at particular points in the curriculum whilst others grasp concepts with comparative ease. What might account for this variation in student performance and, more importantly, what might teachers do in relation to the design and teaching of their courses that might help students overcome such barriers to their learning? As students from a much wider range of educational backgrounds now enter higher education these issues are becoming of increasing importance across all disciplines. A further and related concern is why certain concepts within disciplinary fields appear particularly 'troublesome' to students. What makes particular areas of knowledge more troublesome than others, and how might we help our students not to avoid the troublesomeness, but to feel more confident in coping with it, resolving it and moving on, with the confidence of expectation that there will be further troublesome episodes of learning along the way, but that they will survive them, and maybe even come to enjoy the challenge?

This book discusses these concerns from the new perspective of 'threshold concepts'. It can be read, and probably will be read, we hope, in a number of ways depending of course on what suits the interests and purposes of the reader. The first five chapters in Part I attempt to outline a conceptual framework linking the idea of threshold concepts with notions of troublesome knowledge and liminality. Chapters 6–13 in Part II offer insights into how this might come into view within the perspectives of specific disciplines. The concluding chapter tentatively opens up considerations and implications of this conceptual framework for curriculum design. We hope others will engage in this process and take up these curriculum issues in new ways in their own fields.

The opening chapter presents the original seminal paper by Jan Meyer and Ray Land which introduced the notion that there might be concepts in any discipline that have a particularly transformative effect on student learning. The notion of a *threshold concept* was originally introduced into discussions on learning outcomes as a particular basis for differentiating between core learning outcomes that represent 'seeing things in a new way' and those that do not. A threshold concept is thus seen as something distinct within what university teachers would typically describe as 'core concepts'. Furthermore, threshold concepts may represent, or lead to, what Perkins (1999) described as 'troublesome knowledge' – knowledge that is conceptually difficult, counter-intuitive or 'alien'. Within all subject areas there seem to be particular concepts that can be considered as akin to a portal, opening up a new and previously inaccessible way of thinking about something. A threshold concept represents a transformed way of understanding, or interpreting, or viewing something without which the learner cannot progress. As a consequence of comprehending a threshold concept there may thus be a transformed internal view of subject matter, subject landscape, or even world view, and the student can move on. However, such transformation, though necessary for progress within the subject, may prove troublesome to certain learners for a variety of reasons, not the least of which is that such transformation entails a letting go of earlier, comfortable positions and encountering less familiar and sometimes disconcerting new territory.

Such transformation can also entail a shift in the learner's identity. The result may be that the student remains stuck in an 'in-between' state in which they oscillate between earlier, less sophisticated understandings, and the fuller appreciation of a concept that their tutors require from them. In Chapter 2 Meyer and Land look more closely at the nature of this in-between state which they term a state of 'liminality', from the Latin meaning 'within the threshold'. One outcome is that students present a partial, limited or superficial understanding of the concept to be learned which the authors characterise as a form of 'mimicry'. This characterisation is without negative intent, as the mimicry might be a purposive coping strategy in the wrestle for understanding and clarity. A more serious outcome is that students can become frustrated, lose confidence and give up that particular course. It is the hope of the contributors to this volume that within our various subject areas we can devise ways of helping students to overcome such obstacles – to create 'holding environments' to support students through such conceptual difficulty – that they may move on and succeed.

To complicate matters further, in some instances students may grasp concepts but the barrier to their learning appears to lie at a deeper level of understanding, where the student finds difficulty in appreciating what David Perkins, in Chapter 3, has termed 'the underlying game', or an 'epistemic game'. He defines an episteme as 'a system of ideas or way of understanding that allows us to establish knowledge'. It might also be seen as a 'way of knowing'. Epistemes are 'manners of justifying, explaining, solving problems, conducting enquiries, and designing and validating various kinds of products or outcomes'. However as Perkins goes on to show, through his rather endearing student character Betty Fable, learners often encounter difficulties playing these games. This is partly because concepts, in his analysis, can often make 'double trouble', on the one hand functioning as 'categorisers' and on the other functioning as 'elements in activity systems of problem solving and enquiry'. To help students like Betty cope better with this he advocates a constructivist approach that he terms 'surfacing and animating', to help them 'not simply to know about the game but to play the game knowingly'. It's high time, he argues, 'that we got pragmatic about constructivism'.

> Get those tacit presumptions out on the table at least for a while, both the teacher's and the learners'. When Betty had to discuss her ideas about falling objects or simplification, this surfaced her tacit presumptions and allowed her teachers to examine them with her. And not just as objects of discursive analysis but as systems of activity to engage. The idea is not simply to know about the game but to play the game knowingly.

Playing the game knowingly can be seen as, and indeed requires, a form of metacognition. Anastasia Efklides, in Chapter 4, makes the case from the perspective of cognitive psychology, that metacognition cannot be reduced to metacognitive knowledge and metacognitive skills only. Another facet of metacognition is metacognitive *experiences*, that is, online feelings, judgements or estimates, as well as task-related knowledge. Metacognitive experiences, she argues, monitor cognitive processing and trigger control decisions. They also feed back on the person's self-concept and causal attributions regarding performance outcome. Thus, metacognitive experiences influence self-regulated learning in the short and long run. The ways through which metacognitive experiences influence the learning of threshold concepts are multiple. They offer online awareness of task-specific cognitive procedures, of cognitive load, of the effort demanded, and of features of task processing – whether it runs smoothly or is interrupted. Finally, they offer awareness of the evaluation process of the outcome of task processing. This awareness triggers control decisions supporting or undermining the person's engagement with learning tasks. Metacognitive experiences can convey accurate information about task-processing demands but they can be flawed, as in cases where the person has no previous knowledge or experience with a concept or a task. She discusses the factors influencing the accuracy of metacognitive experiences and goes on to propose possible ways in which teachers might overcome the disadvantages of flawed metacognitive experiences.

In Chapter 5 Peter Davies examines particular issues in the application of threshold concepts to learning and teaching. One difficulty that he identifies lies in identifying *which* concepts in a subject should be regarded as 'threshold concepts'. If 'threshold concepts', as mentioned earlier, are to be distinguished from previous ideas such as 'core concepts' should they be identified by a distinctive procedure? The argument he develops in his chapter suggests an affirmative answer to this question. He follows this argument with an exemplification of a possible way forward in the context of teaching and learning Economics. A second difficulty, he suggests, lies in identifying *when* learners have internalised a threshold concept. How can learners and teachers recognise the difference between a deeply embedded and a superficial understanding of a threshold concept?

Charlotte Taylor, a biologist, observes how troublesome knowledge in her discipline often appears to be associated with processes. This might, she suggests in Chapter 6, reflect the dynamic nature of the discipline, as Biology works with knowledge 'which incorporates change as an integral component'. But she is concerned that the clear distinction between process concepts and abstract concepts in Biology are often encompassed in the same threshold concept. Her 'dissection' of the troublesome nature or threshold experience pertaining to biological concepts has led her to conclude that many of these troublesome elements seem to derive from teaching approaches adopted in early undergraduate Biology courses, in which 'a traditional approach to these concepts has relied on an exposition of the facts as a necessary grounding in the topic'. However, she goes on to suggest, it may be that conceptual thresholds might be more easily surmounted if a different approach to the concept – a holistic approach – is adopted. 'Using a more abstract manifestation' Taylor argues 'allows a holistic view of the concept and its context in a larger picture of living systems.' In this way, she claims, students will be better able to make linkages between what she characterises as 'islands of isolated knowledge'.

> If we are to accommodate such patterns of learning in Biology we will need to construct learning experiences which clearly identify the threshold experience before moulding a variety of learning experiences and opportunities around this core.

In Chapter 7 Martin Shanahan and Jan Meyer focus on a specific concept in order better to identify how discipline specific ways of thinking can alter the learner's view of the world. They consider 'opportunity cost' as an example of a threshold concept in the discipline of Economics. Opportunity cost is the value placed on the best rejected alternative when an individual makes choices. In this chapter they argue that the categories of knowledge that underlie, and to some extent create, 'troublesome knowledge' may be used as a framework, or as 'markers' by which to examine students' articulation of a threshold concept. The authors present analyses of the variation in introductory *students'* articulation of 'opportunity cost' over the course of one semester. The study that forms the basis of this chapter provides a practical example of how variation in students' initial understanding of a threshold concept can be externalised and examined, and in a manner that can inform university teaching. Issues of measurement, articulation and learner development are also identified. There appear to be important implications for the manner in which students are initially introduced to threshold concepts. A key conclusion presented by Shanahan and Meyer is that, in the learning of threshold concepts, 'first impressions matter'. Efforts to make threshold concepts 'easier' by simplifying their initial expression and application may, in fact, set students onto a path of 'ritualised' knowledge that actually creates a barrier that results in some students being prevented from crossing the 'threshold' of a concept.

Nicola Reimann and Ian Jackson also explore aspects of threshold concepts in Economics. In the case study that they present in Chapter 8, they explore students' developing understanding of two threshold concepts within the context of a small first year Microeconomics module. Like the authors of Chapter 7, they also choose to consider opportunity cost, with the notion of elasticity as a second example. They employed questions about authentic scenarios, set in students' everyday lives, to investigate whether students' thinking had changed as a consequence of learning and teaching about the two threshold concepts. The authors collected data in three stages consisting of (repeated) written responses to these questions, as well as interviews with students and staff. The chapter discusses the usefulness of such questions as diagnostic tools as well as the impact of the teaching–learning environment on students' understanding of the two threshold concepts. The use of the questions seems to have provided the lecturer in charge of the particular module with a clearer focus for his teaching and helped him to connect his teaching more explicitly to the student perspective. Distinct differences between the two threshold concepts emerged, both in relation to the teaching and the students' answers to the questions. Previous knowledge of the concepts acquired elsewhere and a curriculum which deals with a sequence of a large number of concepts appeared to have an impact on the level of effort and engagement students displayed in relation to the threshold concepts investigated. While in interviews conducted after having been taught about the two concepts students did not change their minds about their initial answers to the two questions, the second answers elicited at the end of the module seemed to suggest that some students' economic reasoning had become somewhat more sophisticated. The insights gained in this case study seem to suggest that threshold concepts can provide a novel and useful perspective for investigating and enhancing teaching–learning environments, though the authors, cautiously, advocate that further research of this kind that investigates the student perspective is required.

Within the field of cultural studies Glynis Cousin proposes 'Otherness' as a threshold concept, and draws on illuminative evidence gathered from a number of teachers and students of cultural studies in UK universities in order to expose issues associated with its teaching and learning. As she points out, this concept has troublesomeness more-or-less built-in, because of its inherent stability as a concept:

> There is no settled view about the meanings of Otherness. The instability of the concept is part of its territory. Indeed it would undermine the teaching and learning of Otherness were it to be treated as a truth to be unpacked since mastery includes a grasp of the debate about its explanatory scope and limitations.

These issues apply to a range of social science and humanity subjects where explorations of Otherness are made in relation to ethics, social difference and exclusion, democracy, equality, identity formation, representation and oppression. Her discussion centres on the distinctive ways in which Otherness qualifies as a threshold concept and on the strong affective dimension involved in its learning. In particular, she suggests that students with greater experiential proximity to the aspects of Otherness under examination *may* bring more emotional capital to their understandings of them. While there are no easy laws of causation to explain the distribution of emotional experiences, her conversations with teachers raise interesting questions about the emotional positioning of their students, and the bearing this has on their receptivity to the learning of Otherness. This positioning implies that the design of curriculum for the teaching of Otherness needs to be particularly sensitive to the emotional questions it stirs. In addressing the affective difficulties of learning Otherness, she mobilises Perkins's notion of troublesome knowledge to explore forms of learner resistance that not only may prevent students from moving beyond a 'pre-liminal' state in their approaches to learning, but may also alert teachers to the difficulties that attend harnessing students' own experiences to their learning. She offers, as 'heuristic devices', four ideal typical affective learner positions. These are spectator or voyeur, the defended learner, the victim-identified learner and self-reflexive learners. Whilst not suggesting that students conform to these types in any static or pure form, or indeed that these exhaust an understanding of learner positionality, she also raises questions about the ways in which variation in students' mastery of Otherness may be concealed by a conventional academic assessment regime (set essays and examinations). She argues, moreover, that there is 'a tricky curriculum path to be trod in order to give voice to those who endure injuries of oppression while discouraging over-identification with such injuries'.

Ursula Lucas and Rosina Mladenovic (Chapter 10) working respectively in the United Kingdom and Australia, investigate two threshold concepts in depth within their discipline of introductory accounting. These are depreciation, and the relationship between profit and cash. Their research illustrates the nature of the different types of understandings of these concepts as evidenced by students. The two authors distinguish between 'authorised' and 'alternative' conceptions of threshold concepts. Authorised conceptions, they argue, are those endorsed and maintained by the disciplinary community and within textbooks. Alternative conceptions of events and transactions are independent of authorised conceptions. They arise from intuitive or everyday (common-sense) understandings of a concept such as profit or depreciation. They might on occasion be substituted for, or provide an alternative to, the authorised conceptions. Often, where students hold these alternative conceptions, they do not recognise that these conceptions are in opposition to the authorised conceptions promulgated within the course. Thus a particularly important (or higher level of) threshold concept may be to *recognise the difference between authorised and alternative conceptions*. Their discussion raises interesting issues in relation to threshold concepts, suggesting that such a didactic thrust within the prevailing pedagogy may limit accounting education. Threshold concepts, they maintain, need to be placed within a context. Confusions, misunderstandings and misconceptions tend to arise because students, and lecturers, do not acknowledge that learning might be viewed as acquiring the skill of 'contextual appreciation' (Linder 1993). For example, a particular conception of depreciation might be appropriate for use in an accounting context, but inappropriate for use in a personal context. It follows from this that the student, and the lecturer, have to recognise, and accept, that there are different ways of viewing both accounting and the concepts within it. In other words, there has to be an acceptance of diversity and, thus, uncertainty. This may be potentially 'troublesome' for the individual. Thus the teaching of introductory accounting may require pedagogic approaches that move away from the didactic and support students in dealing with this troublesome knowledge.

Maggi Savin-Baden in Chapter 11 draws on research into problem-based learning undertaken across different disciplines but largely in the areas of health and social care. She argues that there are a number of similarities between the notion of 'disjunction' and the concept of troublesome knowledge. In particular she argues that problem-based learning is itself a threshold concept that gives rise to disjunctions in the lives of staff and students. By disjunction she refers to the idea of becoming 'stuck' in learning. Disjunction can be both enabling and disabling in terms of its impact on learning and can be seen as the kind of place that students might reach after they have encountered a threshold concept that they have not managed to breach. Many staff and students, she reports, have described disjunction as being a little like hitting a brick wall in learning and they have used various strategies to try to deal with it. These include retreating from the difficulty and opting out of any further learning, using strategies to avoid it, temporising and waiting for an event or stimulus that will help them to move on or engaging with it directly in an attempt to relieve their discomfort. She goes on to argue that although disjunction occurs in many forms and in diverse ways in different disciplines, it does seem to be particularly evident in curricula where problem-based learning has been implemented. This may be, she suggests, because problem-based learning programmes prompt students to critique and contest knowledge early on in the curriculum and thus they encounter knowledge as being troublesome earlier than students in more traditional programmes. However, it might also be that problem-based learning encourages students to shift away from linear and fact-finding problem-solving. Instead they move towards forms of problem management that demand the use of procedural and personal knowledge as students are asked to engage with strategy or moral dilemma problems. Thus it might be that disjunction is not only a form of troublesome knowledge but also a 'space' or 'position' reached through the realisation that the knowledge is troublesome. Disjunction might, therefore, be seen as a 'troublesome learning space' that emerges when forms of active learning (such as problem-based learning) are used that prompt students to engage with procedural and personal knowledge.

Philosophy proves to be a further interesting domain in which to speculate upon conceptual difficulty. Jennifer Booth (Chapter 12), drawing on her experience of teaching this subject, concludes that it is a hard discipline to introduce to students for two reasons. First, the subject matter or body of knowledge with which it deals will often be entirely new to the student, particularly in the United Kingdom, where she teaches. In Britain, she points out, students rarely study philosophy at school level and thus come to university with a lack of resources with which to approach the subject. The second and more analytical reason why philosophy is hard to introduce to students is that in order to understand this new body of philosophical material students often must re-evaluate or distort parts of their understanding about the world which they hitherto thought to be infallible. Philosophical knowledge is not, she maintains, something one can simply 'accumulate' and store neatly in its own cortical punch pocket. Often previous beliefs or understandings will need to fall by the wayside while other more radical ideas take their place. This, she has found, is something that students find instantly problematic. It is for these reasons that ideas within philosophy may strike new students as being rather hard to grasp, appearing as knowledge which is 'troublesome' both conceptually and affectively. As an example of this troublesomeness she identifies and discusses 'representation' as a threshold concept in the learning and teaching of philosophy, and, as a means of helping students master this concept, she goes on to explore the possibilities afforded by the Socratic method of teaching.

Within the empirical sciences Simon Bishop (Chapter 13) discusses an approach he has developed to assist students grasp complex threshold concepts and cope with troublesome knowledge, either individually, or in a larger group, through the use of analogy. Analogies, he explains, seek to identify similarities in things that are otherwise dissimilar, and to make a link or build a bridge between seemingly unrelated ideas. Because of this, he argues, analogies can be a valuable tool in helping students to connect with complex new subjects based on the knowledge or experience that they already possess. One of the great strengths of using analogy in teaching is that it can significantly speed up the learning process and help students to bridge thresholds of understanding in a single step. Combined with the diversity that the appropriate use of analogies can add to the learning experience, there is much evidence, he maintains, to support their use. However, he also cautions that there are numerous pitfalls lying in wait for the unwary teacher who may make use of this tool inappropriately or without careful design. Analogies in education, he advises, should be carefully crafted to fit the circumstances in which they are used and in no sense will one solution fit every problem. Tremendous care must be taken in designing and applying analogies as part of an education strategy or there exists the risk that the analogy will only serve to obstruct the learning process. He goes on to explore the underpinning mechanisms of analogy that support the process of learning and provides guidance as to when and how this tool should be used.

In the concluding chapter Ray Land, Glynis Cousin, Jan Meyer and Peter Davies bear in mind David Perkins's recommendation that 'it's high time that we got pragmatic about constructivism'. They attempt to draw on the observations and insights of the earlier chapters to open up the implications for course design of considering learning environments in terms of threshold concepts. They expound nine 'considerations' that they feel are important in the design and subsequent evaluation of curricula in higher education. These considerations, the authors feel, are a necessary move towards recognising the importance of identifying ways for enabling learners to negotiate more successfully the kinds of complex transitions that have been discussed earlier in the book. Some of these considerations, they acknowledge, might be seen to 'rattle the cage', to some extent, of 'a linear approach to curriculum design that assumes standard and homogenised outcomes'.

We hope then that threshold concepts have thus emerged as a set of transferable or portable ideas across disciplinary contexts, which offer new insights into teaching and learning in higher education and a new theoretical framework which is both explanatory and 'actionable', that is, capable of translation into action. We feel that *Overcoming Barriers to Student Understanding* provides new perspectives for enhancing learning and teaching environments in higher education with potential application to other educational sectors. In particular we hope that, by offering case studies of how threshold concepts and troublesome knowledge have been addressed within specific disciplinary settings, the book will provide perspectives on rendering courses more congruent with the experience and understanding of students. This will give rise also to future questions as to how threshold concepts might be best *assessed*. The chapters are intended to help us conceptualise how students approach, engage in and emerge from potentially transformative and troublesome episodes in learning. This draws attention to the variation within student learning before, during and subsequent to episodes of learning. We hope others will be attracted to participate in the exploration of these engaging issues, and join us in future enquiry. We are of course already invaluably indebted to our colleagues who have contributed their time and expertise to the chapters in this volume, and to the editorial staff at RoutledgeFalmer for their encouragement and patience.

Ray Land and Jan H. F. Meyer
Glasgow and Durham
November 2005

References

Freud, S. (1990) 'The "Uncanny" ', *Sigmund Freud: Art and Literature*, trans. James Strachey. The Penguin Freud Library, vol. 14, series ed. Albert Dickson. Harmondsworth: Penguin Books.

Linder, C. J. (1993) 'A Challenge to Conceptual Change', *Science Education*, 77: 293–300.

Perkins, D. (1999) 'The Many Faces of Constructivism', *Educational Leadership*, 57(3), November.

Acknowledgements

Chapter 1 is a substantially expanded and revised version of a 2003 article originally published as Meyer, J.H.F. and Land, R. 'Threshold Concepts and Troublesome Knowledge – Linkages to Ways of Thinking and Practising' in *Improving Student Learning – Ten Years On*, C. Rust (ed.), OCSLD, Oxford. The Conclusion, similarly, is a substantially expanded and revised version of a 2005 article originally published as Land, R., Cousin, G., Meyer, J.H.F. and Davies, P. 'Threshold Concepts and Troublesome Knowledge (3): Implications for Course Design and Evaluation' in *Improving Student Learning – Equality and Diversity*, C. Rust (ed.), OCSLD, Oxford. We are deeply grateful to the Oxford Centre for Staff and Learning Development for their kind permission to reuse substantial material in these chapters.

Chapters 1, 2, 8 and 9 were prepared as part of the work of the Enhancing Teaching–Learning Environments in Undergraduate Courses (ETL) project, which is funded by the Teaching and Learning Research Programme of the UK Economic and Social Research Council (http://hwww.tlrp.org). The project was undertaken by a team drawn from the universities of Coventry, Durham and Edinburgh. Members of the project team were Charles Anderson, Liz Beaty, Adrian Bromage, Glynis Cousin, Kate Day, Noel Entwistle, Dai Hounsell, Jenny Hounsell, Ray Land, Judith Litjens, Velda McCune, Jan Meyer, Jennifer Nisbet, Nicola Reimann and Rui Xu. Further information about the project is available on its website (http://www.ed.ac.uk/etl).

Chapter 3, by David Perkins, is a substantially expanded and revised version of a 1999 article entitled 'The Many Faces of Constructivism', originally published in *Educational Leadership* 57(3), 6–11. Some of the ideas presented here were developed as part of the Understandings of Consequence Project, supported by the National Science Foundation, Grant No. REC-9725502 to Tina Grotzer and David Perkins, co-principal investigators. Any opinions, conclusions, or recommendations expressed here are those of the author and do not necessarily reflect the views of the National Science Foundation.

Chapter 4, by Anastasia Efklides draws on the author's keynote address entitled 'Metacognition and Affect: What Can Metacognitive Experiences Tell Us about the Learning Process?' at the Tenth Conference of the European Association for Research on Learning and Instruction, Padova, Italy, 2003.

Part I

Towards a theoretical framework

Threshold concepts and troublesome knowledge

An introduction

Jan H. F. Meyer and Ray Land

Introduction

A threshold concept can be considered as akin to a portal, opening up a new and previously inaccessible way of thinking about something. It represents a transformed way of understanding, or interpreting, or viewing something without which the learner cannot progress. As a consequence of comprehending a threshold concept there may thus be a transformed internal view of subject matter, subject landscape, or even world view. This transformation may be sudden or it may be protracted over a considerable period, with the transition to understanding proving troublesome. Such a transformed view or landscape may represent how people 'think' in a particular discipline, or how they perceive, apprehend, or experience particular phenomena within that discipline (or more generally). It might, of course, be argued, in a critical sense, that such transformed understanding leads to a privileged or dominant view and therefore a contestable way of understanding something. This would give rise to discussion of how threshold concepts come to be identified and prioritised in the first instance. However, first we require examples.

A simple illustrative example can be taken from the kitchen. Cooking is fundamentally a process of using heat (in various degrees and sources) to effect desired outcomes. In physics one encounters the concept of *heat transfer* and its mathematical formalisation (as an equation) that represents heat transfer as a function of something called the temperature gradient. It is not necessary to have a sophisticated understanding of physics to have this principle quite simply illustrated. Imagine that you have just poured two identical hot cups of tea (i.e. they are at the same temperature) and you have milk to add. You want to cool down one cup of tea as quickly as possible because you are in a hurry to drink it. You add the milk to the first cup immediately, wait a few minutes and then add an equal quantity of milk to the second cup. At this point which cup of tea will be cooler, and why? (Answer is the second cup because in the initial stages of cooling it is hotter than the first cup with the milk in it and it therefore loses more heat because of the steeper temperature gradient.) When the physics of heat transfer is thus basically grasped by people in terms of things specific to what goes on the kitchen, it will fundamentally alter how they perceive this aspect of cooking, and they might consequently even filter out what to look for (the signified!) when they watch the better class of television cookery programmes; for example, a focus on the pots and pans that are *selected* by the chef in context (the heat source in relation to the cooking process to be applied as a function of time and its regulation to the ingredients) rather than simply on the ingredients and, superficially, the 'method'. So it could be said that, as a stand alone example, heat transfer or, more precisely, controlling the rate of heat transfer, is a threshold concept in cookery because it alters the way in which you *think* about cooking. And, in the special case where barbecuing is the method of cooking (where heat transfer is via radiation) you also have to take into account the inverse square law, which explains why so many people find barbecuing a 'troublesome' notion. We shall return to the notion of troublesomeness later.

Threshold concepts and troublesome knowledge within subject disciplines

Our interviews and wider discussions with practitioners in a range of disciplines and institutions have led us to conclude that a threshold concept can of itself inherently represent what Perkins (1999) refers to as *troublesome knowledge* – knowledge that is 'alien', or counter-intuitive or even intellectually absurd at face value. It increasingly appears that a threshold concept may on its own constitute, or in its application lead to, such troublesome knowledge.

From a *student* perspective let us consider some examples from Pure Mathematics: first that of a *complex number* – a number that is formally defined as consisting of a 'real' and an 'imaginary' component and which is simply expressed in symbolic (abstract) terms as $x + iy$, where x and y are real numbers (simply put, the numbers we all deal with in the 'real' world; for example numbers we can count on our fingers), and i is the square root of minus 1 ($\sqrt{-1}$). In other words i is a number which when squared (multiplied by itself) equals minus one (-1). So a complex number consists of a real part (x), and a purely imaginary part (iy). The idea of the imaginary part in this case is, in fact, absurd to many people and beyond their intellectual grasp as an abstract entity. But although complex numbers are apparently absurd intellectual artefacts they are the gateway to the conceptualisation and solution of problems in the pure and applied sciences that could not otherwise be considered.

Second, in Pure Mathematics the concept of a *limit* is a threshold concept; it is the *gateway* to mathematical analysis and constitutes a fundamental basis for understanding some of the foundations and application of other branches of mathematics such as differential and integral calculus. Limits, although not inherently troublesome in the same immediate sense as complex numbers, lead in their application to examples of troublesome knowledge. The limit as x tends to zero of the function $f(x)=(\text{sine } x)/x$ is in fact one (1), which is counter-intuitive. In the simple (say, geometric), imagining of this limit is the ratio of two entities (the sine of x, and x) both of which independently tend to zero as x tends to zero and which are also (an irrelevant point, but a conceptual red herring if the threshold concept of a limit is not understood) respectively equal to zero when x equals zero. So the troublesome knowledge here then (based on mathematical proof) is that something which is getting infinitesimally small divided by something else doing the same thing is somehow approaching one in the limiting case.

That mathematicians themselves are aware of issues that surround threshold concepts is evident from the work of Artigue (2001, p. 211) who refers to a 'theory of epistemological obstacles' and, by way of summary, gives as a first example of such obstacles: 'the everyday meaning of the word "limit", which induces resistant conceptions of the limit as a barrier or as the last term of a process, or tends to restrict convergence to monotonic convergence.' The idea is then developed by way of more complex examples that, as forms of knowledge, 'epistemological obstacles' constitute 'resistant difficulties' for students.

Within Literary and Cultural Studies the concept of *signification* can prove problematic, even 'subversive' in that it undermines previous beliefs, and leads to troublesome knowledge insofar as the non-referentiality of language is seen to uncover the limits of truth claims. For example, the recognition (through grasping the notion of signification) that all systems of meaning function like signifiers within a language (that is that terms derive meaning from their relationship to each other, rather than in any direct empirical relationship with a 'reality') leads on to an understanding that there are *no positive terms*. Hence the basis of many systems of meaning, including positivist science and the basis of many religious and moral systems, falls into question. This can be a personally disturbing and disorienting notion leading to hesitancy or even resistance in learners. Other aspects of post-structuralist practice such as techniques of *deconstruction* for analysing literary texts (with a strong emphasis on the ironic, the contradictory, the ludic) often appear counter-intuitive, looking for *absences*, or what is not there, in order to gain insights into how the text is currently structured by a prevailing set of (occluded or tacit) values or priorities.

One final illustrative example from Economics will suffice, again from the *student* perspective. The concept of *opportunity cost* has been put forward as one of many examples of a threshold concept in the study of economics. Martin Shanahan (as quoted in Meyer and Land 2003, pp. 414–15) assesses the transformative effect of this concept as follows:

'Opportunity cost is the evaluation placed on the most highly valued of the rejected alternatives or opportunities' (Eatwell *et al.* 1998, Vol. 3,

p. 719). Fundamental to the discipline of economics is the issue of choice: choosing between scarce resources or alternatives. Economists are interested in how individuals, groups, organisations, and societies make choices, particularly when faced with the reality that resources and alternatives are limited. No-one can have everything, and in most cases the 'constraints' faced by the chooser can be quite severe and binding. People choose, for example, how to allocate their time, their work or leisure; firms choose between different methods of production and combinations of inputs; societies choose between different legal regimes, levels of exports or imports etc. Fundamental to the economic way of approaching the issue of choice is how to compare choices. Thus 'The concept of opportunity cost (or alternative cost) expresses the basic relationship between scarcity and choice' (Eatwell *et al.*, *ibid.*); for this reason it is a fundamental (or threshold) concept in Economics.

Thus opportunity cost captures the idea that choices can be compared, and that every choice (including not choosing) means rejecting alternatives. A student who has a good grasp of this concept has moved a long way toward breaking out of a framework of thinking that sees choices as predetermined, or unchangeable. They have also moved toward seeing 'two sides' of every choice, and in looking beyond immediate consequences, and even just monetary 'costs' towards a more abstract way of thinking.

Thus to quote Eatwell *et al.* for a final time (*ibid.*), 'Opportunity cost, the value placed on the rejected option by the chooser, is the obstacle to choice; it is that which must be considered, evaluated and ultimately rejected before the preferred option is chosen. Opportunity cost in any particular choice is, of course, influenced by prior choices that have been made, but with respect to this choice itself, opportunity cost is *choice-influencing* rather than *choice-influenced*' (emphasis in original). Thus, if 'accepted' by the individual student as a valid way of interpreting the world, *it fundamentally changes their way of thinking about their own choices, as well as serving as a tool to interpret the choices made by others.*

Characteristics of a threshold concept

A threshold concept is thus seen as something distinct within what university teachers would typically describe as 'core concepts'. A core concept is a conceptual 'building block' that progresses understanding of the subject; it has to be understood but it does not necessarily lead to a qualitatively different view of subject matter. So, for example, the concept of *gravity* – the idea that *any* two bodies attract one another with a force that is proportional to the product of their masses and inversely proportional to the distance between them – represents a threshold concept, whereas the concept of a *centre of gravity* does not, although the latter is a core concept in many of the applied sciences.

Our discussions with practitioners in a range of disciplinary areas have led us to conclude that a threshold concept, across a range of subject contexts, is likely to be:

a   *Transformative*, in that, once understood, its potential effect on student learning and behaviour is to occasion a significant shift in the perception of a subject, or part thereof. In certain powerful instances, such as the comprehension of specific politico-philosophical insights (for example, aspects of Marxist, feminist or post-structuralist analysis) the shift in perspective may lead to a transformation of personal identity, a reconstruction of subjectivity. In such instances transformed perspective is likely to involve an affective component – a shift in values, feeling or attitude. In this regard there are correspondences with Mezirow's (1978) work on 'perspective transformation'. A threshold concept may also involve a performative element. Sproull (2002) points out how the gaining of *aquatic confidence* in Sports Science students leads to a dramatically enhanced appreciation of water as a sporting and exploratory environment. This would be an interesting example of an enactive concept in Bruner's sense (Bruner 1966).

b   Probably *irreversible*, in that the change of perspective occasioned by acquisition of a threshold concept is unlikely to be forgotten, or will be unlearned only by considerable effort. As a conveniently graphical metaphor, the post-lapsarian state of Adam and Eve after their expulsion from Eden in the Book of Genesis illustrates how new (and in this case troublesome) knowledge, symbolised by the cunning (i.e. 'conynge', knowing) serpent, radically transforms their landscape as they pass through the threshold from innocence to experience (new understanding). They gain freedom, responsibility and autonomy, though this is not a comfortable transition. As they look back to the Gate at the East of Eden their return across the threshold is barred by Cherubim 'and a flaming sword which turned every way' (Genesis 3: 24) to prevent return to the tree of knowledge. Though they have learned, and grown, their transformed state initially feels like loss. Respondents within our study have pointed to the difficulty experienced by expert practitioners looking back across thresholds they have personally long since crossed and attempting to understand (from their own transformed perspective) the difficulties faced from (untransformed) student perspectives.

c   *Integrative*, that is it exposes the previously hidden interrelatedness of something. Note that if we re-examine the earlier example of opportunity cost from the novice perspective we may observe that while it satisfies (a) and (b) above, it may not be integrative. Davies (2002) provides the following useful insight:

One way of seeking to identify a threshold concept in economics might be to examine discourse on social and economic policy between economists and non-economists. We might infer that a powerful, integrative, idea used by an economist but not by a colleague from another discipline is characteristic of a community of practice rather than a general level of education. For example, Adnett and Davies (2002) show how non-economists have tended to view parental quest for a 'good education' for their children as a simple zero-sum game whereas an economist would anticipate some supply-side responses and peer effects within and beyond school which make the prediction of game outcomes far more difficult. An economist is working here with a concept of general equilibrium which is not a typical feature of educated common-sense. Ideas like this may be thought troublesome not only because their integrative nature makes them difficult to learn, but also because they make the world appear a more problematic and troublesome place.

Davies (2002) also reminds us, in a salutary fashion, that 'any threshold concept can only integrate so much'.

d   Possibly often (though not necessarily always) *bounded* in that any conceptual space will have terminal frontiers, bordering with thresholds into new conceptual areas. It might be that such boundedness in certain instances serves to constitute the demarcation between disciplinary areas, to define academic territories:

> Within the field of Cultural Studies a threshold concept that has to be understood early is the breakdown of the barrier between high and popular culture. This is fundamental to the Cultural Studies approach. This is a significant departure from practice in English Literature where that concept not only doesn't really exist but if it did (i.e. if you crossed that threshold) it would undermine the discipline of Eng. Lit. itself.
>
> (Bayne 2002)

Another respondent, working within Veterinary Sciences, informed us that where students encountered severe conceptual difficulty such areas of the curriculum were quietly dropped. In this sense the conceptual thresholds served to trim the parameters of the curriculum.

e   Potentially (though not necessarily) *troublesome*, for the reasons discussed below.

Forms of troublesome knowledge

> 'When troubles come, they come not single spies.'
>
> (*Hamlet*, IV. v. 83–4)

The notion of a threshold concept might remain merely an interesting issue of cognitive organisation and perspective were it not for the strong indication from our data that such concepts often prove problematic or 'troublesome' for learners. Kennedy's discussion of the concept of 'sampling distribution' in Econometrics appears to identify one such threshold concept that is possibly 'troublesome' for students.

> Upon completion of introductory statistics courses, the majority of students do not understand the basic logic of classical statistics as captured in the concept of repeated samples and a sampling distribution. They know how to do mechanical things such as compute a sample variance, run a regression, and test a hypothesis, but they do not have a feel for the 'big picture'. They have learned a bunch of techniques, but to them they are just that, a bunch of techniques, and they know they can pass the course by remembering how these techniques work. They view statistics as a branch of mathematics because it uses mathematical formulas, so they look at statistics through a mathematical lens. What they are missing is the statistical lens through which to view the world, allowing this world to make sense. The concept of sampling distribution is this statistical lens. My own experience discovering this lens was a revelation, akin to the experience I had when I put on my first pair of eyeglasses – suddenly everything was sharp and clear.
>
> (Kennedy 1998, p. 142)

Given the centrality of such concepts within sequences of learning and curricular structures their troublesomeness for students assumes significant pedagogical importance. How might we best assist our students to gain understanding of such concepts? What might account for the variation in student facility to cope (or not) with these learning thresholds?

Perkins (1999, and with a more recent discussion in Chapter 3 of this volume) has defined troublesome knowledge as that which appears counter-intuitive, alien (emanating from another culture or discourse), or incoherent (discrete aspects are unproblematic but there is no organising principle). He suggests that knowledge might be troublesome for different reasons.

Ritual knowledge

Ritual knowledge, suggests Perkins (1999), has 'a routine and rather meaningless character'. It feels, he argues, 'like part of a social or an individual ritual: how we answer when asked such-and-such, the routine that we execute to get a particular result'.

> Names and dates often are little more than ritual knowledge. So are routines in arithmetic ... such as the notorious 'invert and multiply' to divide fractions. Whereas inert knowledge needs more active use, ritual knowledge needs more meaningfulness (of course, knowledge can be both inert and ritualized).
>
> (Perkins 1999, p. 7)

Diagrams, which are extensively used in Economics to represent complex relationships may well provide an example of the kind of ritualised knowledge that Perkins identifies here. Though students may have learned with some facility how to plot and represent economic relationships, and may well be able to explain the diagrammatic representation of a model, they may not understand the mathematical functional complexity that lies behind the representation.

Inert knowledge

Inert knowledge, suggests Perkins, 'sits in the mind's attic, unpacked only when specifically called for by a quiz or a direct prompt but otherwise gathering dust'. He cites passive vocabulary – words that are understood but not used actively – as a simple example.

> Unfortunately, considerable knowledge that we would like to see used actively proves to be inert. Students commonly learn ideas about society and self in history and social studies but make no connections to today's events or family life. Students learn concepts in science but make little connection to the world around them. Students learn techniques in math but fail to connect them to everyday applications or to their science studies.
>
> (Perkins 1999, p. 8)

This failure to connect may well relate back to the integrative characteristic of threshold concepts. As Davies (2002) pointed out: ' "Integration" is troublesome because you need to acquire the bits before you can integrate, but once you've got the bits you need to be persuaded to see them in a different way.'

Sproull (2002) provides an example of how students find difficulty both in integrating and in making connections between conceptually difficult topics and 'the world around them'. He reports the way in which *metabolism* acts as a troublesome threshold concept within Exercise Physiology. The function of metabolism, as presented within a standard course text on Exercise Physiology, apparently proves troublesome for Sports Science students who are often unable to make integrative understandings with the sports-related knowledge, activities and practices that they encounter elsewhere in their programme. In this sense their knowledge of metabolism remains 'inert'. As a bridging device to foster integrative understandings Sproull uses an autobiographical work on running by a Cambridge scientist (Newsholme and Leech 1985) to scaffold and make accessible the concept of metabolism in a sporting context, which then has the transformative potential to open up the understanding of these students in crucial ways in relation to the ways in which human bodies perform in sporting contexts. In this way the inert, superficial, mimetic use of the language of a threshold concept becomes enlivened.

Conceptually difficult knowledge

Perkins argues that conceptually difficult knowledge is encountered as troublesome in all curricula but perhaps particularly in Mathematics and Science. A mix of misimpressions from everyday experience (objects slow down automatically), reasonable but mistaken expectations (heavier objects fall faster), and the strangeness and complexity of scientists' views of the matter (Newton's laws; such concepts as velocity as a vector, momentum, and so on) stand in the way. The result is often a mix of misunderstandings and ritual knowledge: students learn the ritual responses to definitional questions and quantitative problems, but their intuitive beliefs and interpretations resurface in quantitative modelling and in outside-of-classroom contexts. As one Economist reported to us:

> I think data analysis is very, very difficult . . . You pick up an empirical piece of analysis. There is an immense amount of work involved in getting your head round the data, deciding on the correct estimation techniques – you know, will the estimation techniques actually match to the theory you are trying to test? And I think this is just an incredibly difficult thing to teach undergraduates. The more I think about it – the more difficult I think that is.

Another respondent wondered whether there might be a difference between the relative difficulties of subjects according to their use of threshold concepts, in particular the degree of integration required. He cited as example the perceived contrast in conceptual difficulty between Economics and Business Studies in the UK A level curriculum (Davies 2002).

Alien knowledge

Perkins characterises 'foreign' or 'alien' knowledge as that which 'comes from a perspective that conflicts with our own. Sometimes the learner does not even recognize the knowledge as foreign' (1999, p. 9). A threshold concept that is counter-intuitive for many novice Physics students is the idea, formalised in Newton's second law of motion, that a force acting on a body produces acceleration rather than simply velocity or 'motion'. Formally put, Newton's second law states that force equals mass times acceleration. That this is 'troublesome knowledge' is reflected in the difficulty that students have in answering a question along the following lines: if a car is travelling along a road at a constant speed (i.e. velocity, or rate of change of displacement with respect to time, is constant over time) then what is the resultant force acting on the car? (Answer is zero.) McCloskey (1983, cited in Perkins 1999) makes a similar point about understanding objects in motion, arguing that 'Learners find it hard to accept that objects in motion will continue at the same rate in the same direction unless some force, such as friction or gravity, impedes them. They find it hard to believe that heavier objects fall at the same rate as lighter ones, air resistance aside.'

Tacit knowledge

Perkins suggests that there might be other sources of troublesomeness in knowledge, emanating perhaps from the *complexity* of the knowledge, its seeming *inconsistency* or paradoxical nature or because it contains *subtle distinctions*, such as that between weight and mass. He invites further categories, one of which (not mentioned by Perkins) we would identify as *tacit* knowledge, that which remains mainly personal and implicit (Polanyi 1958) at a level of 'practical consciousness' (Giddens 1984) though its emergent but unexamined understandings are often shared within a specific community of practice (Wenger 1998). The need, for example, for student automotive designers to grasp concepts of 'fluid surfacing', 'double curvature' or other important aspects of spatial and three-dimensional understanding would be examples of threshold concepts that often remain tacit or implicit within the practice of the design community.

Manning (2002) provides a further example from Music, which students within Western musical traditions find troublesome.

> Students who study the art and practice of Western music learn from very early on the concept of *equal temperament*, that is the basic notion of the musical octave and its division thereof into what is perceived as twelve equal steps in terms of pitch. Thus the interval between two adjacent notes on the keyboard, known as a semitone is logarithmically always the same, no matter what pairing is selected. This process of learning, however, is for the most part implicit, and it is rare indeed for either teacher or student to study this concept in any depth at primary or secondary level. The notion of keys, both major and minor, the function of harmony, and the principles of modulation are thus introduced without

any real regard for the reasons why equal temperament has been so axiomatic for the development of classical music, from the 17th century to the present day.

Some elements of doubt as to the robustness of this seemingly all-embracing concept may become apparent to more observant students, but it is rare that explanations are either sought or offered. Those who sing in choirs might, for example, notice that a well-tuned chord does not quite accord to the corresponding intervals produced by conventional keyboard instruments and that problems of intonation can prove particularly acute in the case of unaccompanied vocal works that modulate through many keys. It might also occur to string players that the established practice of tuning strings in 'perfect' fifths, such that no beating can be detected when adjacent strings are played simultaneously, also differs from the equivalent keyboard intervals. In the main, however, these discrepancies are merely accommodated within the overall framework of equal temperament.

What is interesting about Manning's account is how it shows that the source of troublesomeness might often be a compounding of the different kinds of knowledge discussed above. 'When troubles come,' Shakespeare warned us, 'they come not single spies, But in battalions' (*Hamlet*, IV. v. 83–4). The troublesomeness Manning identifies with students' understanding of equal temperament in music compounds both tacit knowledge and alien knowledge, where what appears counter-intuitive in new knowledge is overridden by existing tacit understanding.

As the study of music becomes increasingly multicultural, possible clues as to the existence of other tuning systems are sometimes encountered, but the tendency to Westernise such cultures in terms of popular music once again asserts the dominance of equal temperament. The chance hearing, perhaps, of an Indonesian gamelan orchestra may lead a student to observe that the gongs appear to be 'out of tune', but it is rare indeed that they recognise the significance of alternative tuning systems in the development of other musical genres in Asia and beyond.

Thus it is that an understanding of tuning methodologies and their evolution through history and across the world becomes a threshold concept for an advanced understanding of pitch organisation in music. This aspect of music study will be encountered by tertiary level students in the context of: i) the study of late renaissance and early baroque Western music, when the evolution of harmonic structures necessitated the development of tuning systems that could sustain modulation to more remote keys, ii) the study of ethnomusicology, and iii) the manipulation of timbre in the context of electroacoustic music. Recognition that the structure and organisation of music involves acoustic principles that not only are concerned with the different timbres of instrumental and electronic sources but also their associated tuning systems elevates the analysis of music and modes of composition to new levels of understanding of the processes involved.

(Manning 2002)

Troublesome language

Language itself, as used within any academic discipline, can be another source of conceptual troublesomeness. Specific discourses have developed within disciplines to represent (and simultaneously privilege) particular understandings and ways of seeing and thinking. Such discourses distinguish individual communities of practice and are necessarily less familiar to new entrants to such discursive communities or those peripheral to them (Wenger 1998). The discursive practices of a given community may render previously 'familiar' concepts strange and subsequently conceptually difficult. The use of the term 'culture' within first year Social Anthropology, for example, is reported as problematic in this way (Knottenbelt 2002). Moreover, the inherently arbitrary and non-referential nature of language compounds conceptual difficulty through obliging those seeking to teach or clarify concepts to deploy further terms, metaphors and concepts in an endless play of signification (Derrida 1978). 'There is no concept which exists outside systems of thought and language; there is no concept which is not involved in the infinite play of meaning. In order to function socially we do make temporary determinations of meaning but meaning itself is never determinate' (Land and Bayne 1999, p. 738). Eagleton (1983, p. 129) points out that language:

> instead of being a well-defined, clearly demarcated structure containing symmetrical units of signifiers and signifieds, now begins to look much more like a sprawling limitless web where there is a constant interchange and circulation of elements, where none of the elements is absolutely definable and where everything is caught up and traced through by everything else.

As an example of such conceptual difficulty Hodgkin (2002), discussing education in the visual arts, reports the difficulty of understanding the concept of 'art' itself, locating the concept 'somewhere in the gap that exists between history, scholarship and the feeling of being on the edge of tears'. Reimann (2002) draws attention to the particularly problematic (and complex) example of foreign language learning, where language is also the content.

> If 'foreign' knowledge is troublesome, will learning foreign languages, including knowledge and insights about foreign cultures ('otherness'), always be troublesome? Does this perhaps contribute to the reputation of

languages as difficult subjects? Also, in foreign language learning, issues of content and of language merge. The language *is* the content. Students get very disconcerted when they come across ways of expressing familiar concepts in a different way, for example numbers. Surely saying *eighty-four* is more 'natural' – better than *quatre-vingt-quatre* or *vierundachtzig*? Is this particularly troublesome?

Here we see the notion of alien knowledge compounded with the inherently problematic nature of language itself – another instance of troubles coming not as single spies.

Ways of thinking and practising

Threshold concepts would seem to be more readily identified within disciplinary contexts where there is a relatively greater degree of consensus on what constitutes a body of knowledge (for example Mathematics, Physics, Medicine). However, within areas where there is not such a clearly identified body of knowledge it might still be the case that what might be referred to as 'ways of thinking and practising' within a discipline also constitutes a crucial threshold function in leading to a transformed understanding. One of our respondents identified the threshold function of a way of thinking and practising within the teaching of Economics:

> we have to instil in students a kind of acceptance of modelling which is quite fundamental to the way in which we approach most of our analysis . . . we want our students to start to think about problems, issues. You get them to formulate, if not explicitly at least implicitly, some kind of formal analytical structure or model that simplifies things but then allows someone to think through a problem in a very structured way. That's something fundamental I think.

Another economist from a large modern English university offered a similar view:

> Within Economics I sense that sometimes students see abstract models as abstract models and don't see the link between them and the real world, so that students would be quite happy talking about problems of inflation, unemployment and so on, but as soon as you say 'Good, let's have a look at the model', they sort of switch off. They think that's a completely separate issue. 'I don't want to do the model, I just want to talk about inflation or unemployment.' So the idea that models which look abstract – can be looked at abstractly – actually talk about the real world, perhaps that is a crucial factor. I mean they tend to put models into one box and then the discussion about the policy issues in another box. They don't

necessarily see that the two must be linked. Perhaps that's a threshold issue.

(Respondent 3)

And finally we may consider an extract from a book on the teaching of undergraduate Economics:

> When the dust settles, most students leave the introductory course never having fully grasped the essence of microeconomics. Thus the opportunity cost concept, so utterly central to our understanding of what it means to *think* like an economist, is but one among hundreds of other concepts that go by in a blur.
>
> (Frank 1998, p. 14, emphasis added)

Conclusion

The intention of this chapter has been to open up discussion of threshold concepts as an important but problematic factor in the design of effective learning environments within disciplines and to indicate the linkages to ways of thinking and practising within these disciplines. It is our contention that where threshold concepts exist within curricula there is a likelihood, owing to their powerful transformative effects, that they may prove troublesome for students. Difficulty in understanding threshold concepts may leave the learner in a state of *liminality* (Latin *limen* – 'threshold'), a suspended state in which understanding approximates to a kind of mimicry or lack of authenticity. Palmer (2001), in a discussion of liminality and hermeneutics, reminds us that the insights gained when the learner crosses the threshold might also be unsettling, involving a sense of loss: 'The truth or insight may be a pleasant awakening or rob one of an illusion; the understanding itself is morally neutral. The quicksilver flash of insight may make one rich or poor in an instant' (Palmer 2001, p. 4).

A further significant issue is that threshold concepts might be interpreted as part of a 'totalising' or colonising view of the curriculum. Such a view would point to the effects of power relations within curricula with threshold concepts serving to provide a measure, and exert a 'normalising' function in the Foucaldian sense (Foucault 1979, 1980). '*Whose* threshold concepts?' then becomes a salient question. These are non-trivial concerns and merit further consideration.

These issues notwithstanding, conversations with colleagues in various disciplines have suggested that the idea of a threshold concept remains a powerful one to the extent even of being used to benchmark curricula. It appears, however, that threshold concepts might be more readily identifiable in some disciplines (such as Physics) than in others (such as History). Wherever present they constitute an obvious, and perhaps neglected, focus for evaluating teaching strategies and learning outcomes. This chapter has drawn primarily from the perspectives of teachers in higher education. A research question is also opened up on the degree to which threshold concepts, as perceived by teachers, are experienced by students, and with what *variation*. If it is accepted that threshold concepts represent experiential entities in the minds of students, might threshold concepts usefully provide a micro-perspective for examining learning environments? These questions will form the basis of subsequent chapters in the second part of this volume which draw on the perspectives of both students and teachers in a variety of disciplines in higher education.

References

Adnett, N. and Davies, P. (2000) 'Education as a positional good: implications for market-based reforms of state schooling', *British Journal of Educational Studies*, 50(2): 189–202.

Artigue, M. (2001) 'What can we learn from educational research at the university level?' in Holton, D. (ed.) *The Teaching and Learning of Mathematics at University Level*, Dordrecht: Kluwer Academic Publishers.

Bayne, S. (2002) Personal communication, Queen Margaret University College, Edinburgh.

Bruner, J. (1966) *Toward a Theory of Instruction*, Cambridge, MA: Harvard University Press.

Davies, P. (2002) Personal communication with the authors, University of Staffordshire.

Derrida, J. (1978) 'Structure, sign and play in the discourse of the human sciences', cited in Lodge, D. (ed.) (1988) *Modern Criticism and Theory*, London: Longman.

Eagleton, T. (1983) *Literary Theory: An Introduction*, Oxford: Blackwell.

Eatwell, J., Milgate, M. and Newman, P. (eds) (1998) *The New Palgrave. A Dictionary of Economics*, London: Macmillan.

Foucault, M. (1979) *Discipline and Punish: The Birth of the Prison*, Harmondsworth: Penguin.

Foucault, M. (1980) *Power/Knowledge*, New York: Pantheon.

Frank, R.H. (1998) 'Some thoughts on the micro principles course', in Walstad, W.B. and Saunders, P. (eds) *Teaching Undergraduate Economics: A Handbook for Instructors*, Boston, MA: Irwin/McGraw-Hill, pp. 13–20.

Giddens, A. (1984) *The Constitution of Society*, Cambridge: Polity Press.

Hodgkin, H. (2002) Annual Edinburgh Festival Lecture, University of Edinburgh.

Kennedy, P. (1998) 'Using Monte Carlo studies for teaching econometrics', in Becker, W. and Watts, M. (eds) *Teaching Economics to Undergraduates. Alternatives to Chalk and Talk*, Cheltenham, Northampton/MA: Edward Elgar.

Knottenbelt, M. (2002) Personal communication, University of Edinburgh.

Land, R. and Bayne, S. (1999) 'Computer-mediated learning, synchronicity and the metaphysics of presence', in Collis, B. and Oliver, R. (eds) *ED-MEDIA 1999: Proceedings of 11th Annual World Conference on Educational Multimedia, Hypermedia and Telecommunications*, Charlottesville, VA: American Association for the Advancement of Computing in Education.

McCloskey, M. (1983) 'Naive theories of motion', in Gentner, D. and Stevens, A.L. (eds) *Mental Models*, Hillsdale, NJ: Erlbaum (cited in Perkins 1999).

Manning, P. (2002) Personal communication, University of Durham.

Meyer, J.H.F. and Land, R. (2003) 'Threshold concepts and troublesome knowledge: Linkages to ways of thinking and practising within the disciplines', in Rust, C. (ed.) *Improving Student Learning Theory and Practice – 10 Years On*, Oxford: OCSLD, pp. 412–24.

Mezirow, J. (1978) 'Perspective transformation', *Adult Education*, 28(2): 100–9.

Newsholme, E. and Leech, T. (1985) *Runner: Energy and Endurance*, fourth edition, Roosevelt, NJ, Oxford, London: Walter. L. Meagher.

Palmer, R.E. (2001) *The Liminality of Hermes and the Meaning of Hermeneutics*, MacMurray College, http://www.mac.edu/~rpalmer/liminality.html (last modified 29 May 2001).

Perkins, D. (1999) 'The many faces of constructivism', *Educational Leadership*, 57(3), November.

Polanyi, M. (1958) *Personal Knowledge*, London: Routledge.

Reimann, N. (2002) Personal communication, University of Durham.

Sproull, J. (2002) Personal communication, University of Edinburgh.

Wenger, E. (1998) *Communities of Practice: Learning, Meaning and Identity*, Cambridge: Cambridge University Press.

Threshold concepts and troublesome knowledge

Issues of liminality

Jan H. F. Meyer and Ray Land

Introduction: threshold concepts revisited

In Chapter 1 the generative notion of *threshold concepts* was introduced. It has been argued that the acquisition of such concepts may also prove to be 'troublesome' for a variety of reasons and that such acquisition is likely to be characterised by transition through a state of 'liminality'. In thus beginning to develop and link a set of ideas around the notion of threshold concepts the integrative nature of the notion itself has also been illustrated. This chapter sets out to develop more extensively the notions of liminality within the context of threshold concept acquisition.

Chapter 1 introduced the basic idea that in certain disciplines there are 'conceptual gateways' or 'portals' that lead to a transformed view of something – 'the world looks different' when such thresholds have been crossed. Or it may be that one sees features in a familiar landscape that were previously not discernable. Certain threshold concepts acquired in the study of Economics for example allow one to distinguish for the first time, within a hitherto undifferentiated landscape, phenomena that are amenable to economic analysis. This new and previously inaccessible view of something may also prove to be troublesome for a variety of reasons.

The visual metaphor of a threshold concept represented by a portal or 'space' that needs to be approached and negotiated is a productive one because it invites a consideration of how the portal initially comes 'into view', how it is approached, negotiated, and perhaps even experienced as a transition in terms of sense of self.

Troublesomeness revisited

The following transcript, from an interview with a History lecturer, exemplifies the way in which a troublesome form of knowledge, though important and 'quite exciting' nonetheless 'can in a way seem very alien', and how it can be 'surprisingly difficult to get students to think about it':

LECTURER: The importance of personal contact and personal relationships, like impressing upon students how little could be done in this society, even by people of power, without them actually getting on their horse or whatever and going and seeing someone else, and dealing with and impressing people face to face. The language of personal power expressed through things like dress and symbols and rituals. It can in a way seem very alien. It's surprisingly difficult to get students to think about it and to be self-conscious about the way in which the manner of someone's dress could have affected their social role and could have helped them articulate and then force a particular social role. But it is quite exciting because I think it's something they could then go on and take with them into looking at cultural history and social history in other periods. It might even make them more aware of how power works in our own society, it's not that alien. The role of law too, there is a tendency for people who don't really know anything about mediaeval Europe to talk about mediaeval kings as though they're 20th Century dictators, and getting students to think about the society as a society in which people are supposed to have rights and in which law is quite important also gives an interesting perspective on later periods in European history. So, as a very general concept, we don't have a methodology in the way that some of the social sciences have methodology, but I think there are key concepts that are quite difficult and students don't seem to find them particularly easy to approach. You can get students to grapple with them and they can kind of light up whole periods of the past . . . .

INTERVIEWER: . . . Would you see that as applying to this module, would there be anything like those threshold concepts?

LECTURER: I think so, but I don't think there will be just two or three because we're trying to do something very multi-faceted, we're trying to embrace a whole society and culture and forms of political life so I think you could identify key concepts but I think there would be quite a lot of them. I do think that there are concepts that as I say if students can grasp, they illuminate the period but they would be concepts of the kind that I've just described.

Threshold concepts as discursive and reconstitutive

In developing the notion of threshold concepts Meyer and Land (2005) have initially given further consideration to their *discursive* nature. The acquisition of transformative concepts, it is argued, brings with it new and empowering forms of expression that in many instances characterise distinctive ways of disciplinary *thinking*. This discursive aspect of threshold concepts might provide an enabling and motivating source of new insight – 'action poetry' in Perkins's (2002) phrase, or it might present what Brousseau

(1983, 1997) has termed an 'epistemological obstacle', a source of trouble-someness, impeding and frustrating further development. Whatever the effect, the implication is that any reconceptualisation implies a discursive reconfiguration.

Meyer and Land argue furthermore that the discursive nature of threshold concepts entails a reconstitution of the learner's subjectivity.

> This might have powerful effects, as, for example, when first year students of Cultural Studies report their recognition of the implications of the concept of 'hegemony' for the ways in which their personal choices and behaviour might be culturally constrained, determined or gendered. Alternatively this *reconstitutive* effect of threshold concepts might entail a less discernible, cumulative process of skill acquisition, as when a mature student of French, patiently struggling to understand the use of the subjunctive mood, reports nonetheless a sense of slowly increasing confidence in her emerging identity as a speaker of French.
>
> (Meyer and Land 2005, p. 375)

The emphasis here is on the indissoluble interrelatedness of the learner's identity with thinking and language (reading, writing, listening, talking). For example, in the context of Medical Studies:

> students acquire a point of view and terminology of a technical kind, which allow them to talk and think about patients and diseases in a way quite different from the layman. They look upon death and disabling disease, not with the horror and sense of tragedy the layman finds appropriate, but as problems in medical responsibility.
>
> (Becker *et al.* 2005, p. 421)

There are here, as we shall see, both epistemological and ontological (states of 'being') considerations.

Threshold concepts lead not only to transfigured thought but to a trans-figuration of identity and adoption of an extended or elaborated discourse. The elemental aspects of such discourses may be signalled by shifts in syntax and semantics that in some cases are quite far removed from threshold concepts themselves. Consider, for example, the fact that mathematics is the *lingua franca* of many disciplines. The meaning of mathematics is invariant. And yet within many disciplines mathematics takes on a particular syntax and may even adopt non-standard conventions. What $y = mx + c$ is for one person is $y = a + bx$ for another. The coefficient of x, be it labelled m, b, or something else may, by disciplinary convention, be taken as always represent-ing a particular entity. Thus, a slope, or gradient may be designated m, a regression coefficient b, and a coefficient of proportionality something else. Students are often confused by unfamiliar symbolic ways of expressing essentially the same thing. And unfamiliar symbolism may shroud, even present a barrier to, a threshold concept.

In similar vein there is a mathematical convention when plotting functional relationships in two dimensions on orthogonal axes, namely, that the independent variable is plotted on the horizontal axis (usually labelled the *x-axis*) and the dependent variable on the vertical axis (usually labelled the *y-axis*) Economists for some strange reason find it helpful to do it the other way round when they graphically illustrate the relationship between 'price' and 'quantity' (the 'supply' curve) and, in particular, when they illustrate the concept of *elasticity* as in 'the price elasticity of demand'. And 'elasticity', it should be noted, is a term used by economists and physicists in completely different senses. The variation here is in terms of semantics; to an economist 'elasticity' refers to the *responsiveness* of the demand quantity of a good to its price, while to a physicist it refers to the *restoration* property of a material which, having been distorted, will cause it to assume its original shape.

Liminality

Central to the acquisition of threshold concepts is a consideration of what it might mean to be 'in the threshold'. The interest here is in variability in that state of being that may be thought of as *liminal*. Much has been written about the emotional and behavioural oscillation of men (in particular) undergoing the third stage of the 'midlife transition' or 'midlife crisis' – a spectacle, often tragic in its outcome, often entertaining to behold, that Carl Jung (1875–1961) describes in terms of 'liminality'. During this liminal stage there is uncertainty about identity of self and purpose in life.

Meyer and Land (2005), drawing more specifically on the writing of van Gennep (1960) and Turner (1969), develop the argument that acquiring a threshold concept may be likened in some disciplines to a 'rite of passage'. The term 'liminality' (from the latin *limen*, boundary or threshold) was also adopted by Turner to characterise the transitional state of space or time within which rituals are conducted. It should come as no surprise that this notion of a 'rite of passage' resonates strongly in many disciplines with entry into their communities of practice. As one medical graduate (anon.) commented, going through medical school is 'like getting your hand caught in a meat grinder. It just keeps grinding and scooping up more of you as it goes. You gradually get bundled into a processed package and pop out as a doctor'. The experience is characterised as a matter of survival. 'If you don't conform you're out' (Coombs 1978, p. 3).

The comparison of liminality to rituals or rites of passage is useful for a number of reasons as elaborated by Meyer and Land (2005). First, there is the proposition that the condition of liminality may be *transformative* in function; there may be a change of state or status.

In becoming medical students, the boys enter upon one of the longest rites of passage . . . that series of instructions, ceremonies, and ordeals by which those already in a special status initiate neophytes into their charmed circle.

(Becker *et al.* 2005, p. 4)

This point raises some interesting thoughts about what it means, for example, when a student for the first time becomes conscious of the fact that they are, or are beginning to *think* like, an accountant, chemist, economist, historian, lawyer, mathematician, physicist, statistician, and so on. Teachers within the disciplines are certainly aware of particular patterns of thought and insights that have such ontological significance. For example, a colleague (Mears 2005), in analysing the transcript of an interview with one of her students on a particular learning episode in History, commented that 'in taking owner-ship of the material' in a particular way, her student was 'thinking like a historian'. The student (student A) had observed that 'when you really under-stand it, you've come as far as you can with your interpretation of it but you'll never really know [what happened]'. Mears recognised this as distinct-ive to the practice of historians: 'formulating an opinion, based on the critical analysis of complex sources, yet acknowledging it was contingent and subject to debate and challenge'. In a subsequent communication she commented further that:

the specific case student A was talking about (the abduction of Elizabeth Canning in 1753) is a particularly problematic incident in which, despite the wealth of evidence, there are so many holes and problems with that evidence that a 'definitive answer' (if there is any such thing in History) is difficult, if not impossible, to achieve. Student A recognised this and, though the case was extreme that allowed her to do so, I think it helped put into sharper relief what being a historian was all about (and hence become one!). It may be that this student may undergo times of 'stuck-ness' or 'mimicry', perhaps when she can't apply what she has learned to do in one case in another, perhaps less extreme, situation. But I felt that she had passed through (if that is the right word) a key, big threshold concept from which there would be no real turning back. I think, if pressed, most historians would be able to define what they would think of as threshold concepts for History . . . but because History tends to be rather anti-theory, or at least sceptical of theories like postmodernism and deconstruction etc, we might not have the jargon that other disciplines have to describe it!

Second, as a result of the ritual the participating individual acquires new knowledge and subsequently a new status and identity within the community. This is clearly true of the professions and their (often) self-regulatory status as gatekeepers of exclusive professional practice across vast tracts of special-ised knowledge (see, for example, Goodlad 1993). But there are also examples outside professional practice. Neo-classical Economics is basically about the study of people, their wants and needs, and the choices they make regarding these in the face of scarcity. Neo-classical economic theory is open to serious criticism on a number of charges *and yet* a serious study of it arguably repre-sents the indisputable, and internationally ubiquitous, undergraduate rite of passage to becoming an economist. The point here is that if you want to critique neo-classical Economics your argument is a lot more credible if you have already passed through this rite of passage.

A third consideration is that the transformation can be protracted, over periods of time, and involve *oscillation* between states, often with temporary regression to earlier status. This regression may be viewed as a form of 'com-pensatory mimicry'. Within educational settings it would appear that, on the part of the learner, there may be an inability to achieve the new (transformed) status, occasioning similar forms of 'mimicry' or entry into what Ellsworth (1997) calls 'stuck places'. But there would seem to be no rewinding of the transformative process although there may well be sporadic attempts at mim-icking what has already been lost. It is tempting to equate such mimicry with the 'surface approaches' to learning identified by commentators working within phenomenographic traditions. In student learning terms mimicry, it seems, may involve both attempts at understanding *and* troubled misunder-standing, or limited understanding, and perhaps not merely an intention to reproduce information in a given form. We might speculate that a student in a 'stuck place', having glimpsed the outline of a threshold portal and perhaps only vaguely aware of what lies beyond it, but conscious of the failure to cross it, may engage in two forms of mimicry. The first is compensatory mimicry, in an assuage of self that something *is* understood – witness the novice student who rehearses what is known (but irrelevant) in learning for examinations, rather than what is required to be known for them. The second is conscious mimicry, when the student is aware that what is required is beyond grasp, other than through the mimicry of pretension.

Einstein at the party

A brief digression here provides another way of considering liminality within learning. There exists a (very possibly apocryphal!) story that occasionally circulates within senior Mathematics courses and which concerns Albert Einstein when he was wrestling with the mathematical formalisation of general relativity. The bones of the story are that Einstein met one Gregorio Ricci-Curbastro, of the University of Padua, 'at a party'. Ricci was the inventor of a domain of mathematics called *tensor calculus* and in 1900 he published a fundamental paper on the subject with his student Levi-Civita. Now in 1900 Einstein had only just graduated as a teacher of Mathematics and

Physics. He published a paper proposing the special theory of relativity in 1905 (the same year, incidentally, in which he was awarded his doctorate) and sought after that date to extend the special theory to phenomena involving acceleration. Round about 1907 it appeared that he had not heard about tensor calculus. As the story is relayed (and which, of course, may well be accurate!), Einstein, in a somewhat anxious state, was complaining to Ricci at 'the party' about the fact that he was *stuck*. Ricci explained to him what tensor calculus could do, and Einstein immediately saw it as a solution for his problems. In fact tensor calculus became the 'language', or discourse, of general relativity. It is interesting to speculate here that Einstein may well have been in a liminal state, temporarily suspended by the lack of a formal mathematical vehicle through which to express and progress his thinking, rather than facing what we have referred to in Chapter 1 as 'boundedness'. Having reached the stage of development that he had in relation to his existing thinking about relativity, he could not go backwards – could not, as it were, unlearn or reverse out of his stuckness – but as he had no doubt worked out a considerable amount in his head, he could not go forwards either without acquiring the language of tensor calculus. In addition to the boundedness we can also identify in this account the other characteristics we have associated with threshold concepts, namely a quality of irreversibility, of integration (of existing mathematical formulations), of discursiveness (the formal language of tensor calculus) and clearly of transformation.

However, let us remember that general relativity is very much a BIG threshold concept in Physics. Einstein, in this instance, was not traversing a threshold already in existence, *he was creating the threshold*, and perhaps to a certain extent creating his own liminality. It is feasible that this form of liminality may be quite common to the process of conducting fundamental research, which creates new thresholds rather than extending or elaborating the domains (boundedness) of existing ones. Indeed it might be argued that all creative movements forward in research share a similar quality of liminality as that which appears within the Einstein story.

Troublesomeness and liminality

An insight into the interplay between troublesomeness and liminality is provided by Guest (2005), also in the context of conducting student learning interviews within a disciplinary context

> in which students are most likely to learn about religious movements that are outside of their own experience (including sectarian groups, controversial 'cults' and groups associated with violence and fundamentalism) . . . presented as objects of social scientific interest; that is, they are addressed as cultural phenomena alongside more traditional religious

groups, without privileging the truth claims of any, nor offering any theological critique ... the module highlights the pluralism of the contemporary religious field (Bourdieu 1991), and encourages students to take seriously movements which might otherwise be treated as fringe, deviant or fanatical. In this respect the module may offer an approach that could be presented as 'troublesome' in that it emphasises ... the cultural contingency of religion ... the multiplicity of religious phenomena; and ... the complexity of religion (Juergensmeyer 2003). All challenge, and potentially undermine, understandings of reality which discern truth solely within a singular religious tradition.

He writes that, for one of his students,

the troublesome aspect identified is the absolute and uncompromising conviction of fundamentalist religious believers, which the student finds disturbing, and yet strangely alluring at the same time. He seems to find such unquestioning belief counter-intuitive and yet has some admiration for the conviction and commitment that is associated with it. Hence, the emerging, new perspective is complex: neither affirming nor condemning, neither confirming existing preconceptions nor proving them to be without grounds.

In contrast, for another student,

the 'troublesome' aspect of the course is our coverage of movements which alert the student to the pluralism of the religious landscape, and the decreasing social significance of the Roman Catholic Church, to which he is deeply committed. However, he appears able to consider these movements as objective areas of interest and incorporate them into his existing knowledge without any profound disruption to the learning process. One key factor here could be the social scientific approach to the topics that I encourage on this module: the sense of critical distance from the objects of study – presented descriptively and without judgement – allows students to develop their knowledge without directly challenging their personal religious convictions. Instructive here is case study #2, which suggests a contrasting form of intellectual engagement demanded by other theology modules. When the learning process overlaps with personal religious practice – as with the process of interpreting the Bible – then clashes of method are all the more likely to emerge.

Pre-liminal variation and epistemological obstacles

According to Meyer and Land liminality

> can provide a useful metaphor in aiding our understanding of the
> conceptual transformations students undergo, or find difficulty and anx-
> iety in undergoing, particularly in relation to notions of being 'stuck'.
> 'Stuck places' may of course occasion difficulty by presenting epistemo-
> logical obstacles (Brousseau 1983, 1997) that block any transformed
> perspective.
>
> (Meyer and Land 2005, p. 377)

and go on to suggest further that

> as way of helping students, we can distinguish, in theory at least, between
> variation in students' 'tacit' understanding (or lack thereof) of a thresh-
> old concept. We see this situation of what we choose to call *pre-liminal
> variation* as a potentially important and useful means of opening up our
> understanding of why some students will productively negotiate the
> liminal space and why others find difficulty in doing so.
>
> (Meyer and Land 2005, p. 384)

In developing this argument we revisit the threshold concept of 'opportunity
cost' in Economics. This is a good example for the purpose in mind because
the concept, and some of the difficulties surrounding its acquisition, will be
accessible to readers with no prior knowledge of Economics. Two typical
examples of how the concept may be formally defined in the context of
making a choice are 'the cost of the next best but rejected alternative' and 'the
cost of the next best alternative foregone'.

In 2003 an informal survey of students *who had completed* a module in
Microeconomics was carried out at the University of South Australia.
'Opportunity cost' had been formally taught in this module, and students
were asked to provide in their own words a description (for a hypothetical
friend who had missed out that section of the module) of what it meant.
Amongst the many incorrect explanations provided two stand out: 'the value
of a potential opportunity in business' and 'the cost of borrowing funds – the
cost incurred when you borrow money'. How these students reached these
misunderstandings of the concept is an open *research* question that invites a
consideration of how the concept may initially have 'come into view'.

First, and even before a definition is offered, the concept may literally
come 'into view' as two words, spoken, or on a printed page. What might
these words signify to a person who hears or sees them for the first time? In
terms of the everyday use of these commonly used words there is a coupling
of 'opportunity' and 'cost', and one might plausibly entertain notions of

something along the lines of 'the opportunity of cost' or 'the cost of (an) opportunity'.

Asked to explain what she thought the term 'opportunity cost' meant, an innocent colleague with no prior knowledge of Economics but some experience in running a small business suggested two meanings (Ward 2005): 'the premium my supplier will charge when he knows that I need something', and 'how much I am willing to spend on something which I know will yield me a profit in the future'. So immediately we see the potential for *variation* when the concept first 'comes into view' for students of Microeconomics. Does this potential for variation matter? Limited evidence suggests that it may in the light of the students' apparently persistent misconceptions of the concept.

We have, second, the problem that, in terms of its definition, the concept of 'opportunity cost' does not usually refer explicitly to 'opportunity', and has very little to do with the everyday meaning of 'cost' in an accounting sense. Although a definition of the concept can be contrived in a form of the cost of an 'opportunity foregone', this is somewhat clumsy language. Henderson (2005) furthermore points out that 'the word *opportunity* in *opportunity cost* is actually redundant. The cost of using something is already the value of the highest-valued alternative use.' But he does go on to point out that this redundancy has a virtue in reminding us 'that the cost of using a resource arises from the value of what it could be used for instead'. Decoding the meaning of the language being used here, and in the definitions offered earlier, is demanding. We reinforce here an earlier argument related to the concept of a limit in mathematics (Meyer and Land 2005, p. 385) that the choice of language used to introduce threshold concepts, and indeed used in the naming and explanation of the concepts themselves, can be troublesome and can present epistemological obstacles.

Moving to a rather different disciplinary context, Meyer and Land (2003) have commented briefly on the threshold concept status of a *limit* in pure mathematics. In the words of Cornu (1991, p. 153), 'It holds a central position which permeates the whole of mathematical analysis – as a foundation of the theory of approximation, of continuity, and of differential and integral calculus.' Picking up from the second section of this chapter, we can see how Mathematics combines natural and symbolic language in dealing with the abstract. But in *approaching* the formalised symbolic definition of a limit, it has also been recognised by several writers that the natural language form of the term can create 'troublesomeness'. A 'limit' in terms of pre-liminal variation may be thought about in common-sense terms as a boundary, barrier, the end of something, and so on, that is, for example, visible, real, attainable or reachable in some everyday sense. But this interpretation is fundamentally what a limit in mathematics is *not* about – 'limits' are not reached, they are 'tended towards'. Cornu (1991, p. 154), in referring to work by Schwarzenberger and Tall (1978), observes 'that the words "tends to" and "limit" have a significance for the students *before* any lessons begin ... and that students *continue to rely* on these meanings after they have been given a formal definition' (emphasis added).

A third problem might arise from students' experiences of 'choice'. The emphasis of the concept of 'opportunity cost' is on the *economic* cost of making choices. The concept formalises one of the fundamental arguments of Microeconomics that choice involves sacrifice. Both 'choice' and 'sacrifice' are used here in an economic sense, and another potential obstacle to understanding arises for students when the introduction to the concept is trivialised as in, for example, 'the opportunity cost of drinking a cup of coffee'. From a student learning perspective we might also argue that the concept, in formalising the dynamics of economic choice, is also an *integrating* concept insofar as it may bring together for the individual student a range of personal experiences and understandings of economic activity. For some students the definition of the concept may thus simply formalise tacit knowledge and experience that the student already feels comfortable with – what we refer to in the concluding chapter (drawing on Perkins in Chapter 3) as 'the underlying game'. But for other students this might not be the case. What might the *conception of choice* be for a student with a very limited experience of exercising choice in an economic sense, and studying a Microeconomics course in a country that has a communist or statist economy, where the underlying game is far from being accessible? Again, the open *research* question here is whether there are patterns of variation in students' conceptions of 'choice' that will differentially affect their acquisition of the concept.

What we are left with then are formidable challenges in responding to patterns of pre-liminal variation that students may exhibit in the passage of approaching a threshold concept. There are methodological and conceptual issues here that need to be researched. *How*, in terms of method and strategy, may we externalise such variation and how, in conceptual terms, may we address it?

One possible way forward is in terms of *proxies* (for threshold concepts) – engaging novice students with innocent-looking but authentic representations of concepts in a form that they can relate to in varying (pre-liminal) degrees. These proxies in their 'form of engagement' are stripped of their precise, discourse-specific and often 'troublesome' definitions but they retain, where appropriate, the character of what was referred to earlier as the 'underlying game'. Formulating such proxies, as early work by Reimann and Jackson (Chapter 8) indicates, is difficult and may require a considerable process of trial and error.

Another way forward is suggested in the following transcript from an interview with a lecturer in Media Studies. A seemingly successful approach to opening up a troublesome threshold concept – the notion of Culture – is through 'a gradual move' into what appears like a liminal space, through which the students eventually gain ownership of the concept.

LECTURER: If there is a difficult concept I will start for 20 minutes clarifying and writing on the board, asking what they didn't understand in the reading – getting a real framework on the board or in their minds. That would normally be a way of clearing the ground for them to go and work with these ideas. Then there is reading – some extracts or some material from books they have been reading, for example one of the first bits of material I give out is a handout which has various definitions of the word 'culture' and we talk about it in a lot of detail and pick it apart and think about the issues – analyse in depth and usually there will be time for some group work where the students get together and come up with some ideas and then a plenary at the end so students feel that they have gone from being told or directed to having a grasp of it for themselves. That is the pattern – a gradual move. By the end of the session the students will be a lot more in control of it than I will – in a good sense.

Ontological obstacles

In conclusion, then, we may reflect on the presence of ontological as distinct from epistemological obstacles. Ellsworth (1989 and 1997) has argued that the troublesome nature of some student learning, particularly that encountered by students who do not fit the 'mythical norm' that is 'young, White, hetero-sexual, Christian, able-bodied, thin, middle-class, English-speaking, and male' (Ellsworth 1989, p. 323) may stem from an active refusal of learning, or an anxiety about its transformative effects, which is the result of repressed desire or apprehension, emanating from the unconscious, and hence likely to prove inaccessible both to the learner and the teacher. This obviously renders problematic any simplistic schematic attempt to overcome troublesome knowledge by technicist redesign of curricula alone, and challenges easy assumptions that if the learning environment is suitably ordered and con-structively aligned then the intended transformations will ensue. In a now famous critique of Critical Pedagogy she argued that the latter's humanist, rationalist, universalist (and even dialogic) positionings were inadequate to move students on from their stuck places, owing to the incapacity of rationalist approaches to tolerate the unknown and the uncertain (because unknowable), the affective (because non-rational) and the contextualised/local (because non-universal).

> Although the literature recognises that teachers have much to learn from their students' experiences, it does not address the ways in which there are things that I as professor could never know about the experiences, oppres-sions, and understandings of other participants in the class. This situation makes it impossible for any single voice in the classroom – including that of the professor, to assume the position of centre or origin of knowledge or authority, of having privileged access to authentic experience or

appropriate language. A recognition, contrary to all Western ways of knowing and speaking, that all knowings are partial, that there are fundamental things each of us cannot know – a situation alleviated only in part by the pooling of partial, socially constructed knowledges in classrooms – demands a fundamental retheorising of 'education' and 'pedagogy'.

(Ellsworth 1989, p. 310)

This identifies problems located not only within Critical Pedagogy but within other dominant and orthodox conceptualisations of learning within higher education environments, namely tendencies towards the disembodiment and genericisation of the learner, and an assumed lack of an affective and social dimension to their subjectivity. Ellsworth encourages her own teacher education students towards:

cultivating a third ear that listens not for what a student knows (discrete packages of knowledge) but for the terms that shape a student's knowledge, her not knowing, her forgetting, her circles of stuck places and resistances.

(Ellsworth 1997, p. 71)

Lather (1998), similarly, seeking a 'praxis of stuck places', offers a counternarrative located within feminist and poststructural problematics, 'contrasting the rhetorical position of "the one who knows" with a thinking within Derrida's "ordeal of the undecidable" '. She argues for 'a praxis of not being so sure', and advocates the practices of feminist pedagogy:

where the effort is to speak from discontinuities, the failures of language, self deception, guilty pleasures, and vested interests: what Ellsworth calls 'a speech which comes from elsewhere' to provoke something else into happening – something other than the return of the same.

(Lather 1998, p. 492)

A praxis of stuck places might tolerate 'discrepancies, repetitions, hesitations, and uncertainties, always beginning again' (ibid., p. 491). What it refuses is:

the privileging of containment over excess, thought over affect, structure over speed, linear causality over complexity, and intention over aggregate capacities. Ontological changes and category slippages mark the exhaustion of received categories of mind/body, nature/culture, base/ superstructure, and spiritual/secular.

(Lather 1998, p. 497)

Such a praxis of stuck places, we feel, offers rich possibilities for future research.

References

Becker, H.S., Geer, B., Hughes, E.C. and Strauss, A.L. (2005) *Boys in White: Student Culture in Medical School*, New Brunswick, NJ: Transaction Publishers. (Reprint of the 1961 edition published by the University of Chicago Press.)

Bourdieu, P. (1991) 'Genesis and structure of the religious field', *Comparative Social Research*, 13: 1–44.

Brousseau, G. (1983) 'Les obstacles epistemologiques et les problemes en mathematiques', *Recherches en didactique des mathematiques*, 4(2): 165–98.

Brousseau, G. (1997) *Theory of Didactical Situations in Mathematics*, Dordrecht: Kluwer Academic Publishers.

Coombs, R.H. (1978) *Mastering Medicine*, New York: Free Press.

Cornu, B. (1991) 'Limits', in Tall, D. (ed.) *Advanced Mathematical Thinking*, Dordrecht: Kluwer Academic Publishers, pp. 153–66.

Ellsworth, E. (1989) 'Why doesn't this feel empowering? Working through the repressive myths of critical pedagogy', *Harvard Educational Review*, 59(3), August, pp. 297–324.

Ellsworth, E. (1997) *Teaching Positions: Difference Pedagogy and the Power of Address*, New York: Teachers College Press.

Gennep, A. van (1960) *The Rites of Passage*, London: Routledge and Kegan Paul.

Goodlad, S. (1993) *Education for the Professions*, Guildford: SRHE/NFER.

Guest, M. (2005) 'Religious awareness and troublesome knowledge: the relationship between motivation and the learning process among Theology undergraduates', unpublished manuscript, Durham University.

Henderson, D.R. (2005) 'Opportunity cost', in the *Concise Encyclopedia of Economics*, Library of Economics and Liberty. Retrieved 1 July 2005 from: http://www.econlib.org/library/Enc/OpportunityCost.html

Juergensmeyer, M. (2003) 'Teaching about religious violence without trivializing it', *Spotlight on Teaching* (published by the American Academy of Religion), 18(4).

Lather, P. (1998) 'Critical pedagogy and its complicities: a praxis of stuck places', *Educational Theory*, 48(4), Fall, pp. 487–98.

Mears, N. (2005) 'Gender and confidence in the student learning process in History', unpublished manuscript, Durham University.

Meyer, J.H.F. and Land, R. (2003) 'Threshold concepts and troublesome knowledge: linkages to ways of thinking and practising within the disciplines', in Rust, C. (ed.) *Improving Student Learning. Improving Student Learning Theory and Practice – Ten Years On*, Oxford: OCSLD, pp. 412–24.

Meyer, J.H.F. and Land, R. (2005) 'Threshold concepts and troublesome knowledge (2): epistemological considerations and a conceptual framework for teaching and learning', *Higher Education*, 49: 373–88.

Perkins, D.N. (2002) *King Arthur's Round Table: How Collaborative Conversations Create Smart Organizations*, Hoboken, NJ: John Wiley & Sons.

Schwarzenberger, R.L.E. and Tall, D.O. (1978) 'Conflicts in the learning of real numbers and limits', *Mathematics Teaching*, 82: 44–9.

Turner, V. (1969) *The Ritual Process: Structure and Anti-Structure*, London: Routledge and Kegan Paul.

Ward, S.C. (2005) Personal communication, Durham University.

Chapter 3

Constructivism and troublesome knowledge

David Perkins

Betty Fable's first day at the prestigious Constructivist Academy was some-what disorienting. In European History, the teacher challenged each student to write a letter from a French aristocrat to an Italian one, describing a key event of the French Revolution. In Physics, students were to forecast whether heavy objects would fall faster than light ones, how much faster, and why. Then small groups of students designed their own experiments to test their theories. In Algebra, where the class was learning the basic skill of simplify-ing algebraic expressions, the teacher insisted on conducting a discussion about what it means to simplify. Were simplified expressions the same as simplified equations? In English Literature, after the class read Robert Frost's 'Acquainted with the Night', the students discussed how the poem related to episodes in their own lives.

Betty Fable expected all of the faculty at Constructivist Academy to teach in a constructivist way – whatever that was. But what was it? Role-playing, experimenting, analysing, making connections to one's life? Everyone seemed to be asking for something different. She wondered whether they really had their act together, although, she admitted to herself, she seemed to have learned quite a bit.

It is easy to understand Betty Fable's puzzlement. What is constructivism really, especially since it can look so different from incarnation to incarnation? And does it really help? Any educator from kindergarten through university has good reason to ponder such questions, because constructivism in one or another version has become the generally acknowledged way to think about good teaching and learning. Especially, constructivism is the answer when the question is how to deal with problems of understanding. For memorising parts of the periodic table, no one thinks of constructivism (although in fact active constructive approaches to memory are likely to be more effective than rote techniques). However, for understanding how the periodic table makes sense of the chemical properties of elements, constructivism steps up to the table.

All that acknowledged, it also has to be recognised that constructivism brings considerable frustration to the table too. Many talented, dedicated, and experienced educators would score constructivism closer to a pain than a panacea. Often it comes across as more of an ideology than a methodology. And often it just seems too much bother when a good explanation and a couple of rounds of practice would serve just fine. Viewing constructivism as a toolkit rather than a credo provides a deeper reckoning of what constructivism offers. When learning can proceed straightforwardly, fine. When learning comes with warps and kinks, it's good to have ways of straightening them out. Here then are some ideas about constructivism in general, how knowledge makes trouble for learners, and how the constructivist toolkit speaks to those troubles.

What is constructivism in its variety?

No one can live in the world of education long without becoming aware that constructivism is more than one thing – but what accounts for the variety? Philosopher D.C. Phillips (1995) identifies three distinct learner roles in constructivism. We'll call them the active learner, the social learner, and the creative learner.

- *The active learner: knowledge and understanding as actively acquired.* Constructivism generally casts learners in an active role. Instead of just listening, reading, and working through routine exercises, they discuss, debate, hypothesise, investigate, and take viewpoints – a common thread in Betty Fable's first day at Constructivist Academy.
- *The social learner: knowledge and understanding as socially constructed.* Constructivists often emphasise that knowledge and understanding are highly social. We do not construct them individually; we co-construct them in dialogue with others. Instruction in History should make students aware of how historical 'truth' varies with the interest groups – hence in Betty's history class, the letters from the aristocratic perspective. Instruction in Science should lead students to recognise that scientific truths are arrived at by a social critical process that shapes their supposedly objective reality – thus, the group work in Betty's science class.
- *The creative learner: knowledge and understanding as created or recreated.* Often, constructivists hold that learners need to create or recreate knowledge for themselves. It is not enough that they assume an active stance. Teachers should guide them to rediscover scientific theories, historical perspectives, and so on. Betty's history teacher hopes that the letter exercise will help students reconstruct the aristocratic perspective, and her science teacher hopes that the students' theories and experiments will build a strong understanding of why objects fall as they do.

It is natural to ask how the three constructivist roles relate to one another. An active role for the learner is basic, with social and creative aspects common but not inevitable accompaniments. Teachers can organise learning experiences in active ways that do not require learners to engage in testing and building knowledge in a social manner or to invent or reinvent theories or viewpoints. Betty's history teacher, wanting to get at the constructed character of truth, might have introduced the theme with examples and then asked students individually to analyse a portfolio of primary source materials from various constituencies with the theme in mind. Active, yes. Social and creative, no, not in D.C. Phillips's sense, although of course any astute analysis is to some extent creative. The social and creative elements certainly can contribute richly to learning; however, they are perhaps not as constitutive of constructivism as active learning.

Why – and why not – constructivism?

Why has constructivism enjoyed such advocacy for several decades? One reason is simply the search for better ways to teach and learn. With traditional methods, researchers and educators have noted persistent shortfalls in students' understanding and a great deal of passive knowledge across all ages and grades, including the university (Gardner 1991 offers a good synthesis).

A philosophical argument also supports constructivist educational practices. The stimuli that we encounter, including messages from others, are never logically sufficient to convey meaning. To some extent, the individual always has to construct or reconstruct what things mean. It only makes sense to organise learning to reflect this reality.

Another kind of argument looks to psychological sources (e.g. Bruer 1993; Gardner 1991; Perkins 1992a; Duffy and Jonassen 1992; Reigeluth 1999; Wilson 1996; Wiske 1998). Considerable research shows that active engagement in learning typically leads to better retention, understanding, and active use of knowledge. A social dimension to learning – what is sometimes called collaborative or co-operative learning – often, although not always, fosters learning. Sometimes, engaging students in discovery or rediscovery processes energises them and yields deeper understanding.

Such arguments certainly encourage constructivist practices. However, there is another side to the case. These practices often require more time than do more cut-and-dried educational methods – a cost worth paying, enthusiasts say, but many teachers feel the pressures and conclude that they need to make compromises. Asking learners to discover or rediscover principles can foster understanding, but learners sometimes persist in discovering the wrong principles – for instance, an idiosyncratic scientific theory. Strike and Posner (1985) argue that students are unlikely to forsake initial intuitive theories for more sophisticated ones based on the sorts of evidence they can turn up; too many conditions for conceptual change need to be met. Although ardent constructivists may argue that process is all, others believe that one way or another, students need to arrive at an understanding of the best theories propounded by the disciplines. Also, constructivist learning experiences can exert high cognitive demands on learners, and not all learners respond well to the challenge (Perkins 1992b). Constructivist techniques can even seem deceptive and manipulative. Betty Fable might sometimes find herself asking, 'Why don't you just tell me what you want me to know instead of making a big secret of it?' This is not always an unreasonable question.

Finally and relatedly, the learner's stance has tremendous importance. Entwistle (2003) summarises his own and colleagues' research on approaches to learning and studying. Some students adopt a deep approach, motivated by intrinsic interest, focused on building personal understandings, and achieved by building understandings through thoughtful analysis of ideas and evidence. Other students adopt a surface approach, motivated by fear of failure and extrinsic concerns, focused on minimal coping, and accomplished by memorisation and procedural learning. Another distinction concerns studying. Some students approach studying strategically, managing time carefully to attain high grades or other rewards, whereas others are less systematic.

While the teacher's way of organising material and activities influences these stances, students come with their own interests, dispositions, and skills. However constructivist the teaching, students not particularly interested in the topic or having difficulty with it may well adopt an unsystematic surface approach just to get by. Constructivism, in other words, is a choice that not only teachers but learners make. It takes two to tango.

The idea of troublesome knowledge

One approach to getting the most good out of constructivism is to ask what specifically it is good for. What particular educational challenges does it help us to address? The many kinds of knowledge we hope Betty Fable and other learners will master are troublesome in systematic ways. Students all over the world from middle school through university have trouble with Newtonian conceptions of motion. Students all over the world fall into presentism, seeing historical attitudes and choices through contemporary eyes. Students all over the world have trouble with systemic phenomena in Economics, Electronics, Population Dynamics, Biology, and other areas where 'emergent' effects occur as the collective consequence of many small interactions without any single guiding force or agent. However, what is obscure and tedious in the hands of one teacher may prove lucid and lively in the hands of another. Seasoned teachers know what troubles are likely and draw on active, social, and creative learning to address them. This helps to explain why artful constructivism looks different in different settings. It has a diagnostic character, the particular unguent for the ache of the day.

As noted earlier, students' approaches to learning are a powerful influence too. Some students will resort to rote memory and routine procedures as a way of coping. They will try to learn enough about ideas, explanations, and alternative perspectives to pass the test without developing any real insider feel. And pass they may, ending up with knowledge troubled by partial and brittle understandings that do not serve them beyond the compass of the course and its superficial credentials.

To elaborate on all this a bit, let us consider five sorts of trouble – ritual knowledge, inert knowledge, conceptually difficult knowledge, foreign knowledge, and tacit knowledge – and how constructivist teaching practices can help students with them.

Five kinds of troublesome knowledge

Ritual knowledge

Ritual knowledge has a routine and rather meaningless character (Perkins 1992a). It feels like part of a social or individual ritual: how we answer when asked such-and-such, the routine that we execute to get a particular result. Names and dates often are little more than ritual knowledge. So are routines in arithmetic – an analogue of misconceptions in science (Gardner 1991) – such as the notorious 'invert and multiply' to divide fractions.

A constructivist response to knowledge likely to become ritualised strives to make it more meaningful. For example, a teacher can wrap such knowledge in authentic problem-solving activities. Students can explore its rationale and utility through discussion, as in the discussion of simplification in Betty Fable's Algebra class. A teacher can sometimes involve students in surveying a large-scale story or historical episode or controversy that lends meaning to a piece of ritual knowledge. If Columbus 'discovered' America in 1492, what else was going on in the world at about that time? How did Columbus's activities interact in the following decades with other events in Europe and beyond?

Inert knowledge

Inert knowledge sits in the mind's attic, dusted off only when specifically called for by a quiz or a direct prompt (Bransford *et al.* 1989; Bereiter and Scardamalia 1985). A familiar and relatively benign example is passive vocabulary – words that we understand but do not use actively. Unfortunately, considerable knowledge that needs active use proves to be inert. Students commonly learn ideas about society and self but make few connections to today's news, citizenship responsibilities, or family life. Students learn scientific concepts but make few connections to the physical and biological worlds around them. Students learn techniques in Mathematics but fail to relate them to everyday applications or to their science studies. These are all problems with a venerable theme in learning theory called *transfer of learning*:

how knowledge and skill acquired in one context for one purpose impacts performance in other contexts for other purposes. A long history of research shows that transfer – particularly 'far' transfer where the initial learning and target applications differ greatly – occurs only partially and sporadically. However, conditions of learning that foster good initial mastery, diverse practice, and mindful abstraction can enhance transfer substantially (Bransford and Schwartz 1999; Salomon and Perkins 1989).

What is the constructivist response when knowledge is likely to become inert? One strategy is to engage learners in active problem solving with knowledge that makes connections to their world. Betty Fable's English Literature teacher asked her students to make connections between Frost's 'Acquainted with the Night' and episodes in their own lives. For another example, students studying basic machines (levers, pulleys, and so on) might find and analyse examples around their homes. Another approach is to engage students in problem-based learning, where they acquire the target concepts while addressing some medium-scale problem or project (Boud and Feletti 1991; Savery and Duffy 1996). The English Literature students might search out varied poems for a project on the theme 'poems of the nights of our lives'. Science students might build playful gizmos or useful gadgets that use basic machines.

Conceptually difficult knowledge

Serious university study in any discipline stages an encounter with conceptually difficult knowledge. Before students reach the university level they meet conceptually difficult knowledge, most commonly in Mathematics and Science, although it can occur in any subject area. Understanding objects in motion is a good example for students of any level (e.g. McCloskey 1983). Even university students often find it hard to grasp how objects in motion continue at the same rate in the same direction unless some force, such as friction or gravity, impedes them. They find it hard to believe that heavier objects fall at the same rate as lighter ones, air resistance aside. A mix of misimpressions from everyday experience (objects slow down automatically), reasonable but mistaken expectations (heavier objects fall faster), and the strangeness and complexity of scientists' views of the matter (Newton's laws; such concepts as velocity as a vector, momentum, and so on) stand in the way. The result is often a mix of misunderstandings and ritual knowledge. Students learn the ritual responses to definitional questions and quantitative problems, but their intuitive beliefs and interpretations resurface on qualitative problems and outside the classroom. Science education researcher Marcia Linn noted wryly what one student made of a Newtonian principle of motion: 'Objects in motion remain in motion in the classroom, but come to rest on the playground' (Linn 2002).

Perhaps the most common constructivist response is to arrange enquiry processes that confront students with discrepancies in their initial theories – either discrepancies between theory and observations (as in Betty Fable's experiments with falling objects) or logical discrepancies. For example, students commonly believe that a fly standing on a table pushes down but that the table does not push up on the fly, a violation of Newton's third law, which calls for equal and opposite forces. However, they believe that the same table does push up on a bowling ball sitting on it. Imagine the bowling ball shrinking down to fly size and weight. Where, all of a sudden, does the table stop pushing? Discussing such cases provides 'anchoring intuitions' that make the principle clear and provoke students to extend it (Clement 1993).

As with the bowling ball and fly example, it often helps to introduce learners to imagistic mental models or to invite them to invent their own (Gentner and Stevens 1983). It also often helps to engage learners with qualitative problems rather than with the solely quantitative ones that dominate some textbooks. Qualitative problems lead students to confront the character of the phenomenon rather than just to master computational routines. Such strategies may involve asking learners to rediscover the principle in some sense, but not necessarily. The teacher can instead introduce the principles directly and ask learners to test them and to use them to interpret phenomena in an active, exploratory way. Also engaging students in exploration and model building and *then* presenting the official story can be a powerful pattern of learning, yielding results superior both to a straight presentational style and to a straight discovery style (Bransford and Schwartz 1999).

Foreign or alien knowledge

Foreign or alien knowledge comes from a perspective that conflicts with our own. Sometimes the learner does not even recognise the knowledge as foreign. Noted earlier was the example of presentism in historical understanding: Students tend to view past events through present knowledge and values (Carretero and Voss 1994). Harry Truman's decision to drop the atomic bomb on Hiroshima may seem foolish to today's students. Perhaps it was vexed, but viewed through the knowledge and cultural mindsets of the era, it was hardly foolish. Other examples include value systems carried by different nationalities, faiths, and ethnic groups. How indeed did the French aristocracy view the Revolution, the question that Betty Fable encountered in her History class? To pose such a puzzle is not, of course, to recommend the aristocratic view, but it is to recognise that many situations in history, contemporary society, literature, and current science and technology allow multiple serious, sincere, and well-elaborated perspectives that deserve understanding.

What then are constructivist responses to foreign knowledge? We can ask learners to identify and elaborate alternative perspectives. We can provoke compare-and-contrast discussions that map the perspectives in relation to one another. This method may sometimes involve extensive investigation as students set out to research what other perspectives have to say. We can engage students in dialogues and debates that require representing different points of view. We can foster role-playing activities that ask students to get inside mindsets different from their own.

Tacit knowledge

Meyer and Land (2003) suggest that tacit knowledge is another important type of troublesome knowledge. Much of the knowledge we rely upon every day in both commonplace and professional activities is tacit; we act upon it but are only peripherally aware or entirely unconscious of it. The Chomskian machine keeps us speaking grammatically in our mother tongues, although we cannot directly introspect its mechanism or rules. Likewise, we often get the hang of enquiry in a discipline without having a clear reflective conception of what we are doing. For a personal example, I remember when sometime in the course of my university education I first got around to reading the ideas of Gyorgy Polya (1954, 1957) about mathematical problem solving. I had been studying formal Mathematics for years. I was truly startled to discover that I was using quite naturally and intuitively most of the problem-solving heuristics Polya profiled. Without ever labelling or listing them, somehow I had picked them up or cooked them up.

The role of tacit knowledge is one of those good news bad news stories. On the good news side, it is often very efficient for knowledge to function tacitly. Betty does not want to labour through tables of declensions to take her turn in a conversation or review mental lists of problem solving heuristics to do well in Maths. On the bad news side, learners' tacit presumptions can miss the target by miles, and teachers' more seasoned tacit presumptions can operate like conceptual submarines that learners never manage to detect or track. One general constructivist approach to this might be called 'surfacing and animating'. Get those tacit presumptions out on the table at least for a while, both the teacher's and the learners'. When Betty had to discuss her ideas about falling objects or simplification, this surfaced her tacit presumptions and allowed her teachers to examine them with her. And not just as objects of discursive analysis but as systems of activity to engage. The idea is not simply to know about the game but to play the game knowingly.

Of course, these are neither the only ways that knowledge can be troublesome nor the only constructivist responses possible. For instance, knowledge can be hard to remember – complex, with many pieces of information. Surprisingly, even this difficulty invites a constructivist response. Research shows that memory is better served by organising the information actively, looking for internal patterns and relating it to what you already know (Schacter 2001). Simple repetition is much less effective. Or knowledge can be full of seeming inconsistencies and paradoxes, as when art critics or scientists disagree. Or knowledge can be full of subtle distinctions, such as that between weight and mass. Add your own categories and your own constructivist responses, by all means.

How concepts make double trouble

It's natural to look for ritual, inert, conceptually difficult, foreign, and tacit knowledge among the important concepts presented by various disciplines. Indeed, concepts often make double trouble, on the one hand as categorisers and on the other as elements in activity systems of problem solving and enquiry.

Most fundamentally, concepts function as categorisers. They carve up the world we already see and often posit the unseen or even the unseeable. They sort things into plants and animals, living and dead, art nouveau and art deco, democratic and autocratic governments, the deductive and the inductive, velocity and mass and momentum. There is a huge gain right there. As Betty Fable learns a fresh conceptual system, a new world emerges. The pre-Freudian self does not look the same as the Freudian self with its id, ego, and superego; and in a post-Freudian era largely sceptical of these homunculi, the self looks different again. The categorical function of concepts also brings its distinctive troubles. Betty is likely to find a novel parsing of the familiar world confusing and confounding, for instance mixing up id and ego, or mass and weight.

Concepts as categorisers set the stage for a more elaborate function. Associated with clusters of concepts are activity systems or conceptual games that animate them. The Freudian self, if you believe it, provides a broad scaffold for interpretation, diagnosis, and treatment. The Newtonian toolkit provides a resource for analysing and predicting anything from galactic dynamics to the trajectories of artillery shells. Styles of art – Impressionism, Expressionism, Surrealism – provide ways of marking trends and tracing influences.

Although some of what is troublesome about knowledge squarely concerns the categorical function of concepts, much concerns the larger conceptual games around them. It is easy enough for Betty to understand in principle the concept of bias in historical sources but harder to make this knowledge active rather than inert, examining sources in an alert critical way for likely biases and adjusting the most probable story in an effort to correct for their influence. As with inert knowledge, so with ritual, conceptually difficult, foreign, and tacit knowledge – these troubles have as much to do with the activity systems that animate concepts as they do with concepts in their basic categorical functions.

From concept to episteme

Besides recognising the games of enquiry we play with particular concepts, it is important also to lift our eyes above the particular. The disciplines are more than bundles of concepts. They have their own characteristic *epistemes*. Betty Fable probably never heard the word episteme, but she deals with epistemes tacitly all the time. An episteme can be defined as a system of ideas or way of understanding that allows us to establish knowledge. Schwab (1978) and Bruner (1973) among others have emphasised the importance of students understanding the structure of the disciplines they are studying. 'Ways of knowing' is another phrase in the same spirit. As used here, epistemes are manners of justifying, explaining, solving problems, conducting enquiries, and designing and validating various kinds of products or outcomes.

The disciplines bring with them distinctive epistemes. In formal Mathematics theorems are one important product of enquiry and deductive validity within an axiomatic system that provides the principal test of soundness. In much of Science, theories are key products. The empirical disconfirmation of deliberate experiment filters out the bad theories, leaving what we hope are the good ones, although they may be dethroned in turn. In History, explanations for particular notable events and trends – say the Industrial Revolution – are one important kind of product. Evidence comes from not only broad principles but the nuanced and idiosyncratic particulars as evidenced by original sources and filtered by concerns about bias and misrepresentation. In branches of Engineering, effective designs find their validation in not just sets of principles but practical performance from prototypes to wide-scale field tests.

These epistemes make trouble for Betty just as do particular concepts. Learners often encounter difficulties playing the 'epistemic games', as they might be called, that go with the disciplines (Collins and Ferguson 1993; Perkins 1994, 1997). The place of formal deductive proof in Mathematics bewilders students happy with a confirmatory example or two. Literary interpretations that make sense of one or two lines of a poem seem good enough, never mind the rest (Richards 1929). The troubles multiply when learners encounter tacit tensions within a discipline about the right episteme – should we embrace a structuralist or post-modern idiom or what?

Happily, constructivist solutions make sense for troublesome epistemes much as they do for troublesome concepts. For instance, presentism in History, mentioned before as part of the general discussion of troublesome knowledge, is not so much a problem with the particular conceptual arsenal of historical analysis as with learners' naive approach to the *foreign* epistemic game of History, a game that asks people to set aside today's common knowledge and consider motives and perceptions indigenous to a remote period. Constructivist solutions such as deliberate comparison of familiar and foreign ways of thought, and deliberate immersion in foreign ways of thought, can help. Similarly, students of Science and Mathematics often display *ritualised* routines rather than genuine enquiry and problem solving. Authentic problem solving and problem-based learning that foreground the game of the discipline are constructivist practices that can help.

Difficulty with particular disciplinary concepts may derive from difficulty with the underlying episteme. Perkins and Grotzer argue that students' confusions about science concepts reflect not just the concepts per se but also the underlying causal models characteristic of them. For instance, areas of study as diverse as Biology, Climate, History, and Economics involve distributed or decentralised causation with emergent effects, whereas everyday life leads us to look for single principal causes (Grotzer 2003; Perkins and Grotzer 2005). Perhaps tacit knowledge is the most pervasive trouble with epistemes. Many teachers play the epistemic games of their professional disciplines fluently and automatically, and successful students ultimately need to do so as well. The problem is, many students never get the hang of it, or only slowly, because the epistemes receive little direct attention. For Betty and others, surfacing the game through analytic discussion and deliberative practice could make a big difference.

Alan Schoenfeld and his colleagues developed some revealing findings about the power of explicitness in studies of mathematical problem solving at the university level (Schoenfeld 1979, 1980; Schoenfeld and Herrmann 1982). A significant literature had emerged on good practices of mathematical problem solving, including the works of Polya (1954, 1957) mentioned earlier, but efforts to teach these practices had yielded erratic and ambiguous results. A systematic programme of research turned up what might be called the toolkit fallacy: providing the students with the toolkit of explicit heuristics would enable their effective use; instead, it was found that students also needed a self-management strategy to monitor their deployment of heuristics and their progress. Moreover, it was not enough for teachers to work model problems, they had to comment directly on the heuristics as they were deployed so students gained a situated sense of their utility. The combination of a self-management strategy and explicit modelling yielded a dramatic improvement in students' mathematical problem solving.

Threshold concepts

Betty Fable is acutely aware that there is a huge lot out there to learn, and quite grateful that her teachers do not expect her to learn all of it. Meanwhile, her teachers struggle to decide what will prove most meaningful and useful. Through their notion of threshold concepts, Meyer and Land (2003) offer an insightful perspective and a powerful heuristic for looking at this puzzle. Threshold concepts are pivotal but challenging concepts in disciplinary understanding. They act like gateways. Once through the gate, learners come to a new level of understanding central to the discipline. Among the examples mentioned by Meyer and Land are opportunity cost from Economics, limits and complex numbers for Mathematics, and signification within Literary and Cultural Studies.

A threshold concept is not necessarily troublesome by definition, the authors note. However, by definition transformative, a threshold concept is likely to seem foreign and conceptually difficult, get ritualised by students or indeed teachers, and in general present a hurdle. Earlier remarks about concepts in general apply to threshold concepts in particular. Besides their categorical functions, threshold concepts bring into play whole new patterns of enquiry, the games we play with the concepts. For the troubles that makes, the constructivist strategies mentioned earlier offer some assistance.

Also, threshold concepts certainly include more than particularly tough conceptual nuts in the content of a discipline. There are threshold epistemes that shape one's sense of entire disciplines. Certainly aware of all this, Meyer and Land note how learning the language of the discipline involves threshold-like transitions, as do the discipline's ways of thinking and practising.

The notion of limit in Mathematics illustrates both a threshold concept and a threshold episteme, affirming how difficulties with concept and episteme become intertangled. The definition of limit formalises the intuitive idea of getting closer and closer to a target value. A sequence of numbers approaches a particular limit L providing that for any ε (epsilon), however small, there exists a positive integer N such that all members of the sequence further along than N lie within ε of L. Poor Betty Fable! Those εs and Ns and Ls are likely to make her suffer. Betty gets befuddled partly because the definition is conceptually complex, but partly because it reflects the foreign episteme of formal Mathematics. Betty expects definitions to make new ideas sensible and accessible, and by this standard the definition of limit appears convoluted and arcane. But the game is different here. Viewed not as an elucidation but a proof kit, the definition is precise, elegant, and powerful. Does the limit hold? Well, imagine I have an arbitrarily small ε. Can I find that N? If I can, I've proved the limit.

Einstein is said to have quipped that it is not the job of a chemical analysis of a cup of tea to taste like the tea. The same applies to the definition of limits and many others in formal Mathematics. They aim not to 'taste like' their target concepts but to provide a proof kit. Betty will stay befuddled until she gets the hang of this different game.

Pragmatic constructivism

Often, the case made for constructivism seems resoundingly ideological. If learners do not rediscover Greek philosophy or Newton's laws for themselves, they will never truly understand them. To arrive at meaningful knowledge, they must learn through deep enquiry. As the unexamined life is not worth living, so the unexamined fact is not worth believing. And so on.

In contrast, the ideas assembled here are anything but ideological. They constitute a perspective on what makes knowledge troublesome and what constructivism can do about it. They warn that knowledge often has a ritual, inert, conceptually complex, foreign, or tacit character, or makes trouble in other ways. Concepts can prove difficult both in their categorical function and in the activity systems or 'games' of enquiry they support. Not only content concepts but the underlying epistemes of the disciplines make trouble for learners, with confusion about content concepts often reflecting confusion about the underlying epistemes.

In all cases, a constructivist response chosen to suit the challenge can help. Even so, while how to teach is the teacher's choice, how to learn is the student's choice. Despite lucid explanations and engaging activities, those learners who find themselves interested less and struggling more tend to make knowledge troublesome for themselves. Inevitably, the best constructivist teaching becomes an art of intellectual seduction, luring students into learning in ways deeper than those to which they might be disposed. This adds up to a view of learning we might call pragmatic constructivism. It invites us to treat constructivism as a toolbox for problems of learning. Troublesome knowledge of various kinds invites constructivist responses to fit – not one standard constructivist fix. If a particular approach does not solve the problem, try another – more structured, less structured, more discovery-oriented, less discovery-oriented, whatever works. And when knowledge is not particularly troublesome for the learners in question, well, forget about the active, social, creative learners of which D.C. Phillips wrote. Teaching by telling may serve just fine.

We began with Betty Fable's bewilderment about Constructivist Academy. In part, her confusion reflected the disparate constructivist moves she encountered in a day of classes, but it also marked a tension between ideological constructivism and pragmatic constructivism. The term constructivism, with its ideological overtones, suggests a single philosophy and a uniquely potent method – like one of those miracle knives advertised on late-night TV that will cut anything, even tin cans. We can look at constructivism in another way, more like a Swiss army knife with various blades for various needs. Indeed, for many teachers from the early grades to graduate study, the miracle-knife version of constructivism has become as tired over the years as those TV commercials. At Constructivist Academy and elsewhere, it's high time we got pragmatic about constructivism.

References

Bereiter, C. and Scardamalia, M. (1985) Cognitive coping strategies and the problem of inert knowledge. In S.S. Chipman, J.W. Segal and R. Glaser (eds) *Thinking and Learning Skills, Vol. 2: Current Research and Open Questions* (pp. 65–80). Hillsdale, NJ: Erlbaum.

Boud, D. and Feletti, G. (eds) (1991) *The Challenge of Problem-based Learning.* New York: St Martin's Press.

Bransford, J.D. and Schwartz, D.L. (1999) Rethinking transfer: A simple proposal with interesting implications. In A. Iran-Nejad and P.D. Pearson (eds) *Review of Research in Education* (Vol. 24, pp. 61–101). Washington, DC: American Educational Research Association.

Bransford, J.D., Franks, J.J., Vye, N.J. and Sherwood, R.D. (1989) New approaches to instruction: Because wisdom can't be told. In S. Vosniadou and A. Ortony (eds) *Similarity and Analogical Reasoning* (pp. 470–497). New York: Cambridge University Press.

Bruer, J.T. (1993) *Schools for Thought: A Science of Learning in the Classroom.* Cambridge, MA: MIT Press.

Bruner, J. (1973) The growth of mind. In J. Anglin (ed.) *Beyond the Information Given* (pp. 437–451). New York: Norton.

Carretero, M. and Voss, J.F. (eds) (1994) *Cognitive and Instructional Processes in History and the Social Sciences.* Hillsdale, NJ: Erlbaum.

Clement, J. (1993) Using bridging analogies and anchoring intuitions to deal with students' preconceptions in physics. *Journal of Research in Science Teaching,* 30(10), 1241–1257.

Collins, A. and Ferguson, W. (1993) Epistemic forms and epistemic games: Structures and strategies to guide inquiry. *Educational Psychologist,* 28(1), 25–42.

Duffy, T.M. and Jonassen, D.H. (eds) (1992) *Constructivism and the Technology of Instruction: A Conversation.* Hillsdale, NJ: Erlbaum.

Entwistle, N.J. (2003) Enhancing teaching–learning environments to encourage deep learning. In E. De Corte (ed.) *Excellence in Higher Education* (pp. 83–96). London: Portland Press.

Gardner, H. (1991) *The Unschooled Mind: How Children Think and How Schools should Teach.* New York: Basic Books.

Gentner, D. and Stevens, A.L. (eds) (1983) *Mental Models.* Hillsdale, NJ: Erlbaum.

Grotzer, T.A. (2003) Learning to understand the forms of causality implicit in scientific explanations. *Studies in Science Education,* 39, 1–74.

Linn, M. (2002) The role of customisation of innovative science curricula: Implications for design, practice, and professional development. Symposium at the annual meeting of the National Association for Research in Science Teaching, New Orleans, LA.

McCloskey, M. (1983) Naive theories of motion. In D. Gentner and A.L. Stevens (eds) *Mental Models* (pp. 299–324). Hillsdale, NJ: Erlbaum.

Meyer, J.H.F. and Land, R. (2003) Threshold concepts and troublesome knowledge: linkages to ways of thinking and practising within the disciplines. In C. Rust (ed.) *Improving Student Learning. Improving Student Learning Theory and Practice – Ten Years On* (pp. 412–424). Oxford: OCSLD.

Perkins, D.N. (1992a) *Smart Schools: From Training Memories to Educating Minds.* New York: Free Press.

Perkins, D.N. (1992b) What constructivism demands of the learner. In T.M. Duffy and D.H. Jonassen (eds) *Constructivism and the Technology of Instruction: A Conversation* (pp. 161–165). Hillsdale, NJ: Erlbaum.

Perkins, D.N. (1994) The hidden order of open-ended thinking. In J. Edwards (ed.) *Thinking: Interdisciplinary Perspectives.* Victoria, Australia: Hawker Brownlow Education.

Perkins, D.N. (1997) Epistemic games. *International Journal of Educational Research,* 27(1), 49–61.

Perkins, D.N. and Grotzer, T.A. (2005) Dimensions of causal understanding: The role of complex causal models in students' understanding of science. *Studies in Science Education*, 41, 117–166.

Phillips, D.C. (1995) The good, the bad, and the ugly: The many faces of constructivism. *Educational Researcher*, 24(7), 5–12.

Polya, G. (1954) *Mathematics and Plausible Reasoning* (2 vols.). Princeton, NJ: Princeton University Press.

Polya, G. (1957) *How to Solve It: A New Aspect of Mathematical Method* (2nd edn). Garden City, NY: Doubleday.

Reigeluth, C. (ed.) (1999) *Instructional Design Theories and Models: Volume II.* Mahwah, NJ: Erlbaum.

Richards, I.A. (1929) *Practical Criticism: A Study of Literary Judgment.* New York: Harcourt, Brace.

Salomon, G. and Perkins, D.N. (1989) Rocky roads to transfer: Rethinking mechanisms of a neglected phenomenon. *Educational Psychologist*, 24(2), 113–142.

Savery, J.R. and Duffy, T.M. (1996) Problem-based learning: An instructional model and its constructivist framework. In B.G. Wilson (ed.) *Constructivist Learning Environments: Case Studies in Instructional Design* (pp. 130–143). Englewood Cliffs, NJ: Educational Technology Publications.

Schacter, D.L. (2001) *The Seven Sins of Memory: How the Mind Forgets and Remembers.* New York: Houghton Mifflin.

Schoenfeld, A.H. (1979) Explicit heuristic training as a variable in problem solving performance. *Journal for Research in Mathematics Education*, 10(3), 173–187.

Schoenfeld, A.H. (1980) Teaching problem-solving skills. *American Mathematical Monthly*, 87, 794–805.

Schoenfeld, A.H. and Herrmann, D.J. (1982) Problem perception and knowledge structure in expert and novice mathematical problem solvers. *Journal of Experimental Psychology: Learning, Memory, and Cognition*, 8, 484–494.

Schwab, J. (1978) *Science, Curriculum, and Liberal Education: Selected Essays* (I. Westbury and N.J. Wilkof, eds). Chicago, IL: University of Chicago Press.

Strike, K. and Posner, G. (1985) A conceptual change view of learning and understanding. In L.H.T. West and A.L. Pines (eds) *Cognitive Structure and Conceptual Change* (pp. 211–232). New York: Academic Press.

Wilson, B.G. (ed.) (1996) *Constructivist Learning Environments: Case Studies in Instructional Design.* Englewood Cliffs, NJ: Educational Technology Publications.

Wiske, M.S. (ed.) (1998) *Teaching for Understanding: Linking Research with Practice.* San Francisco, CA: Jossey-Bass.

Chapter 4

Metacognition, affect, and conceptual difficulty

Anastasia Efklides

Introduction

The title of this chapter refers to two distinct categories of phenomena, namely metacognition and affect, and their relation with conceptual difficulty. The term 'metacognition' stands for what we call *cognition of cognition* (Flavell, 1979), whereas the term 'affect' represents emotions and other mental states that have the quality of pleasant–unpleasant, such as feelings, mood, motives, or aspects of the self e.g. self-esteem. These two sets of phenomena are related to learning as extant research has shown. However, most of the studies focus on aspects of metacognition and affect that are independent from each other, e.g. emotions or motives, on the one hand, and metacognition on the other. The emphasis of this chapter is different: it is on metacognitive experiences (ME), which are the joint product of metacognition and affect, and are distinct from emotions or other affective states as well as from other forms of metacognition (see Figure 4.1). The relationship of ME with threshold concepts is denoted by the third component of the chapter's title. Our research is predominantly focusing on mathematical concepts some of which – e.g. ratio – can be considered threshold concepts in the sense that they are critical for the acquisition of a range of other notions in mathematics.

In what follows, I shall refer to metacognition and its various facets, namely metacognitive knowledge, metacognitive skills, and ME. Then, I will focus on ME and their conceptualization, on the effects of several factors on them, particularly of affective ones, as well as on the function of ME and their relevance to the learning process, particularly in cases of threshold concepts. Finally, I shall discuss the implications of this evidence for instruction.

The main point of this chapter is that ME form an indispensable part of the learning process and they contribute to it both directly by activating control processes and indirectly by influencing the self-regulation process that determines whether the student will get engaged in threshold concepts or not.

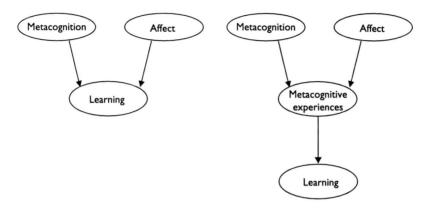

Figure 4.1 Metacognition, affect, and learning: two different approaches.

The various facets of metacognition

It has been repeatedly argued that metacognition is a fuzzy concept and needs to be 'refined, clarified, and differentiated' (Flavell, 1987, p. 28). Following Nelson (1996; Nelson and Narens, 1994), we can define metacognition as a model of cognition, which acts at a meta-level and is related to the object-world (i.e. cognition) through the monitoring and control function. The meta-level is informed by the object-world through the monitoring function and modifies the object-world through the control function (see Figure 4.2). In the relevant literature one can identify three distinct facets of metacognition, namely metacognitive knowledge, metacognitive experiences, and metacognitive skills.

- *Metacognitive knowledge* is declarative knowledge about cognition. It is knowledge we derive from long-term memory (Flavell, 1979; Hertzog and Dixon, 1994). It comprises knowledge or beliefs about the *person* him/herself and the others as cognitive beings, and their relations with various cognitive tasks, goals, actions, or strategies. It also comprises knowledge of *tasks* (i.e. categories of tasks and their processing) as well as knowledge of *strategies* (i.e. when, why, and how to deal with a task) (Flavell, 1979). Besides this, it involves knowledge (i.e. beliefs, theories) about the various *cognitive functions*, such as memory or thinking, regarding what they are and how they operate (e.g. metamemory, see Flavell, 1979; Wellman, 1983; for theory of mind, see Fabricius and Schwanenflugel, 1994). Finally, it comprises knowledge of the *criteria of validity of knowledge*, what is called 'epistemic cognition' (Kitchener, 1983).
- *Metacognitive experiences* (ME) are what the person experiences during a cognitive endeavor. Metacognitive experiences form the *online awareness*

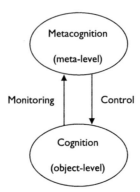

Figure 4.2 The conceptualization of metacognition following Nelson (1996).

of the person as s/he is performing a task (see also 'concurrent metacognition': Hertzog and Dixon, 1994). They comprise feelings, judgments or estimates, as well as online task-specific knowledge, i.e. awareness of the instructions and features of the task at hand associated with metacognitive knowledge that pertains to the processing of the task (Efklides, 2001; Flavell, 1979). Metacognitive experiences differ from metacognitive knowledge because they are present at working memory, they are specific in scope, and they are affectively charged. The affective character of ME is particularly evident in metacognitive feelings. Metacognitive feelings and metacognitive judgments or estimates are the exemplars of ME par excellence (Efklides, 2001).

- *Metacognitive skills* are what the person deliberately does to control cognition. It is procedural knowledge. It involves the executive processes of metacognition (Brown, 1978). For example, monitoring of the comprehension of task requirements, planning of the steps to be taken for problem solving, checking, regulation of processing when it fails, and evaluation of the outcome of the processing (Veenman and Elshout, 1999). Metacognitive skills differ from metacognitive knowledge of strategies because metacognitive knowledge is declarative knowledge that does not automatically lead to appropriate control behaviors. Metacognitive skills also differ from ME because ME monitor online processing and they provide input that activates control processes, such as effort regulation or use of cognitive and metacognitive strategies (i.e. metacognitive skills).

In educational research the emphasis has traditionally been on metacognitive knowledge and metacognitive skills. However, to the dismay of researchers it was found that teaching of metacognitive skills does not generalize to other tasks easily and metacognitive knowledge of strategies correlates moderately (from 0.23 to 0.42) with the use of strategies (Georgiadis and Efklides, 2000; Schneider, 1985). Furthermore, there are students with learning difficulties who do not benefit from the teaching of metacognitive skills at all (Brown, 1978; Brown and Lawton, 1977; Vauras *et al.*, 1999). This suggests that it is not only metacognitive knowledge that activates metacognitive skills and secures effective use of strategies. Other aspects of metacognition may also be involved; ME represent one of the missing links as experimental research on metamemory has shown (Nelson and Narens, 1994; Reder, 1987).

Besides metacognition, the person's self-concept in a knowledge domain (Dermitzaki and Efklides, 2000, 2002), affect, and motivation also contribute to the exercise of control processes as research on self-regulation has shown (Borkowski *et al.*, 2000; Georgiadis and Efklides, 2000; Pintrich *et al.*, 1991). This viewpoint places strategy use in a self-regulation context, and this is correct. Nevertheless, what is still missing is the understanding of the mechanism that underpins the self-regulatory process. Our approach aims at showing the relevance of ME to self-regulation. In this way we can understand better the monitoring and control functions of metacognition and how they are related to cognition, affect, and volition.

Metacognitive experiences

Metacognitive experiences (ME) are the interface between the person and the task. They monitor the person's response to the task at hand, the fluency of cognitive processing, and the extent to which the goal set has been accomplished (Efklides, 2001, 2002a; Frijda, 1986). One of the most well-studied ME is feeling of knowing (Koriat, 1994; Nelson, 1984). It is related to the tip of the tongue phenomenon (Hart, 1965), i.e. to the feeling that we have something in memory but cannot retrieve it. Other ME are the feeling of familiarity (Whittlesea, 1993), the judgment of learning (Leonesio and Nelson, 1990), the feeling of difficulty (Efklides *et al.*, 1997, 1998; Efklides *et al.*, 1999), the feeling of confidence (Costermans *et al.*, 1992), the judgment of solution correctness and the feeling of satisfaction (Efklides, 2002a). All the above ME are expressions of the monitoring of cognitive processing from the moment the task is presented to its conclusion (see Table 4.1).

Specifically, feeling of familiarity monitors the fluency of cognitive processing with respect to stimulus recognition and provides the information that processing is possible or not. Feeling of difficulty monitors the interruption of processing and summons the need for corrective action. Judgment of learning and judgment of solution correctness along with feeling of confidence and feeling of satisfaction monitor the outcome of processing. Judgment of solution correctness focuses on the quality of the answer, i.e. correct or incorrect. Feeling of confidence monitors how the person reached the answer – fluently or with interruptions, and feeling of satisfaction monitors whether the answer meets the person's criteria and standards as regards the quality of the answer (Efklides, 2002a).

The above clustering of ME around the three basic phases of cognitive

Table 4.1 A model representing phases of cognitive processing and the corresponding ME and MS

Cognitive processing	Metacognitive experiences	Metacognitive skills

Stimulus recognition
Processing of task
   instructions
	Feeling of familiarity
	Feeling of knowing
	Estimates of when and where
	   the information was acquired
	   (source memory)
		Monitoring of
		   comprehension

Planning	Feeling of difficulty	Planning Allocation of resources

Use of cognitive strategies/
   carrying out the planned
   action
	Feeling of difficulty
	Estimate of effort
	Estimate of time spent on
	   the task
		Checking
		Regulation of processing
		Use of metacognitive
		   strategies

Response	Judgment of learning Judgment of solution correctness Feeling of confidence Feeling of satisfaction	Evaluation of outcome

processing, that is, *initiation, planning and execution*, and *output*, is based on evidence coming from our work. We have found that ME are interrelated and form systems, so that changes in one of the ME changes the others as well (Efklides, 2002a, b). Specifically, feeling of familiarity is interrelated with estimate of recency and of frequency of previous encounters with the stimulus as well as with other source memory attributions (Efklides *et al.*, 2000; Efklides *et al.*, 1996; Mitchell and Johnson, 2000). Feeling of difficulty correlates with estimate of effort expenditure and time (to be) spent on the task, while estimate of solution correctness with feelings of confidence and satisfaction (Efklides, 2002b). Furthermore, feeling of familiarity influences feeling of difficulty (Efklides *et al.*, 1996) and feeling of difficulty contributes to the estimate of solution correctness and feeling of confidence (Figure 4.3) (Efklides, 2002a).

Factors influencing metacognitive experiences

In our research we have focused basically on feeling of difficulty as experienced during maths problem solving. However, as ME are interrelated and form systems, we have also included in our studies measures of other ME as well. Based on the assumption that ME form the interface between the person and the task, we investigated the effects of task difficulty and a person's characteristics on ME.

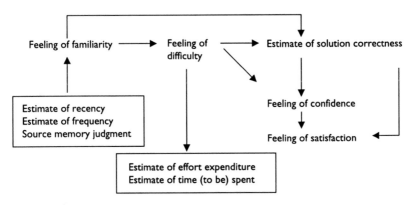

Figure 4.3 Relations between metacognitive experiences.

Task difficulty

Task difficulty is usually defined in terms of performance success (Brehm and Self, 1989). However, there are various sources of task difficulty, such as task complexity, task conceptual demands, and task context. Task complexity is defined by the number of operations, or steps, required for its processing. Task conceptual demands are defined by the cognitive demands of the concepts involved in the task – e.g. from a developmental point of view, acquisition of rational numbers follows the acquisition of integers and operation on integers. Task context is defined by the presentation form, by the structuring of the task, by the environmental noise, etc. (Efklides *et al.* 1997, 1998; Paas and van Merrienboer, 1994).

Feeling of difficulty monitors task difficulty but cannot be reduced to it. We found that judgments of feeling of difficulty (i.e. rating on a scale how much difficulty the person experienced), in the main, reflect the complexity or processing demands of tasks. Specifically, the objectively more difficult tasks give rise to higher feeling of difficulty than less difficult tasks (Efklides *et al.*, 1997, 1998; Efklides, 2002b). Yet, feeling of difficulty may be flawed. In other words, there can be 'illusions of feeling of difficulty'. Thus, objectively difficult tasks (in terms of mean performance on them) are perceived as easy depending on whether they look familiar or not. This often happens only at the beginning of task processing. When students, for instance, go on to solve the problem and monitor the qualities of processing, i.e. fluency or disruption, they change their initial feeling of difficulty judgment (Efklides, 2002b; Efklides *et al.*, 1996).

Similar types of 'illusions' have been identified with respect to feeling of familiarity (Whittlesea, 1993), feeling of understanding (Stark *et al.*, 2002), and judgment of one's level of performance (Krueger and Mueller, 2002). It seems that the more ignorant or unskilled one is in a domain, the more unaware one is of the conceptual and processing demands of the task. This implies that the goals – and standards – set for task processing and perform-ance are lower than the true demands of the task and this has an impact on the judgment of feeling of difficulty and of the effort invested on the task. (Whether the overestimate of performance of the low scorers is a metacogni-tive deficit or a product of a general better-than-average heuristic is an inter-esting issue, pertaining to the processes underlying the formation of ME (see Efklides, 2001; Krueger and Mueller, 2002).)

However, despite the 'illusions' people may have about their cognition, monitoring of processing fluency or interruption is continuous and updated from the beginning of task processing to its end. The judgments of ME are revised based on inferential processes that make use of information from task features and prior task knowledge (i.e. familiarity and metacognitive know-ledge) as well as on features of the actual task processing (that is, fluency or interruption of processing). We should point out here that there are students who do not revise their feeling of difficulty judgment in light of actual task processing. This happens when they rely on other persons guiding them how to deal with the task (Efklides *et al.*, 1999). What is also highly interesting is the finding that young children of 5 to 6 years of age also show sensitivity to task difficulty but only in tasks with which they have previous experience (Gonida *et al.*, 2003).

Instructional mode

Instructional mode is another factor that has an impact on feeling of dif-ficulty and other ME. Instructional mode regards task presentation, task structure, practicing on the task, use of worked-out examples, providing explanations, etc. In a study we performed with worked-out examples (Efklides *et al.*, 2006) we found that they facilitated performance on maths problems as compared to traditional presentation of the problems without any form of assistance. However, depending on the type of worked-out example we used, there were different effects on students' performance, self-explanations, and ME. This was due to the fact that various types of worked-out examples imposed different levels of *extraneous* cognitive load, that is, load caused by task-presentation form (Paas and van Merrienboer, 1994). The traditional way of presenting problems with the initial problem space and the goal state only given is imposing more extraneous load than worked-out examples do because it requires more memory search and use of working memory capacity (van Merrienboer *et al.*, 2002)

According to cognitive load theory (Sweller, 1988), tasks have inherent cognitive load called *intrinsic* load caused by the task processing demands. Conceptual difficulty and complexity can be considered as sources of intrinsic cognitive load (Efklides *et al.*, 1997, 1998). Threshold concepts can be conceived as instances of high intrinsic load. Therefore, acquisition of threshold concepts may be inhibited if extraneous cognitive load is also high.

Extraneous cognitive load is added to intrinsic cognitive load and interferes with learning when the task-processing demands exceed the person's capacity; feeling of difficulty and estimate of effort reflect the task-processing demands on capacity. However, the evidence coming from our study (Efklides *et al.*, 2006) suggests that students of the control group failed the task not because extraneous cognitive load was high but because they did not realize the conceptual difficulty of the task and its demands on capacity. Therefore, they did not invest effort on the task.

Worked-out examples, on the other hand, increased awareness of the task-processing demands and facilitated performance. The use of explicit sub-goals guiding the solution process had the best effect on performance, but increased cognitive load much more than another type of worked-out example we used that presented a heuristic schema for the solution of the problem. This type of worked-out example had equally good results as regards performance, but the experienced difficulty and estimate of effort expenditure was much lower than in the case of the sub-goals solution.

Task context

Task context has to do with the task 'environment', in which the task is embedded. The structuring of task sequence, for example, can impact feeling of difficulty because it provides a basis for comparison. We found that judgments of feelings of difficulty are comparative in nature, because tasks that precede or follow moderate them (Efklides *et al.*, 1997, 1998). Another contextual factor is the affective tone of task instructions, that is whether they stress the difficulty or the interestingness of it. Affective cues in task presentation and instructions contribute to the moderation of feeling of difficulty (Efklides and Aretouli, 2003).

Affective context

The affective context, as created by task instructions, the person's mood, or the feedback provided, influences the reported ME. Specifically, in three studies of ours we found that affective context is important but it interacts with the type of task and with person factors such as self-concept. In the first study (Efklides and Aretouli, 2003) we found that girls with *low* self-concept in maths, as compared to boys with similar self-concept and level of performance in maths, responded more favorably to instructions stressing the 'interestingness' of the task, whereas boys to instructions stressing the 'difficulty' of the task. Specifically, girls reported higher feeling of liking, lower feeling of difficulty and estimate of effort, and higher judgment of solution correctness, feeling of confidence and feeling of satisfaction in the context of 'interest' than in the context of 'difficulty'. The opposite occurred for boys. Furthermore, there was no gender effect in ME in the case of drawing tasks.

In another study (Efklides and Petkaki, 2005), we tested the effect of mood induction on maths performance and ME. Negative mood mainly predicted the initial or prospective ME, such as feeling of difficulty, estimate of effort expenditure, and estimate of solution correctness, whereas positive mood predicted interest. However, as students got engaged in problem solving, there was self-regulation of affect, so that all the reported ME *after* problem solving were predicted by both positive and negative mood, except for feeling of satisfaction that was predicted only by positive mood.

Finally, in a third study (Efklides and Dina, 2004) we tested the effect of positive (success) or negative (failure) extrinsic feedback on maths performance and ME. We found that the valence of extrinsic feedback had an immediate impact on the ME reported after it was provided, as well as after a period of time when students were asked to solve the problems again. Students who received positive extrinsic feedback – irrespective of their actual performance – reported higher effort expenditure and higher feeling of satisfaction in the second testing than in the first one. The opposite happened with students who received negative extrinsic feedback. Our findings suggest that the positive or the negative affect generated by extrinsic feedback activated self-processes that had an effect on students' interpretation and attributions of their ME. These self-processes along with a re-assessment of task-processing demands led to the modulation of the reported ME in the second testing, despite the fact that the task was the same.

All these findings suggest that threshold concepts may fail to be evaluated as such if the task presentation mode or the task context increase the cognitive load for their processing or mask their significance in case other secondary task features take over the person's attention. Students' negative affect may also exaggerate the difficulty felt and decrease the satisfaction gained from engagement with the task.

Person characteristics

However, 'task effects' is not the only factor that impacts ME. Cognitive ability as well as personality factors seem to have an effect on reported feeling of difficulty and other ME. In our research we found that there is low to moderate correlation between domain-free and domain-specific cognitive ability, on the one hand, and feeling of difficulty and other ME, on the other (Efklides *et al.*, 1997, 1998; Efklides *et al.*, 2006; Efklides and Petkaki, 2005). There is also an indirect effect of domain-specific cognitive ability on all ME through its relationship with domain-specific self-concept (Efklides and Tsiora, 2002). Dispositional factors, such as anxiety trait and nAch (need for achievement) (Efklides *et al.*, 1997, 1998; Metallidou and Efklides, 1998) may also have an effect on ME. However, dispositional factors interact with objective task difficulty, and their effects are small.

Self-concept

Self-concept and its facets, namely self-perception, self-esteem, self-efficacy, and others' perception of one's ability seem to be critical for ME. We found (Dermitzaki, 1997; Dermitzaki and Efklides, 2000, 2001) that self-efficacy influenced the estimate of solution correctness, self-perception influenced feeling of difficulty, while others' perception of one's self influenced the reported estimate of effort and use of strategies.

Metacognitive person knowledge

Metallidou (1996; Metallidou and Efklides, 1998) showed that metacognitive knowledge of one's self as cognitive processor affects the judgment of solution correctness and feeling of satisfaction, but not feeling of difficulty.

Overall, our research suggests that the more students get engaged in a knowledge domain the more aware they become of their ME and of their capability to deal with task demands. Also, students become able to calibrate the ME vis-à-vis performance on each particular task and its conceptual, procedural, or context demands. However, the effects of extant domain-specific self-concept, personality dispositions (ability included), and situation-specific factors make the calibration of ME difficult to achieve.

Relations of metacognitive experiences with performance

One of the basic criteria for the determination of the accuracy of a reported ME is its relationship with performance (Efklides, 2002b; Nelson, 1996). In our studies we found that feeling of difficulty consistently covaries with performance and so do the ME that monitor the outcome of processing. However, feeling of difficulty correlates with performance mainly in the case of tasks of moderate difficulty (Efklides *et al.*, 1998). It seems that in the case of very familiar or very easy tasks, where processing is automatic, there is no awareness of processing features. Therefore, judgments of feeling of difficulty may be based on irrelevant or extrinsic cues, such as mode of task presentation or other situational characteristics that do not have a real effect on performance. In the case of very difficult tasks, the reported feeling of difficulty is also highly fallible, because there is no or very little actual processing that could provide cues for the determination of one's feeling of difficulty (see Koriat, 1994, for feeling of knowing). Thus, the person experiences high feeling of difficulty that cannot be attributed to some specific feature of the task processing.

The relationship of estimate of solution correctness, of feeling of confidence and of feeling of satisfaction with performance is not so much influenced by task difficulty as feeling of difficulty is. It is influenced by person factors such as cognitive ability, self-concept, and gender (Dermitzaki and Efklides, 2001; Efklides and Aretouli, 2003; Metallidou, 1996). This is particularly evident in maths, where girls, at least in younger ages, perform similarly with boys, report similar level of feeling of difficulty with that of boys, and yet they are less confident and less satisfied with their performance than boys are (Efklides *et al.*, 1996). This, however, does not occur in the case of other school subjects, such as drawing, where no negative stereotype exists about girls (Efklides and Aretouli, 2003).

It can be concluded, then, that metacognitive feelings and other metacognitive judgments are products of inferential processes based on complex interactions of task, person, and context factors. Context effects may range from those of the socio-cultural environment to situational, task, and affective context (Dermitzaki and Efklides, 2001; Volet and Jarvela, 2001). Furthermore, ME themselves form an *intrinsic context* that affects other ME both during task processing and later on, when the person comes across the same or similar tasks.

The function of metacognitive experiences

Monitoring

As we have already mentioned, ME monitor cognitive processing and its outcome. The way this is done is still not known. Its complex feedback loops and inferential processes are similar in many respects to those involved in social judgments (Efklides, 2001; Koriat and Levy-Sadot, 1999; Yzerbyt *et al.*, 1998). Yet, what the person is aware of is the outcome of the monitoring process in the form of metacognitive feelings and estimates/judgments or task-related knowledge that are present in working memory. In particular, the metacognitive feelings through their hedonic quality inform the person of whether processing is running smoothly and fluently or not as well as whether the processing outcome matches the person's concerns or not.

There are two things we should point out here: first, metacognitive feelings are momentary and transient and therefore they often go unnoticed; they may hardly reach awareness – to the extent processing has no interruptions (for the rapid feeling of knowing see Reder, 1987). If, however, they persist and are salient enough to draw the person's attention, then they become conscious and call for conscious control decisions (Efklides, 2001; Koriat and Levy-Sadot, 1999). Thus, metacognitive feelings are nonconscious and nonanalytic as to their formation but trigger conscious analytic processes once they reach awareness.

Second, because the processes that give rise to metacognitive feelings and estimates/judgments are nonconscious, it is often very difficult for the person to explain why they are feeling that way. Thus, the person may feel difficulty in task processing and still not be able to explain where the difficulty is coming from. That is, the person cannot exactly describe which aspect of the problem gave rise to the feeling of difficulty. Consequently, they have to infer this information. Extant metacognitive knowledge regarding the task plays a crucial role here. Lack of previous knowledge or expertise with a task leads often to superficial or wrong attributions, whereas more experienced persons are better able to identify the processing features that are relevant to the ME experienced. This explains why the reasons the students give about how they solve a problem hardly correlate with the ratings of their ME (Efklides *et al.*, 2006).

Control

Monitoring is of no use unless it triggers control processes. Research on metamemory as well as our research on maths problem solving has shown the relevance of ME to strategy use and to knowledge of strategies (Efklides *et al.*, 1999; Nelson and Narens, 1994; Reder, 1987). Metacognitive experiences contribute to control decisions in two ways: (a) directly, by activating cognitive and metacognitive strategies; (b) indirectly, by providing information to the database of metacognitive knowledge. This metacognitive knowledge regards the task (e.g. task complexity or conceptual demands); the person (e.g. the person's relations with the task, namely successful/unsuccessful solution of the tasks, difficulty experienced); and strategy (e.g. strategies used, conditions related to strategy use, etc.). Then, the metacognitive knowledge is used to guide strategy selection and use in the future.

In the first case, ME by monitoring task-demands, on the one hand, and task-related procedural information activated in memory, on the other, trigger the cognitive processes needed for the processing of the task. This can be done rapidly, without explicit, analytic awareness of the processes or cognitive strategies activated (Reder, 1987). Regulation of effort and time as well as commands for the initiation or termination of processing are also examples of this direct effect of ME on control processes (Nelson and Narens, 1994).

The triggering of online control processes can also be carried out explicitly at a conscious level, when the person becomes aware of feeling of difficulty, of feeling of understanding, or of feeling of knowing, of judgment of learning, etc. The conscious/analytic activation of cognitive strategies in this case is mediated by metacognitive knowledge regarding cognitive strategies and the conditions for their use (Efklides *et al.*, 1999). Metacognitive skills are also involved if the person deliberately monitors and regulates the application of cognitive strategies (see Hacker, 1998; Veenman and Elshout, 1999).

It can be concluded, then, that ME trigger online control decisions as the person deals with a task (direct effect) and indirectly by informing and updating metacognitive knowledge that is used in subsequent encounters with similar tasks.

Self-concept and causal attributions

A third function of ME is their contribution to self-concept and to attributions regarding task performance. In this way they affect the person's motivation. Specifically, Dermitzaki and Efklides (2001, 2002) showed that ME in maths and verbal problems are influenced by the person's respective domain-specific self-concept, that is the self-concept specific to the domain of knowledge in which the task belongs. Efklides and Tsiora (2002) showed that ME also feed back on the domain-specific self-concept and modify it via a task-specific self-concept. This is due to the fact that ME provide to the person intrinsic feedback about their own capability to deal with specific tasks – e.g. difficulty experienced, effort expended, confidence and satisfaction felt. In this way the person maintains self-consistency and stability of self.

Metallidou and Efklides (2001), on the other hand, showed that ME also contribute to the causal attributions regarding one's own performance. In this study that involved maths problem solving we found that feeling of confidence after task processing had been completed contributed to the attribution of ability. Also, the experienced need for 'thinking' or 'doing computations' in order to solve the problem, which indicates working memory activity, contributed to the attribution of effort. This suggests that it is mental load that is critical for the attribution of effort. Feeling of difficulty along with estimates of effort and time or 'need for having previous practice with a task' contributed to the attribution of task difficulty. The experienced 'need for help from others' contributed to the attribution of luck. Therefore, the sources upon which causal attributions are drawing are partly performance outcome and, partly, metacognitive feelings or estimates and metacognitive knowledge regarding the task and the relations of the person with it. It remains to be seen if and how these attributions influence the person's self-concept and future involvement with similar tasks.

Metacognitive experiences and the learning process

Up to now we have shown that ME are the interface between the person and the task and form an integral part of the self-regulation process. They monitor cognitive processing as it takes place and trigger online control processes in light of perceived task demands, the context, the person's ability and affective state as well as self-processes. Furthermore, they contribute to long-term self-regulation of learning via their effect on self-concept, attributions, and metacognitive knowledge.

However, such a description of the function of ME provides only the general framework of the relations of ME with the learning process. In order to understand the exact ways in which ME contribute to learning we need to look at the details of the interactions of ME with control and regulation processes. Specifically, we need to remember three things: first, that all ME are inferential in nature. Second, that metacognitive feelings and metacognitive judgments/estimates are hard to analyze and to locate their true determinants. Third, that ME can trigger control processes either directly and rapidly without the mediation of analytical processes, or indirectly, via the person's metacognitive knowledge, based on analytical and reflective processes.

Metacognitive experiences, context, and learning

What does the inferential character of ME imply for learning? It implies that even small changes in the phrasing or in the context of the task may have an effect on ME. Social psychology work on familiarity and judgment formation has underscored this (Yzerbyt et al., 1998). Our research on the manipulation of the affective context of the task is another example (Efklides and Aretouli, 2003; Efklides and Dina, 2004; Efklides and Petkaki, 2005). This kind of data may explain, for instance, why the teacher's enthusiasm can have an effect on students' learning: it increases situational interest particularly among the less able students and, by lowering the perception of difficulty or effort needed, increases their engagement with the task. Thus the teacher's enthusiasm helps students gain in confidence and satisfaction.

Adult or peer collaboration and/or teachers' scaffolding (Vygotsky, 1978), that is, the social context and practices of learning, can also help students overcome the initial feeling of difficulty and engage with a learning task. Scaffolding helps them 'learn' from their own experiences and regulate their effort. If, on the other hand, the adult or the peer group provides ready-made answers purporting to enhance performance rather than mastery, then students do not learn to regulate their effort because they do not update their ME in face of actual problem-solving demands.

Another strategy that can be used to alleviate the difficulty experienced in task processing is the increase of the familiarity with the task; it helps students enter the learning process, because they think the task is not so difficult. Of course, students will subsequently revise their judgment of feeling of difficulty as processing goes on, but this is helpful because they come to realize that 'looking familiar' does not necessarily mean availability of procedures or knowledge.

Metacognitive experiences and effort

Feeling of difficulty, on the other hand, as well as judgment of learning, is related to effort (Efklides, 2002b; Nelson and Leonesio, 1988). A highly unfamiliar and/or complex stimulus that raises high feelings of difficulty suggests lack of available responses, and therefore task processing and effort is abandoned. Moderate difficulty, as implied by existing familiarity with the stimulus – even an illusory one – increases effort because it suggests that interruption of processing can be restored. Low feeling of difficulty, on the other hand, implies no need for increased effort. One consequence of this fact, in teaching practice, is the following: if we provide students only with tasks that are easy – that is, tasks very similar to what we taught – or even moderate in difficulty, then these tasks after limited practice become very familiar. The result is that feeling of difficulty decreases and no further effort is invested. Providing students with more difficult tasks, however, makes them aware that effort needs to be sustained (Bjork, 1994).

The use of worked-out examples is another means to alleviate students' mental effort caused by intrinsic and extraneous cognitive load. Worked-out examples also impose cognitive load, called *germane cognitive load* (Sweller *et al.*, 1998). Germane cognitive load, although it is added to intrinsic and extraneous cognitive load, is beneficial to learning because it helps students integrate a problem-solving schema that they can use on other occasions as well. Worked-out examples increase germane cognitive load but their efficiency is limited if they do not decrease extraneous cognitive load. Otherwise, the high overall (intrinsic, extraneous, and germane) cognitive load exceeds students' capacity and may have adverse affects on learning.

Indeed students' affective responses and ME along with performance are good indicators of the efficiency of the instructional method. However, the teacher's perception of students' ME may be incorrect because teachers often think that failing students experience difficulty although this is not necessarily true (Salonen *et al.*, 2005). Students may not feel difficulty if they are not aware of task demands or have illusions of understanding. Besides the factors that impact short-term task-specific effort, learning also requires persistence, that is, long-term effort in face of obstacles. Feeling of confidence seems to contribute to persistence in learning.

Feeling of confidence and learning

Feeling of confidence is related (a) to feeling of difficulty, (b) to performance, and (c) to estimate of solution correctness. This implies that for a person who has no epistemic knowledge, i.e. criteria for judging the properties of knowledge and of processing outcome, the only cue that is available for building his/her feeling of confidence is feeling of difficulty. As a consequence, students who have limited knowledge base and reach an answer quickly and with no experience of difficulty, feel very confident in their response although it is wrong – this leads to overconfidence and lack of further effort. On the other hand, a person who has the required knowledge base as well as criteria for judging their knowledge, also feels little difficulty, and high confidence; unlike the previous group, however, their performance is correct. Further investment of effort in this case will be associated with epistemic criteria rather than just the metacognitive feelings experienced. Finally, persons, who have adequate knowledge base but do not have a readily available response to the task or do not have relevant epistemic knowledge to judge their response, experience difficulty, invest effort, and may come to a correct response. Yet, although the response is correct the person does not feel confident – this leads to underconfidence. Underconfidence may undermine in the long run the effort to be invested to the task.

What seems to help people moderate their confidence is the repeated practice with a task, so that the experienced difficulty decreases and they can accurately judge the correctness of their response. A characteristic example of this phenomenon is young students who start counting and use their fingers to reach the answer. Teachers and parents put pressure on young students to learn the mathematical facts and reach the response using their memory rather than external means. This demand makes the child experience difficulty because the relevant knowledge is not readily available. Therefore, children use at this point of learning memory search as well as counting with fingers (see Siegler, 1986). The use of counting with fingers ceases when it is no longer needed, that is, when the answer comes fluently and the children feel confident in their answer. Indeed, extended experience with related tasks is the 'medicine' for overconfidence as well. Becoming aware of interruptions of processing – i.e. experiencing difficulty – where overconfidence dictates that no such difficulty should exist, makes the person more able to calibrate their judgment of confidence (see also Allwood and Granhag, 1996).

Feeling of satisfaction and learning

A related issue is the satisfaction one feels after engaging in the processing of a task. Feeling of satisfaction is associated with judgment of solution correctness and confidence. However, it also involves judgment that performance meets certain criteria or standards that go with the goal (Efklides, 2001, 2002a). These criteria are personal, social, or epistemic. As a consequence, the relationship of feeling of satisfaction with performance and with the other relevant ME may vary depending on whether the person does have such standards or not, on how imperative the standards are, on situational considerations, or even on social criteria and on gender. For example, girls are known to be less confident and less satisfied than boys in maths even when their performance is equal to boys' (Metallidou and Efklides, 1998; Pajares and Valiante, 2002).

The non-epistemic criteria for satisfaction can be found in young children or people who are unskilled. They experience a strong feeling of satisfaction because they produced an answer, even if it is wrong, and producing an answer brought them closer to their goal; this discrepancy reduction produced positive affect perceived as satisfaction (Carver et al., 1996). Thus, although young children correctly judge the difficulty of a task, and this judgment is predicted by their performance (Gonida et al., 2003), the satisfaction they express is not predicted by their performance. This is probably so because they put their own goals or standards onto the task – i.e. a game in this particular study. Indeed what children often do when they fail a task is to change and adapt the task goal to their own level of capability, so that finally they are wrong in their response but satisfied with themselves because they did manage to reach their goal. The opposite probably happens with perfectionists, who put so high standards that they can hardly ever meet them.

Accuracy of metacognitive monitoring and learning

Another issue that is important for learning is the relation of ME with performance, that is the accuracy of metacognitive monitoring (Thiede *et al.*, 2003). This issue has created a lot of discussions (Pressley and Schneider, 1998) because there is mixed evidence about it. However, there are some implications that are worth mentioning. For example, awareness of feeling of difficulty is most accurate at moderate difficulty tasks (Efklides *et al.*, 1997, 1998). Thus, for experts who work on difficult tasks without processing interruption, feeling of difficulty is low and so is the experience of effort. As a consequence, they do not analyze their thought processes and ME. It is exactly the opposite with novices, who experience great difficulty but cannot explain where the difficulty comes from. This creates a ME asymmetry between experts and novices, or teachers and students, or parents and children having a bearing on the control processes that are to be activated. The question is: can experts predict what the ME of novices are and adapt their explanations and/or their instruction to the novices' needs? More research is needed in this direction (Salonen *et al.*, 2005).

Conclusions

The aim of this chapter was to show the relevance of ME to learning of threshold concepts. The argument is that lack of engagement with threshold concepts is partly a cognitive phenomenon and partly metacognitive. Students, on the one hand, may have or not have the cognitive background to process threshold concepts and to integrate them into their conceptual repertory and, on the other, their ME 'misinform' them over the processing demands of such concepts.

Specifically, our research has shown that the more students get engaged in a knowledge domain, the more aware they become of their capability to deal with the concepts and procedures specific to that domain. They also become aware of the features and processing demands of the tasks that presuppose these concepts. Thus, they make informed decisions how to regulate their learning in order to advance their skills or quit learning efforts. Students who continue to work are the 'ideal' students. These students realize the importance of threshold concepts and invest effort on them based on intrinsic feedback and intrinsic motivation from their ME.

'Ideal students' are, however, the very minority. The majority of students will follow different routes. One route is followed by students who, despite their competence in a knowledge domain, underestimate their capability, overestimate the difficulty experienced and effort invested, lack confidence and, finally, gain no satisfaction from engagement with task in that domain. These students will not work on threshold concepts or they will only do it if they have to. Yet, they will not capitalize on their work.

Another route is the one followed by students with low domain-specific knowledge who overestimate their performance and underestimate the difficulty of the threshold concepts and the effort needed to process them. Thus, when they fail, they do not know how to deal with it and give up any attempt to work with these concepts.

Our presentation of the nature and function of ME tried to make clear how closely connected is cognition, metacognition, motivation, and affect. The relationship of ME with self-concept and causal attributions shows that what is task-specific can become part of the person's dispositional characteristics and have long-term effects on students' willingness to learn and to regulate their learning. Affect preceding or following engagement with learning tasks can also impact the ME and interest in the short and long run. Thus, situational affect can promote or undermine interest in a domain and through it involvement with learning tasks.

Yet, it would be wrong to assume that students' ME are totally individual phenomenon based only on students' interaction with the task. Interaction with peers and teachers is also important. The role of teachers is multifaceted and impacts on students' cognition, affect, and ME. These effects are produced by the teachers' personality as well as by their instructional methods and the cognitive load they impose on students. This implies that student engagement with threshold concepts is the teacher's as much as the student's responsibility. Future research will elucidate the conditions that can make the teacher mentor of their students' learning.

References

Allwood, C. M. and Granhag, P. A. (1996) Considering the knowledge you have: Effects of realism in confidence judgments. *European Journal of Cognitive Psychology*, 8, 235–256.

Bjork, R. A. (1994) Memory and metamemory considerations in the training of human beings. In J. Metcalfe and A. Shimamura (eds), *Metacognition: Knowing about Knowing* (pp. 185–205). Cambridge, MA: Bradford.

Borkowski, J. G., Chan, L. K. S. and Muthukrishna, N. (2000) A process-oriented model of metacognition: Links between motivation and executive functioning. In G. Schraw and J. C. Impara (eds), *Issues in the Measurement of Metacognition* (pp. 1–43). Lincoln, NE: Buros Institute of Mental Measurements.

Brehm, J. W. and Self, E. A. (1989) The intensity of motivation. *Annual Review of Psychology, 1989*, 109–131.

Brown, A. L. (1978) Knowing when, where and how to remember: A problem of metacognition. In R. Glaser (ed.), *Advances in Instructional Psychology* (pp. 77–165). New York: Halsted Press.

Brown, A. L. and Lawton, S. C. (1977) The feeling of knowing experience in educable retarded children. *Developmental Psychology*, 13, 364–370.

Carver, C. S., Lawrence, J. W. and Scheier, M. F. (1996) A control-process perspective on the origins of affect. In L. L. Martin and A. Tesser (eds), *Striving and Feeling* (pp. 11–52). Mahwah, NJ: Erbaum.

Costermans, J., Lories, G. and Ansay, C. (1992) Confidence level and feeling of knowing in question answering: The weight of inferential process. *Journal of Experimental Psychology: Learning, Memory, and Cognition*, 18, 142–150.

Dermitzaki, I. (1997) The relations and the dimensions of self-concept and level of cognitive development with school performance [in Greek]. Unpublished doctoral dissertation, Aristotle University of Thessaloniki, Greece.

Dermitzaki, I. and Efklides, A. (2000) Self-concept and its relations with cognitive and metacognitive factors regarding performance in specific domains of knowledge. *Psychology: The Journal of the Hellenic Psychological Society*, 7, 354–368.

Dermitzaki, I. and Efklides, A. (2001) Age and gender effects on students' evaluations regarding the self and task-related experiences in mathematics. In S. Volet and S. Jarvela (eds), *Motivation in Learning Contexts: Conceptual Advances and Methodological Implications* (pp. 271–293). Amsterdam: Elsevier.

Dermitzaki, I. and Efklides, A. (2002) The structure of cognitive and affective factors related to students' cognitive performance in language and maths. *Psychology: The Journal of the Hellenic Psychological Society*, 9, 58–74.

Efklides, A. (2001) Metacognitive experiences in problem solving: Metacognition, motivation, and self-regulation. In A. Efklides, J. Kuhl, and R. M. Sorrentino (eds), *Trends and Prospects in Motivation Research* (pp. 297–323). Dordrecht, The Netherlands: Kluwer.

Efklides, A. (2002a) The systemic nature of metacognitive experiences: Feelings, judgments, and their interrelations. In M. Izaute, P. Chambres, and P.-J. Marescaux (eds), *Metacognition: Process, Function, and Use* (pp. 19–34). Dordrecht, The Netherlands: Kluwer.

Efklides, A. (2002b) Feelings as subjective evaluations of cognitive processing: How reliable are they? *Psychology: The Journal of the Hellenic Psychological Society*, 9, 163–184.

Efklides, A. and Aretouli, E. (2003) Interesting, difficult, or an exercise for the mind? The effect of the affective tone of the instructions on metacognitive experiences and self-concept [in Greek]. In A. Efklides, A. Stogiannidou, and E. Avdi (Vol. eds), *Scientific Annals of the Faculty of Philosophy, School of Psychology, Aristotle University of Thessaloniki: Vol. 5. Volume in memory of M. Maniou-Vakali* (pp. 287–322). Thessaloniki, Greece: Art of Text.

Efklides, A. and Dina, F. (2004) Feedback from one's self and from the others: Their effect on affect. *Hellenic Journal of Psychology*, 1, 179–202.

Efklides, A. and Petkaki, C. (2005) Effects of mood on students' metacognitive experiences. *Learning and Instruction*, 15, 415–431.

Efklides, A., Kiorpelidou, K. and Kiosseoglou, G. (2006) Worked-out examples in mathematics: Effects on performance and metacognitive experiences. In A. Desoete and M. J. Veenman (eds), *Metacognition and Mathematical Problem Solving.* Hauppauge, NY: Frank Columbus Nova Science.

Efklides, A., Pantazi, M. and Yazkoulidou, E. (2000) Factors influencing the formation of feeling of familiarity for words. *Psychology: The Journal of the Hellenic Psychological Society*, 7, 207–222.

Efklides, A., Papadaki, M., Papantoniou, G. and Kiosseoglou, G. (1997) The effects of cognitive ability and affect on school mathematics performance and feelings of difficulty. *American Journal of Psychology*, 110, 225–258.

Efklides, A., Papadaki, M., Papantoniou, G. and Kiosseoglou, G. (1998) Individual differences in feelings of difficulty: The case of school mathematics. *European Journal of Psychology of Education*, 13, 207–226.

Efklides, A., Samara, A. and Petropoulou, M. (1996) The micro- and macro-development of metacognitive experiences: The effect of problem-solving phases and individual factors. *Psychology: The Journal of the Hellenic Psychological Society*, 3(2), 1–20.

Efklides, A., Samara, A. and Petropoulou, M. (1999) Feeling of difficulty: An aspect of monitoring that influences control. *European Journal of Psychology of Education*, 14, 461–476.

Efklides, A. and Tsiora, A. (2002) Metacognitive experiences, self-concept, and self-regulation. *Psychologia: An International Journal of Psychology in the Orient*, 45, 222–236.

Fabricius, W. V. and Schwanenflugel, P. J. (1994) The older child's theory of mind. In A. Demetriou and A. Efklides (eds), *Intelligence, Mind, and Reasoning: Structure and Development* (pp. 111–132). Amsterdam: North Holland.

Flavell, J. H. (1979) Metacognition and cognitive monitoring – A new era of cognitive-developmental inquiry. *American Psychologist*, 34, 906–911.

Flavell, J. H. (1987) Speculations about the nature and development of metacognition. In F. E. Weinert and R. H. Kluwe (eds), *Metacognition, Motivation and Understanding* (pp. 21–29). Hillsdale, NJ: Erlbaum.

Frijda, N. (1986) *The Emotions.* Cambridge: Cambridge University Press.

Georgiadis, L. and Efklides, A. (2000) The integration of cognitive, metacognitive, and affective factors in self-regulated learning: The effect of task difficulty. *Psychology: The Journal of the Hellenic Psychological Society*, 7, 1–19.

Gonida, E., Efklides, A. and Kiosseoglou, G. (2003) Feeling of difficulty and confidence during preschool and early school age: Their relations with performance and image of cognitive self. *Psychology: The Journal of the Hellenic Psychological Society*, 10, 515–537.

Hacker, D. J. (1998) Definitions and empirical foundations. In D. J. Hacker, J. Dunlonsky, and A. C. Graesser (eds), *Metacognition in Educational Theory and Practice* (pp. 1–23). Mahwah, NJ: Erlbaum.

Hart, J. T. (1965) Memory and the feeling-of-knowing experience. *Journal of Educational Psychology*, 56, 208–216.

Hertzog, Ch. and Dixon, R. A. (1994) Metacognitive development in adulthood and old age. In J. Metcalfe and A. Shimamura (eds), *Metacognition: Knowing about Knowing* (pp. 227–251). Cambridge, MA: Bradford.

Kitchener, K. S. (1983) Cognition, metacognition and epistemic cognition: A three level model of cognitive processing. *Human Development*, 4, 222–232.

Koriat, A. (1994) Memory's knowledge of its own knowledge: The accessibility account of feeling of knowing. In J. Metcalfe and A. Shimamura (eds), *Metacognition: Knowing about Knowing* (pp. 115–136). Cambridge, MA: Bradford.

Koriat, A. and Levy-Sadot, R. (1999) Processes underlying metacognitive judgments. Information-based and experience-based monitoring of one's own knowledge. In S. Chaiken and Y. Troppe (eds), *Dual Process Theories in Social Psychology* (pp. 483–502). New York: Guilford.

Krueger, J. and Mueller, R. A. (2002) Unskilled, unaware, or both? The better-than-average heuristic and statistical regression predict errors in estimates of own performance. *Journal of Personality and Social Psychology*, 82, 180–188.

Leonesio, R. J. and Nelson, T. O. (1990) Do different metamemory judgments tap the same underlying aspects of memory? *Journal of Experimental Psychology: Learning, Memory, and Cognition*, 16, 464–470.

Metallidou, P. (1996) Cognitive abilities and cognitive-affective aspects of the self in adolescence: Structure and development [in Greek]. Unpublished doctoral dissertation, Aristotle University of Thessaloniki, Greece.

Metallidou, P. and Efklides, A. (1998) Affective, cognitive, and metamemory effects on the estimation of the solution correctness and the feeling of satisfaction from it [in Greek]. *Psychology: The Journal of the Hellenic Psychological Society*, 5, 53–70.

Metallidou, P. and Efklides, A. (2001) The effects of general success-related beliefs and specific metacognitive experiences on causal attributions. In A. Efklides, J. Kuhl, and R. Sorrentino (eds), *Trends and Prospects in Motivation Research* (pp. 325–347). Dordrecht, The Netherlands: Kluwer.

Mitchell, K. J. and Johnson, M. K. (2000) Source monitoring: Attributing mental experience. In E. Tulving and F. I. M. Craik (eds), *The Oxford Handbook of Memory* (pp. 179–195). Oxford: Oxford University Press.

Nelson, T. O. (1984) A comparison of current measures of the accuracy of feeling-of-knowing predictions. *Psychological Bulletin*, 95, 109–133.

Nelson, T. O. (1996) Consciousness and metacognition. *American Psychologist*, 51, 102–116.

Nelson, T. O. and Leonesio, R. J. (1988) Allocation of self-paced study time and the 'labor-in-vain effect'. *Journal of Experimental Psychology: Learning, Memory, and Cognition*, 14, 676–686.

Nelson, T. O. and Narens, L. (1994) Why investigate metacognition? In J. Metcalfe and A. Shimamura (eds), *Metacognition: Knowing about Knowing* (pp. 1–25). Cambridge, MA: Bradford.

Paas, F. G. W. C. and van Merrienboer, J. J. G. (1994) Variability of worked examples and transfer of geometrical problem-solving skills: A cognitive-load approach. *Journal of Educational Psychology*, 86, 122–133.

Pajares, F. and Valiante, G. (2002) Students' self-efficacy in their self-regulated learning strategies: A developmental perspective. *Psychologia: An International Journal of Psychology in the Orient*, 45, 211–221.

Pintrich, P. R., Smith, O. A., Garcia, T. and McKeachie, W. J. (1991) *A Manual for the Use of the Motivated Strategies for Learning Questionnaire (MLSQ)*. Ann Arbor, MI: The Regents of the University of Michigan.

Pressley, M. and Schneider, W. (1997) *Introduction to Memory Development during Childhood and Adolescence*. Mahwah, NJ: Erlbaum.

Reder, L. M. (1987) Strategy selection in question answering. *Cognitive Psychology*, 19, 90–138.

Salonen, P., Vauras, M. and Efklides, A. (2005) Social interaction: What can it tell us about metacognition and co-regulation in learning? *European Psychologist*, 10, 199–208.

Schneider, W. (1985) Developmental trends in the metamemory – memory behavior relationship: An integrative review. In D. L. Forrest-Pressley, G. E. MacKinnon, and T. Gary Waller (eds), *Metacognition, Cognition, and Human Performance: Vol. 1. Theoretical Perspectives* (pp. 57–109). San Diego, CA: Academic.

Siegler, R. S. (1986) *Children's Thinking*. Englewood Cliffs, NJ: Prentice Hall.

Stark, R., Mandl, H., Gruber, H. and Renkl, A. (2002) Conditions and effects of example elaboration. *Learning and Instruction*, 12, 39–60.

Sweller, J. (1988) Cognitive load during problem solving: Effects on learning. *Cognitive Science*, 12, 257–285.

Sweller, J., van Merrienboer, J. J. G. and Paas, F. G. W. C. (1998) Cognitive architecture and instructional design. *Educational Psychology Review*, 10, 251–296.

Thiede, K. W., Anderson, M. C. M. and Therriault, D. (2003) Accuracy of metacognitive monitoring affects learning of texts. *Journal of Educational Psychology*, 95, 66–73.

van Merrienboer, J. J. G., Schuurman, J. G., de Croock, M. B. M. and Paas, F. G. W. C. (2002) Redirecting learner's attention during training: Effects on cognitive load, transfer test performance and training efficiency. *Learning and Instruction*, 12, 11–37.

Vauras, M., Kinnunen, R. and Rauhanummi, T. (1999) The role of metacognition in the context of integrated strategy intervention. *European Journal of Psychology of Education*, XIV, 555–569.

Veenman, M. and Elshout, J. J. (1999) Changes in the relation between cognitive and metacognitive skills during the acquisition of expertise. *European Journal of Psychology of Education*, XIV, 509–523.

Volet, S. and Jarvela, S. (eds) (2001) *Motivation in Learning Contexts: Conceptual Advances and Methodological Implications*. Amsterdam: Elsevier.

Vygotsky, L. S. (1978) *Mind in Society. The Development of Higher Psychological Processes*. Cambridge, MA: Harvard University Press.

Wellman, H. M. (1983) Metamemory revised. In M. Chi (ed.), *Trends in Memory Development Research: Contributions to Human Development* (pp. 31–51). Basel, Switzerland: Karger.

Whittlesea, B. W. A. (1993) Illusions of familiarity. *Journal of Experimental Psychology: Learning, Memory, and Cognition*, 19, 1235–1253.

Yzerbyt, V. Y., Dardenne, B. and Leyens, J.-Ph. (1998) Social judgeability concerns in impression formation. In V. Y. Yzerbyt, G. Lories, and B. Dardenne (eds), *Metacognition: Cognition and Social Dimensions* (pp. 126–156). London: Sage.

Chapter 5

Threshold concepts

How can we recognise them?

Peter Davies

Introduction

Successful undergraduates acquire 'ways of thinking and practising in a subject' (McCune and Hounsell, 2005). They are inducted into ways of understanding the world that are shared by a community of scholars. The idea that undergraduate teaching introduces students to a 'way of thinking' is often cited. For example, many introductory Economics courses include the following quotation from Keynes (1973, p. 856): 'The theory of economics does not furnish a body of settled conclusions immediately applicable to policy. It is a method rather than a doctrine, an apparatus of the mind, a technique of thinking which helps its possessor to draw correct conclusions.'

However, the phrase 'way of thinking' can be interpreted in several different ways. Most introductory Economics courses refer to certain 'key' or 'fundamental' concepts that contain the 'core of the discipline'. Here, the 'way of thinking' is interpreted as 'applying the key concepts'. A second approach locates a 'way of thinking' in the learner's understanding of particular phenomena. The individual who is 'inside the discipline', who possesses this way of thinking, sees and experiences phenomena in a particular way. Threshold concepts offer a third interpretation that chooses to extend the phrase to 'way of thinking and practising'. This approach can be distinguished from either of the other two in terms of the way it characterises subject learning and in its implications for teaching. In particular, it embraces the processes that members of a subject community typically use in their investigations as well as the particular conceptions that bind understanding in their subject into a coherent way of thinking. Ways of *thinking* in a subject necessarily entail particular ways of *practising*.

It is difficult to provide an account of this relationship without approaching it from the perspective of ways of thinking *or* ways of practising. Scholarship on argument in higher education (e.g. Andrews and Mitchell, 2001) has approached the relationship through the practice of argumentation. The idea of threshold concepts encourages us to approach the relationship from the perspective of ways of thinking. There is much that is shared by these two approaches. Both reject any idea that a subject community's 'way of thinking and practising' can be simply reduced to the acquisition of a set of distinct concepts or skills. It is the way in which such concepts are related, the deep-level structure of the subject which gives it coherence and creates a shared way of perceiving that can be left unspoken. This shared way of perceiving is the ideology a subject, 'the invisible structures and beliefs by which we operate and which appear as natural unchallengeable ways of doing things' (Mitchell, 2001, p. 2).

Both these approaches to 'ways of thinking and practising' also emphasise the sense in which learning is an entrance into a community. The act of learning is an act of identity formation. In coming to see the world in a particular way learners associate themselves with a community of people who share that way of thinking and practising and through this they position themselves in relation to others inside and outside of that community. A student can accumulate knowledge about a community and the ideas that are commonly accepted in that community, but this falls short of acquiring the way in which members of that community see the world. When asked to explain a given theory, or to cite extracts from a body of received knowledge, they may be able to do this perfectly well. But when asked to look around them they do not see the world as viewed by a member of a subject community.

Both approaches also suggest that teaching should encourage a subject-specific pedagogy that aims to expose the 'ground rules' (Sheeran and Barnes, 1991) or, as Perkins (Chapter 3) refers to them in this volume, 'epistemes', so that these become a focus for dialogue between teachers and learners. Whilst the argumentation approach starts with an intention to expose the forms of argument that are considered valid in a subject community, the idea of threshold concepts starts with an intention to reveal integrating ways of thinking that presuppose the validity of certain forms of argument. Without this openness the interaction between teachers and learners is shrouded in a mystery that ultimately deprives many learners of an opportunity to experience the way of thinking and practising that is apparently being offered to them. They just cannot see it.

This chapter concentrates on the processes by which threshold concepts may be identified. The first two sections of the chapter focuses on the teacher or lecturer's identification of threshold concepts in the subject they are introducing to students. In the third section attention switches to the learner's identification of threshold concepts. The common theme through the chapter is that threshold concepts, by their 'taken-for-granted' nature, tend to be obscured from overt dialogue between teachers and learners. Learners who acquire an understanding of threshold concepts do so by reading 'between the lines'. This characteristic of threshold concepts creates difficulties for the task of identification. In trying to overcome these difficulties the chapter uses the subject community of Economics as an example and it begins by *contrasting* the search for threshold concepts with the search for 'key concepts' and variation in understanding of particular phenomena.

Three approaches to defining 'a way of thinking' in a subject

This section compares three approaches to defining a 'way of thinking' in a subject: application of key concepts; a way of understanding particular phenomena; and threshold concepts.

Applying key concepts

In the case of Economics the interpretation of a way of thinking as application of key concepts can be attributed to two bodies of thought. First, the notion that some concepts are 'key' to the discipline is central to accounts of the history of the discipline and debates about its future. For example, during the twentieth century there were sustained debates about whether choice should be depicted as an individual or a social phenomenon (Marchionatti, 2002) and whether choice should be viewed as a subjective experience (Littlechild, 2005). In these debates the concept of opportunity cost was central to dialogue between economists about the nature of their subject. The second influential body of thought has been Bruner's (1960, 1966) application of Piagetian theory to subject understanding and curriculum design. Economics educators enthusiastically took up the idea that the curriculum should be designed as a spiral based upon recurring and deepening understanding of key concepts (e.g. Lumsden and Attiyeh, 1971).

This conjunction brings distinctiveness to the 'applying key concepts' approach to defining a way of thinking in a subject. The key concepts identified by this approach are the outcomes of debate *within* the subject. Scarcity and opportunity cost were identified as key economic concepts through debate intended to establish the primacy of one view of economics rather than another. In subsequent debate economists (e.g. Buchanan, 1979, 1982; Heilbroner, 1987) who have questioned the neo-classical version of the subject argued that other concepts should be regarded as key or fundamental to the subject. This raises a question as to whether economists from different schools of thought share a 'way of thinking'. If they do, then the 'key concepts' identified through internal debate within a subject may not capture this very well. A shared way of thinking does not require debate. It can be left implicit.

A second characteristic of the 'application of key concepts' approach is that learners are introduced to 'key concepts' in a simplified form at the outset of their studies. In later work they progress to learning more complex versions of the same concept and learn how to apply the concepts in a range of contexts. This approach has been identified as problematic in that it leads to teaching that is successful in helping students to learn theoretical representations of concepts, but fails to enable students to apply these concepts in making sense of problems or experience (Lee, 1986; Levačić, 1987). In response to these difficulties, economics educators in the USA developed an economic decision-making framework designed to guide students to apply concepts in the context of an evaluation of costs and benefits (Sumansky, 1986). Economics educators in the UK have tended to look beyond the 'applying concepts' approach in order to deal with this problem. Hodkinson and Thomas (1984) suggested a decision-making framework as the core of economic thought, without any reference to 'applying concepts'. The authors of the Economics 16–19 Project (McCormick *et al.*, 1994) describe the approach set out by Sumansky as 'theory-first'. They advocate a reversal of this process such that students are asked first to analyse examples (or phenomena) in order to expose their current understanding.

Phenomenography and variation in ways of understanding

Phenomenographers avoid the 'theory-application' problem by defining distinct conceptions in terms of relations between the mind of the individual and the world they experience. 'Conceptions are conceived as relational phenomena rather than as inherent qualities in the mind of the thinker or in the objects/phenomena themselves' (Säljö, 1988, p. 44). Variation in students' conception of price remains a frequently cited example of the phenomenographic approach. Two main conceptions were identified. The first treats price as 'the true value of the bun' and the second treats price as the outcome of supply and demand (Dahlgren, 1984).

Answers in category one are described as 'object-orientated' and 'commonly found in everyday situations', whilst answers in category two are described as 'recognising the system dependency of price'. The distinction is characterised in terms of a grasp of a system of relationships and this can be viewed as another approach to defining a 'way of thinking'. The distinction between common-sense and discipline-based ways of understanding the world in Economics is equivalent to those found by other studies in science (Marton, 1988; Bowden *et al.*, 1990). It is difficult to imagine how any individual could experience price in terms of the outcome of supply and demand before the idea of market equilibrium had been developed by the community of economists. Even supposing that an individual achieved this insight, it is inconceivable that anyone else would be able to recognise it as such because a body of language and analysis through which understanding of the idea could be shared had not been developed. That is, ways of understanding a phenomenon are generated through reflection by communities on those phenomena and the creation of a new way of understanding may be influential in establishing a new sense of community identity. Nevertheless, this community identity is likely to be built on a systemic understanding and shared assumptions that go well beyond understanding of an individual phenomenon.

Consequently, analysis of students' talk about one particular phenomenon may only give partial insight into their systematic thinking about relationships. A student who has been taught about the arguments for expecting 'sticky prices' in markets with stable competition might also reply to the question (of the bun) by saying that the price reflected the cost of production. Moreover, a student who accepts neo-classical analysis of markets and competition might respond that the price reflects the cost on the basis of an unstated assumption that the market was fully competitive. That is, the category of 'cost being equal to price' may roughly correspond to three ways of thinking about price.

Without reference to Dahlgren's original interview transcripts it is difficult to judge how these distinctions might have been represented in students' talk or how they were interpreted in the researchers' process of classification. By using a category of description which treats price as determined by cost Dahlgren implies an internal structure which has a unique set of external relations (Marton and Booth, 1997), but this condition is violated where there are competing schools of thought. In these circumstances it is very difficult for researchers to avoid devising categories of description which are suggested by *their own conception* of the nature of a discipline given the dictum that individuals are unaware of the basis of their own perceptions.

Threshold concepts

Threshold concepts provide a third way of describing the 'way of thinking' distinctive to a discipline. Following the approach taken in the introduction to this chapter, the five characteristics of threshold concepts (Meyer and Land, 2003) can be seen in the light of 'joining a community'. The transformative character of threshold concepts reflects the way in which they can change an individual's perception of themselves as well as their perception of a subject. In gaining access to a new way of seeing, an individual has access to being part of a community. The irreversibility of a threshold concept makes it inconceivable that they would return to viewing not only the world around them, but also a subject community and themselves, in the way they did before. The integrative quality of a threshold concept is critical to these first two characteristics. When an individual acquires a threshold concept the ideas and procedures of a subject make sense to them when before they seemed alien. It is the threshold concept that provides coherence. Fourth, a threshold concept necessarily helps to define the boundaries of a subject area because it clarifies the scope of a subject community. Finally, a threshold concept is very likely to be troublesome (Perkins, 1999) because it not only operates at a deep integrating way in a subject, but it is also taken for granted by practitioners in a subject and therefore rarely made explicit.

For example, Adnett and Davies (2002) show how non-economists have tended to view parental quest for a 'good education' for their children as a simple zero-sum game. 'If one child secures a place at a "good school" it is necessarily at the expense of another.' An economist would anticipate some supply-side responses and peer effects within and beyond school. That is, parental choices may lead to a change in the number of 'good schools' as a result of the effect of incentives on schools' behaviour and a redistribution of the benefits of learning with more able students. These uncertainties associated with these effects make the prediction of non-zero sum game outcomes far more difficult. An economist is working here with a concept of general equilibrium which is not a typical feature of educated common sense. Ideas like this may be thought troublesome not only because their integrative nature makes them difficult to learn, but also because they make the world appear a more troublesome place in the sense that it is more complex and difficult to understand.

General equilibrium is a transformative concept because it changes the way an individual thinks about the consequences of economic events. Situations which had previously appeared to be zero-sum games no longer appear so, and the outcomes of a decision can no longer be evaluated on the basis of immediate effects. The systemic effects have to be considered. The concept of general equilibrium is also irreversible and integrative. It is integrative because it provides a framework for thinking about economies as systems and this characteristic makes the concept irreversible. In fact, these first three characteristics seem mutually interdependent. It is because the concept is integrative that it is also transformative and irreversible. It is difficult to imagine how a concept could possess one of these characteristics without the others. General equilibrium also helps to define the boundaries of Economics. Economists who reject the notion of 'closed system' general equilibrium as defined by neo-classical economists nevertheless recognise the interrelatedness of markets. Moreover, versions of Economics that reject neo-classical general equilibrium are defined at least in part as departures from that notion.

The integrative characteristic of the concept also makes it troublesome. The original Brunerian 'fundamental concepts' purport to be self-contained. It is conceivable that a novice learner should be introduced to fundamental concepts at the outset of their study in order to acquire building blocks which will serve as foundations for their later understanding. A threshold concept is conceived in a quite different way. From the point of view of the expert, it is an idea which gives shape and structure to the subject, but it is inaccessible to the novice. In fact, it may be counter-intuitive in nature and off-putting. It can appear to be a denial of the world which the student experiences and it may therefore lead to the student rejecting the subject as 'abstract' and 'meaningless' (Levačić, 1987). Before a student can grasp a threshold object they must first acquire pieces of declarative knowledge and understanding which can later be integrated. The power and value of the threshold concept can only be recognised by a student if they can see how it is able to act in an integrative way.

There are two sources of trouble here for the teacher. First, if a threshold concept is introduced too early it is inaccessible to the student and it can only be learnt in a rote fashion which emphasises its lack of real meaning to the student. Second, once a student has acquired sufficient knowledge and understanding to make it possible for the concept to play an integrative role, the teacher has to help students to re-interpret their current ideas in the light of the threshold concept. This is a major undertaking and, if it fails, the student fails to truly 'get inside' the subject. In either case the teacher and the student may settle for the *appearance* of understanding which is all that can be achieved if the threshold concept is not acquired.

Comparing three definitions of a 'way of thinking' in a subject

At this point we might ask whether these definitions are three ways of looking at the same idea. Does the idea of a 'threshold concept' generate a new perspective on each of the 'key concepts' previously identified in a subject or does it generate a new set of categories altogether? Does the idea of a 'threshold concept' correspond to particular variations in conception identified by phenomenographers? To answer these questions we use an example that has received attention in each of these traditions.

'Opportunity cost' features in nearly all lists of 'key concepts in economics' (for example, Senesh, 1967; Lumsden and Attiyeh, 1971; Scottish Education Department, 1978; Holley and Skelton, 1980) and is usually made prominent in introductory textbooks and lectures. For example an introduction to the study of economics at the University of Lancaster (University of Lancaster, 2005) includes a definition of opportunity cost as 'the evaluation placed on the most highly valued of the rejected alternatives or opportunities'. One instance in which this concept is applied is in the analysis of gains from trade through the principle of comparative advantage (see, for example, Frank and Bernanke, 2005). In Chapter 7 of this volume Shanahan and Meyer demonstrate variation in the way that students integrate their understanding of opportunity cost with their thinking about everyday experience. From this perspective students may be said to have acquired the threshold concept once they have achieved a level of integration that allows them to use opportunity cost in an unself-conscious way in describing their own experience. The remainder of this section aims to complement this perspective by focusing on the way in which students' use of the idea of opportunity cost may be integrated in their understanding of different economic contexts and their adoption of an economist's way of practising.

Opportunity cost is the basis for arguments for free trade. Working from a phenomenographic perspective, Pong (1997) investigated students' conceptions of the benefits from trade. He identifies two conceptions of benefits from trade in students' transcripts. Conception One he terms 'an exchange of commodities' in which countries see mutual advantage in trading given absolute advantage (one country is absolutely more efficient in producing one product whilst another country is absolutely more efficient in producing a second product). He refers to Conception Two as a 'zero-sum game' in which it is conceived that an advantage to one nation from trading must be at the expense of a disadvantage to another.

Both these conceptions fall short of the comparative advantage principle which suggests that trade will be mutually beneficial even if one country is more efficient (has an absolute advantage) in producing each good as long as it is relatively more efficient in producing one good than another. The concept of 'opportunity cost' is implicit in any exposition of 'Conception One' (absolute advantage). Countries face a choice of whether to make or buy. The opportunity cost of making a product they could buy is the value of the production of the alternative product they could make and then sell. However, Pong's evidence suggests that a student can conceive of a phenomenon (such as 'gains from trade') using the idea of opportunity cost without achieving the conception that would be used by an economist working inside the discipline. Why is that?

We can start to answer this by thinking about how an economist would construct the problem in the first place. They would make a series of assumptions to make the problem tractable: think only in terms of two countries, each of which can make either of two products, such that in order to make more of one of the products they have to sacrifice some production of the other product; assume that in each country resources can be switched from production of one product to production of another; assume that a net increase in the production of the two products will be beneficial. The reduction to two countries and products makes the conception of opportunity cost much simpler because there are only two alternatives: production of this good or that good. The production-switching assumption appears strange to students at first sight, especially in view of the examples such as 'guns and butter' typically chosen. It is far from self-evident that cows and grass can be turned with ease to the production of military hardware. The underlying assumption is that in the long run resources can be switched and that therefore it is reasonable to ignore switching costs when developing a basic argument. In other words, the use of opportunity cost in an economist's conception of the gains from trade problem cannot be divorced from an argument (or practice) through which the problem is constructed. The integrating characteristic of the concept of opportunity cost (making it relevant to the analysis of many phenomena) is only brought into play when it is deployed in the context of an economist's way of constructing the world. This way of constructing the world (or ideology in the language favoured by

Mitchell, 2001) is exactly the part of the analysis which typically remains hidden in textbook expositions.

Moreover, the generality of the assumptions which are deployed in textbook expositions of the principle of comparative advantage are particular to one school of thought (albeit the overwhelmingly dominant one, Reimann, 2004) in Economics. In particular, the assumption that production-switching costs can be safely ignored on the basis that it is a 'long-run view' is based on neo-classical theorising of time and uncertainty that is not shared by heterodox economists who are likely as a result to be more openly sceptical of the universal applicability of the comparative advantage principle. That is, insofar as there are different schools of thought within disciplines, there will also be integrating 'school threshold concepts' that *characterise* these schools as well as 'discipline threshold concepts' that distinguish *all* members of a subject community from those in other communities.

Alternative approaches to identifying variation in understanding

We might expect that each definition of a way of thinking and practising in a subject will prompt a different method by which the way of thinking may be identified. This section begins by describing the search methods used to identify key concepts in Economics and those used by phenomenographers, and goes on to consider appropriate methods of searching for threshold concepts.

The process by which 'key' or fundamental concepts were identified by the designers of the 'Master Curriculum Guide' in the USA is described at some length by Sumansky (1986). The process is pithily summed up on the EcEdweb site by the statement that 'Prominent economists and educators worked together to develop a set of fundamental economic concepts that are appropriate for presentation at each of the various levels of pre-college education' (EcEdweb, 2003). This kind of process was replicated in the UK and different economists came up with their own lists of fundamental concepts (e.g. Lumsden and Attiyeh, 1971).

The process of identifying key concepts is treated as synonymous with the identification of the building blocks of the subject as perceived by experts in the field (Sumansky, 1986). Naturally enough, this search has prompted some economists to borrow from the philosophy of science in order to support their claims for identifying the fundamental concepts of the subject. Jeffreys's (1985) deploys Lakatos's (1970) concept of a 'Scientific Research Programme' (SRP) to buttress the argument for regarding the neo-classical foundations of opportunity cost, the margin and efficiency as the key concepts of Economics. Heterodox economists (e.g. Brown, 1981; Cross, 1982; Dow, 1983) come to quite different conclusions on the basis of their application of the SRP idea.

Phenomenographic method begins by aiming to expose the way in which students relate to the world by posing questions about their explanation of a phenomenon within their experience. In the case of conceptions of price, students were asked to explain the price of a bun in the canteen they used. Questions asked during this process aim to expose the way in which the respondent construes the phenomena and the concepts they use to explain it. Responses are recorded and transcribed. Transcripts are then read and re-read to generate categories which describe the conceptions. This inductive process relies on the ability of a team of researchers to identify rather than impose variation through their reading of the transcripts. As noted earlier, it is difficult to see how this process can identify ways of thinking that have yet to be codified by a community of scholars as a separate conceptualisation.

Given the familiarity of most economists with the idea that there are 'fundamental concepts' in their subject, there is a considerable risk that any search for threshold concepts will get derailed by slipping into a familiar discourse. This is a likely outcome if researchers try to find threshold concepts through dialogue with economists about the nature of the subject. An attempt to identify a threshold concept should employ a mode of enquiry that is distinctive and necessary given the characteristics of threshold concepts.

Several possibilities present themselves. Since threshold concepts are conceived as distinctive ways of thinking and practising in a community we might identify them by comparing ways in which different groups of scholars analyse the same set of phenomena. For example, if we compare the approach of economists and sociologists to the analysis of markets for schooling, we find some systematic differences (Adnett and Davies, 1999, 2002). That is, these differences reflect the systems of thought that are brought to bear on the problem. Sociologists tend to treat schooling markets as a zero-sum game: if one child is awarded a place at a 'good school' it is at the expense of another, and so it is assumed that schooling markets encourage positional competition that cannot improve welfare. The way in which economists seek to model school choice as an economic system enables analysis that includes non-zero sum games and this opens up ways of thinking about policy that would otherwise be ruled out. Conversely, the systematic way in which sociologists theorise intergenerational transmission of perceptions and constraints prevents them from assuming that revealed choices reflect individual preferences in a way that is required for the application of mainstream economic analysis.

The difference between economists' and sociologists' ways of thinking in this example is bound up with their ways of practising. For example, the economist's conception of a system of interactions between idealised individuals and producers encourages the application of mathematics to formally model ultimate outcomes. Abstraction from the peculiarity of any one individual or producer is necessary in order to make it possible to examine outcomes from many interactions that do not simply replicate the outcomes that would arise from one producer and one consumer.

Since threshold concepts are meant to reflect the difference in ways of thinking and practising between those who are 'inside' the subject and those who have not yet grasped that way of seeing, we might compare the way in which acknowledged experts in the field (such as teachers of economics) and novices (such as students in their early weeks of an undergraduate degree) analyse a problem that the experts recognise as appropriate for the application of their disciplinary expertise. Since threshold concepts integrate a way of thinking about a range of contexts we might also compare students' responses to different problems to see if there are common identifiable ways of seeing problems and constructing approaches to solving problems that students use in different situations.

Furthermore, since threshold concepts are 'transformative' and 'integrative' they should change the learner's sense of identity in relation to a subject community. When students come to view themselves as part of a community they have reached a point where they have an understanding of how that community thinks and practises. This implies a self-awareness which ought to be susceptible to exposure and external observation. Biographical interviews or reflective diaries of the kind that encourage the description of critical incidents might reveal threshold concepts through moments of realisation of how a subject community thinks and practises.

Finally, our earlier discussion suggests the possibility of different layers of community that are relevant to a student's learning. Whilst we can refer to an economist's way of thinking we can also refer to the way of thinking that is characteristic of a school of thought in Economics. We can also refer to ways of thinking and practising that economists share with those in other disciplines (for example in their use of statistics).

Helping learners to identify threshold concepts

As noted in the introduction, the idea that experts have a particular way of thinking and practising is very familiar to members of subject communities such as Economics. The previous two sections have aimed to show that threshold concepts provide a distinctive and useful way of characterising a way of thinking and practising. This third section suggests ways in which this tacit knowledge can be made explicit for learners. The assumption being made here is that learners are more likely to recognise the way of thinking and practising in a subject if they are explicitly assisted rather than left to pick things up through intuition. The benefits of explicit assistance are likely to accrue disproportionately to learners who have developed weaker metacognitive abilities in terms of 'learning how to learn'.

An immediately apparent problem in trying to make threshold concepts explicit for students is that if these concepts integrate a way of thinking they necessarily operate at a high level of abstraction. The 'spiral curriculum' solution to this problem was to develop ways of representing the concept that were sufficiently simplified to be consistent with each developmental stage of thinking. A contrasting recommendation is suggested for threshold concepts. First, if threshold concepts integrate a way of thinking in a subject then the time to introduce them to students is when they have acquired sufficient subject knowledge such that it is feasible for them to attempt to develop and practise an integrated understanding. That is, understanding of a threshold concept might be assisted by helping students to recognise the way in which subject thinking about two quite different contexts (e.g. 'gains from trade' and 'investment appraisal') is based on a common foundation.

Second, learners might be assisted towards understanding a threshold concept by helping them to focus on, and use, salient characteristics of that concept. This might be illustrated by an example from Business Studies. A characteristic feature of teaching Business Studies in schools and universities is the use of case studies. These present few difficulties for learners in the upper half of the ability range, but school students whose literacy is less developed experience great difficulties in expressing their understanding of case studies in the form of sustained written accounts. Analysis of the components and structure of stories is well developed and business case studies are simply a particular type of story (Davies *et al.*, 2003). By making the components of a story and the use of connectives an explicit requirement, students can be assisted to write their own business case studies in ways that are much more extensive and complex than they could do previously (Davies *et al.*, 2003).

Third, learners might be helped by evaluating their own work in terms of descriptions of levels of thinking and practising that build towards understanding a threshold concept. For example, Table 5.1 presents an example of three descriptions of levels of quality in arguments that have been used by

Table 5.1 Support for school students' self-evaluation of economic arguments

Way of practising	Example
1 Costs or benefits are not connected (like a list)	'People who do not recycle are wasting resources'
2 The balance between costs and benefits is considered (weighing up)	'For it to be worth recycling the cost of recycling must not outweigh the benefits from recycling'
3 The effects of everyone's behaviour on the future balance of costs and benefits is considered (knock-on effects)	'If more and more people recycle plastic then it may make the costs of recycling fall. It would be worth having more locations where you can leave plastic and this will reduce transport costs and it may cost the recycling companies less if the total volume of plastic is increased'

school students to evaluate the quality of their arguments. If we imagine a description of a threshold concept as the highest level in such a table then the lower levels would help to provide learners with a way of evaluating whether their thinking was developing towards understanding of the threshold.

Conclusions

Threshold concepts provide an attractive perspective on learning and teaching because they resonate with several familiar aspects of the experience of teachers: that there are distinctive ways of thinking and practising in subjects; that much of this distinctive way is left tacit in learning and teaching especially in subjects such as Economics where there is a monolithic approach to the subject in school and undergraduate teaching; and that many students learn to reproduce versions of subject knowledge and mimic its application without seeming to grasp the underlying meaning of that knowledge.

However, for threshold concepts to make a significant contribution to learning, teachers must be able to identify these concepts in their subject and they must be able to do so in a way that is different from the methods used by other approaches to conceptual structure. In addition, teachers will need to identify ways of assisting learners to recognise explicitly what is currently left tacit. This chapter has suggested several ways in which each of these challenges might be met. It remains for future work to test whether these suggestions are fruitful or not.

Acknowledgements

I am grateful to Jan Meyer and Jean Mangan for their helpful comments on earlier drafts of this chapter.

References

Adnett, N. and Davies, P. (1999) Schooling quasi-markets: reconciling economic and sociological analyses, *British Journal of Educational Studies* 47(3): 221–234.

Adnett, N. and Davies, P. (2002) Education as a positional good: implications for market-based reforms of schooling, *British Journal of Educational Studies* 50(2): 189–205.

Andrews, R. and Mitchell, S. (2001) (eds) *Essays in Argument* (London: Middlesex University Press).

Bowden, J. A., Dall'Alba, G., Laurillard, D., Martin, E., Marton, F., Masters, G., Ramsden, P., Stephanou, A. and Walsh, E. (1990) Phenomenographic studies of understanding in physics: displacement, velocity and frames of reference, paper presented by Bowden, J.A. to the AERA Annual meeting, Boston, April.

Brown, E. (1981) The neoclassical and post-Keynesian research programmes: the methodological issues, *Review of Social Economy* 39: 111–132.

Bruner, J. (1960) *The Process of Education* (New York: Random House).

Bruner, J. (1966) *Towards a Theory of Instruction* (Oxford: Oxford University Press).

Buchanan, J. (1979) *What Should Economists Do?* (Indianapolis, IN: Liberty Press).

Buchanan, J. (1982) The domain of subjective economics: between predictive science and moral philosophy, in I. Kirzner (ed.) *Method, Process and Austrian Economics* (Lexington, MA: Lexington Books).

Cross, R. (1982) The Duhem-Quine thesis, Lakatos and the appraisal of theories in macroeconomics, *Economic Journal* 92: 320–340.

Dahlgren, L-O. (1984) Outcomes of learning, in F. Marton, D. Hounsell and N. Entwistle (eds) *The Experience of Learning* (Edinburgh: Scottish Academic Press).

Davies, P., Bentham, J., Cartwright, S. and Wilson, J. (2003) Developing narrative skills through case studies, *Curriculum Journal* 14: 217–232.

Dow, S. (1983) Substantive mountains and methodological molehills: a rejoinder, *Journal of Post-Keynesian Economics* 5: 304–308.

EcEdweb (2003) Economic concepts high school graduates should know, available at http://ecedweb.unomaha.edu/ec-cncps.htm (25 May 2003).

Frank, R. H. and Bernanke, B. S. (2005) Principles of microeconomics (second edition) (Online Learning Center with Powerweb) available at http://highered.mcgraw-hill.com/sites/0072554096/student_view0/chapter_2/key_concepts.html (last accessed 19 February 2005).

Heilbroner, R. (1987) Fundamental economic concepts – another perspective, *Journal of Economic Education* 18: 111–120.

Hodkinson, S. and Thomas, L. (1984) *Economics in the General Curriculum* (London: University of London, Institute of Education).

Holley, B. and Skelton, V. (1980) *Economics Education 14–16* (London: NFER).

Jeffreys, D. (1985) The nature of economic knowledge, in G. B. J. Atkinson (ed.) *Teaching Economics* (third edition) (London: Heinemann), pp. 11–31.

Keynes, J. M. (1973) *Total Collected Writings*, vol. XII (London: Macmillan).

Lakatos, I. (1970) The methodology of scientific research programmes, in I. Lakatos and A. Musgrave (eds) *Criticism and the Growth of Knowledge* (Cambridge: Cambridge University Press).

Lee, N. (1986) Putting the heart back into economic man, *Economics* 22: 92–95.

Levačić, R. (1987) What changes should be made to the 'A' level economics syllabus for the 1990's? *Economics* 23: 100–105.

Littlechild, S. C. (2005) Buchanan and Shackle on cost, choice and subjective economics, available at http://www.gmu.edu/jbc/fest/files/littlechild.htm

Lumsden, K. and Attiyeh, R. (1971) The core of basic economics, *Economics* 9: 33–40.

McCormick, B., Vidler, C. and (ed.) Thomas, L. (1994) *Teaching and Learning the New Economics* (London: Heinemann).

McCune, V. and Hounsell, D. (2005) The development of students' ways of thinking and practising in three final-year biology courses, *Higher Education* 49: 255–289.

Marchionatti, R. (2002) What don't economists know that Marshall knew a century ago? University of Torino Departmento die Economie Working Paper 02/2002 available at http://www.cesmep.unito.it/WP/2_WP_Cesmep.pdf (accessed 15 January 2005).

Marton, F. (1988) *Phenomenography and 'The Art of Teaching All Things to All Men'*, Fenomenografiska notiser 8, (Göteborg: Institutionen för pedagogik Göteborgs Universitet).

Marton, F. and Booth, S. (1997) *Learning and Awareness* (Mahwah, NJ: Lawrence Erlbaum).

Meyer, J. H. F. and Land, R. (2003) Threshold concepts and troublesome knowledge: linkages to ways of thinking and practising within the disciplines, in C. Rust (ed.) *Improving Student Learning. Improving Student Learning Theory and Practice – Ten Years On* (Oxford: OCSLD), pp. 412–424.

Mitchell, S. (2001) Some key concepts in argument, in R. Andrews and S. Mitchell (eds) *Essays in Argument* (London: Middlesex University Press).

Perkins, D. N. (1999) The many faces of constructivism, *Educational Leadership* 57: 3.

Pong, W-Y. (1997) Students' ideas of price and trade, *Economic Awareness* 9: 6–9.

Reimann, N. (2004) First-year teaching and learning environments in economics, *International Review of Economics Education* 2(1) available online http://www.economicsnetwork.ac.uk/iree/i3/reimann.htm (accessed 19 February 2005).

Säljö, R. (1988) Learning in educational settings: methods of enquiry, in P. Ramsden (ed.) *Improving Learning: New Perspectives* (London: Kogan Page).

Scottish Education Department (1978) *Economics in SI and SII – A Feasibility Study* (Edinburgh: HMSO).

Senesh, L. (1967) Teaching economic concepts in the primary grades, in N. Lee (ed.) *Teaching Economics* (first edition) (London: Heinemann).

Sheeran, Y. and Barnes, D. (1991) *School Writing* (Buckingham: Open University Press).

Sumansky, J. (1986) The evolution of economic thought as revealed through a history of the Master Curriculum Guide: Framework for Teaching the Basic Concepts, in S. Hodkinson and D. Whitehead (eds) *Economics Education: Research and Development Issues* (London: Heinemann).

University of Lancaster (2005) Introduction, Definitions, Key Concepts (PowerPoint presentation) available at http://www.lancs.ac.uk/people/ecavnb/ec402%20lec1.ppt (last accessed 19 February 2005).

Part II

Threshold concepts in practice

Chapter 6

Threshold concepts in Biology
Do they fit the definition?

Charlotte Taylor

Introduction

Meyer and Land (2003) discuss the definition of a threshold concept as a transformative gateway, possessing certain properties (for example being integrative, and possibly 'troublesome'), that leads to the understanding of new and conceptually more difficult ideas. Such concepts are the key to subsequent higher order learning within a discipline and a lack of ability to progress past such a threshold may lead to ongoing problems in subsequent understanding and application. Many concepts can be seen as 'troublesome' by teachers, for a number of reasons associated with both difficulties in teaching and lack of understanding by students. However, relatively few of these concepts will satisfy key descriptors associated with threshold concepts; namely, instances of 'significantly changing the way of thinking', and a focus on the integrative nature of knowledge. Rather they will constitute a *series* of concepts associated with a progression through levels of understanding (Hegarty-Hazel, 1985). This chapter provides an overview of the debate associated with these ideas, and attempts a subsequent analysis of what is, and what is not, a threshold concept in Biology. Examples of potential threshold concepts are proposed, their defining characteristics analysed, and some problems in fitting the initial definition discussed. Following this, an example of a concept, which appears to fit the concept of *threshold*, is explored to determine the extent, and degree, to which students understand it and demonstrate that they have, or have not, crossed a threshold.

The current study involved a series of interviews with seven academics, from a broad range of research areas of Biology, teaching in four different universities in Australia and the UK. Students enrolled in first-year Biology courses provided access to their written answers to questions about hypotheses for analysis of their understanding of this concept. Providing the introductory definition, described above, to academics in fields as varied as Human and Plant Physiology, Biochemistry, Ecology, and Marine and Freshwater Biology, gives rise to some interesting insights. Initially there is an enthusiastic identification with the idea, and all interviewees immediately suggest candidate concepts for the 'troublesome' label. However, teasing apart these concepts in terms of the reason for the troublesome label and the degree to which such concepts may incorporate learning thresholds proves more challenging.

Common ancestry of concepts

The field of Biology in a university context is very diverse with areas of research often being separated into different departments or faculties such as Environmental Biology, Molecular Biology and DNA technology, Ecology, Marine Studies, Biochemistry, Physiology (both animal and plant), Cell Biology, Evolutionary Biology, and Genetics. Finding common ground in terms of threshold concepts may therefore prove much more difficult than doing so in other scientific disciplines such as Geology or Mathematics, for example. However, it is particularly interesting to note that biologists in very different fields and from different countries, teaching in very different systems, initially all tend to identify similar concepts as problematic in terms of their teaching. These are areas with which teachers and students consistently struggle, and which are recognized as forming a barrier to understanding, the world over. A typical discussion of the idea of thresholds, amongst practitioners in Biology across the range of research areas, focuses initially on higher level concepts which may require a sophisticated understanding *often never reached by undergraduate students*. When different interpretations of the concepts are pared down to the basics from which they arise, a commonality of ancestry is invariably revealed. Three biologists in discussion may each provide an area of difficulty relevant to their area of expertise, for example, nerve impulses in human Biology, the biochemistry of photosynthesis in plants, and water uptake in crops (Merry and Orsmond, personal communication). Each of these areas is associated with opportunities and challenges at the forefront of research in the diverse areas of Neurobiology, Biophysics, and Agricultural Botany. While appearing very different, these areas all rely on an understanding of the fundamentals of *osmosis* – the movement of water across a membrane. An appreciation of the significance of this water movement opens the door to many other concepts within plant and animal Biology, from the subcellular to the whole organism level. Thus, engaging with the threshold concept results in a major shift in the appreciation of biological processes at a number of scales. This is a key element in a sophisticated understanding of the complexities of modern Biology (Hazel *et al.*, 2002). At the same time, such a concept demonstrates the interrelatedness of all aspects of Biology, particularly at the fundamental level, and highlights the way in which such concepts can be integrated into a larger understanding of living systems.

Isolated islands of knowledge

An important characteristic of discussions about the troublesome nature of biological knowledge is the link to the complexity inherent in living systems themselves. Learning in Biology usually requires the development of a gradually increasing awareness and constant re-evaluation of the topics being studied. Truisms taught at early stages are re-examined as further layers of complexity within the topic require a new set of truths to be constructed. While this is undoubtedly the case in all disciplines in science, it has been identified as a threshold in itself within some areas of Biology. Areas such as Ecology, which deal with the dynamics of interactions, require students to constantly work with the concepts of probability and uncertainty as part of their developing understanding of the systems. 'Until students can exist in this state as they engage with new knowledge they remain at a very unsophisticated level of understanding' (Interviewee 1).

A series of similar discussions with other biologists identified a range of other apparent threshold concepts in Biology; for example, the consequences of meiosis, creating hypotheses, the alternation of generations in plants and the stability and continuity of DNA molecules. All are raised in discussion as distinct problems from a teaching perspective and stimulate constant searches for new ways of 'getting the information across so that students show some glimmer of understanding'. Many academics admit that some of these concepts 'may be impossible to teach' at a beginner's level in undergraduate Biology. We persevere however, because it is recognized that progression to other areas of Biology is equally impossible without this understanding. Discussions of this dilemma invariably lead teachers to reflect on the way in which they themselves 'dealt with' learning the concepts, and how they now view them after traversing the threshold. In many cases each piece of knowledge may be perceived as existing on an island and remains isolated, even if well understood, until we put together links to related pieces of knowledge, or concepts (Merry, personal communication). Learning is therefore grounded in building up these links and teachers strive to show students how to make a complex web of composite knowledge and understanding. Poor understanding, or a resistance to indulge in link-building, which many students do display, leads to the islands remaining as isolated, and seemingly irrelevant, bits of information, which may be memorized for exams and never touched again.

Further analysis of the proposed biological threshold concepts reveals some apparent departures from the features which initially defined a threshold concept. In comparison to concepts identified in other disciplines, those in Biology appear relatively complex and introduction to the concept presupposes knowledge in a scientific context. It may be that biological scientific concepts are fundamentally different in terms of learning and understanding. However, this seems unlikely given the outcomes of studies carried out in other areas of science, in particular focusing on concepts in Physics (Crawford *et al.*, 1998). Discussion of this phenomenon has provided interesting insights into understandings of concepts and methods of teaching such concepts. Some interviewees were of the opinion that biological concepts are no more complex than those defined in other disciplines, rather the complexity is created through the approach to teaching and learning the concept and the language in which such discussions are couched. While Physics teachers at early undergraduate levels have made efforts to group the concepts in 'real world' and 'relevant' examples and demonstrations, the teaching in undergraduate Biology may be focusing much more on fact transmission; that is, creating the islands of knowledge.

Process as troublesome

Another explanation of the phenomenon may lie in an apparent pattern which emerges from many interviews with biologists, where troublesome knowledge appeared to be associated very much with *processes* in Biology. While this perception may be to some extent a function of the discipline area interests of the interviewees, it may also reflect the dynamic nature of the discipline – Biology works with knowledge which incorporates change as an integral component. Learning in Biology therefore has to acknowledge change, such that constant reflection on, and re-evaluation of, biological knowledge and ideas are fundamental to an understanding of concepts. The apparent importance of processes in Biology may again be a function of the way in which we approach teaching Biology. There has traditionally been a focus at the early undergraduate level on 'hard facts' rather than a more philosophical approach to the concepts (Lawson *et al.*, 2000). Thus students will memorize details of the process of photosynthesis rather than take the opportunity to think, in a holistic framework, about the significance of photosynthesis in maintaining life on earth. While both teachers and students will identify the concept of the process of photosynthesis as troublesome, it does not necessarily constitute a threshold concept. Instead, an understanding of the detail of this process may foster an appreciation of photosynthesis as an appropriate example of the concept of energy transfer in biochemical processes. The threshold concept thus becomes one of understanding the cyclical and conservative nature of processes in the dynamics of cellular energy conversions.

> Why does putting an enzyme in make it work so much faster, but at the end the enzyme can turn round and do it all again, you don't run out of enzyme? The enzyme's just there, and the classic is with glucose, it stores an enormous amount of energy but as I say to the students 'the sugar bowl never spontaneously combusts in my house, it just sits there and you put the sugar in your tea, and there's all that energy there.' And yet I can put 10 or 12 enzymes in and you can capture all that energy. I find that quite remarkable. In the end, life is enzymes. But I think you need to be

able to see it happen to have the light go on and you understand the concept. We should sit the students down all afternoon with something there without the enzymes, so that they actually see how very slowly it works, and they can see one with enzyme and one without – then they'd appreciate it.

(Interviewee 2)

Meanwhile, a different view of photosynthesis would lead to identifying it as a threshold concept based on its key function in an evolutionary context, since it constitutes

the process which changed the chemistry of the planet. Half of the time on earth we didn't have this and didn't have life forms as we know them. It was the fact that photosynthesis made oxygen. If you look at it conceptually it really is an amazing thing!

(Interviewee 5)

Process and abstraction in threshold concepts

Taking a more holistic view of the disciplinary knowledge allows us to reflect on a set of more *abstract* concepts, which are also troublesome but may more specifically involve a threshold transition. Interestingly, in many cases interviewees identified certain topics in Biology as threshold concepts in both their *process* and *abstract* manifestations. Reflecting on these two ways of viewing a biological concept leads to the question of whether we tend to teach biological concepts with a focus on the *processes*, particularly at the early undergraduate level. If this is the case, students may be more likely to be struggling to engage with details of published information or 'hard facts' about a topic, rather than taking a more philosophical view of the same concept. In this way they may rarely have opportunities to think about the significance of, for example, the process of photosynthesis in the framework of life on earth. In the latter context the concept may not necessarily be identified as troublesome knowledge, but it would fit the definition of a threshold concept since it has a key role in transforming thinking. In this case transformed thinking about the evolutionary and global role of the process of photosynthesis will shift the learning of the details of the process into a new model, and may improve understanding. In a similar vein, Lawson *et al.* (2000) stress the need to focus learning initially on discussion of alternatives, arguments and evidence leading to the acceptance of such facts. The significance of the process of photosynthesis will thus become more obvious when applied to a current environmental problem, for example global warming. It has been suggested (Interviewee 3) that, on being presented with such a problem to solve, students have an opportunity to resurrect their prior understandings and move across a new threshold as they critically evaluate the situation and apply the appropriate knowledge. This may also demonstrate a threshold difference between students and scientists engaging in research who are creating their own challenges to extend frontiers of research. It may be possible to help students in their learning by mirroring this stimulus in scientific research and enquiry. Once students experience this sense of excitement and ownership they may more easily recognize the significance of isolated islands of knowledge and be challenged to make links. As they see more links and move further into the discipline learning becomes more and more contextualized and motivating.

> The students seem to be learning 'through connecting islands of knowledge' when they realise there is a need to do so. When teachers provide them with a new challenge using a biological concept they will go back and link it together with older packages of information, sitting there from earlier lectures, and put them together to make more sense. If that's the case they will be fairly passive and nothing changes until they're challenged – they won't do anything with the knowledge until we come along and dig it up again in a new context.
>
> (Merry, personal communication)

Issues of timing and context

A new challenge in teaching arises at this juncture, since students cross their own threshold *at different times* within the learning of a topic. The role of the teacher in such a passage thus becomes one of presenting a series of carefully crafted challenges, which will facilitate these moves and are presented at appropriate times. It also requires a clear appreciation, on the part of the teacher, of the progress through the learning of the concept, something which may become problematic if students are studying a particular threshold concept during courses in many different areas of Biology during their degree programme. Another problem may be that student misconceptions about the concept may be maintained for longer and may be more difficult to identify. Thus, for many key concepts taught in undergraduate Biology the opportunities for individual students to engage with the concept in a way which transforms their understanding *may never occur*.

Other examples of the more abstract biological concepts include that of *variability*. In an ecological context this phenomenon requires an appreciation of the inherent variability and capacity for change in all living systems. While it can be quantified, and a body of knowledge created which can be transmitted to students in the form of specific case studies, it means different things to different people. Students' preconceptions of this concept will therefore have been moulded in a variety of contexts. However, an understanding of the central role of complexity and variability in our understanding of ecological processes may need to be developed over many years of experiential learning. Only through working with the limitations and complexity of the concept can we incorporate it into our thinking in all instances.

> It's understanding variability and how results you get in one situation may not apply in another situation because of the inherent variability in biological and ecological systems, that take a little while for them to appreciate. Being able to come to terms with that, and being able to work within the framework of that uncertainty – that's the threshold. And if you don't get that you're never going to have a very sophisticated understanding and application of ecology so it's a really interesting thing in terms of contextual understanding.
>
> (Interviewee 1)

Scale

A further example discussed independently by all interviewees involves the question of *scale* in Biology. Again this concept can be clearly defined in many contexts and in the various areas of Biology. In terms of ecological studies it parallels the significance of variability

> because the ways in which you may look at something changes your perception and understanding of it, and the way in which it's working and that can be really important in Ecology.
>
> (Interviewee 1)

An example of this may be an investigation into the distribution of different birds in an area, which may be carried out by observing and counting birds in suburban gardens (Ashley, 2004). However, if the birds in question have territories or feeding ranges larger than this, then no patterns will be found at the scale chosen for the study. If the scale of observations is changed to the level of the street then a clearer pattern of distribution may be apparent. You have to be aware of what is the right scale for the problem.

A discussion in the context of physiology or cell biology, working inside a single cell, may present different problems with the concept of scale.

> You've got to be able to think about water moving in cells and what's going on across membranes and then see the intercellular level, and that feeds into action potentials and then muscles come in and how you move your elbow. Then the whole thing comes together at a level where you can actually see something happen.
>
> (Interviewee 3)

Conversely, when students are looking down a microscope, the concept of how big things are and what you can see comes into play.

> You can't see things which are sub-cellular in most cases, but they expect to be able to see the structure of DNA under the microscope. They can isolate a blob of DNA, as a bit of jelly, put it on a slide and they expect to see strands of DNA.
>
> (Ross, P., personal communication)

Similar conceptual problems are associated with appreciating that very small single-celled organisms can be living and reproducing even though we cannot see them. A recurring theme in these discussions centred around the perception, as described by Lawson (2003), that objects or processes which cannot be viewed directly prove much more difficult to teach and to understand. This is particularly pertinent in the expanding fields of molecular biology and biochemistry.

> Students do have quite a few problems with things to do with biochemistry and what goes on in cells. Biochemistry works so well because you have all these little compartments doing different things which link together and help things work at different levels, it separates processes and maximises the way you can have a multifunctional unit. You can have fat being burnt to produce energy in one part of a cell and somewhere else, in the same cell, it's being made – all because of the compartments. No, wonder they get confused!
>
> (Interviewee 2)

The language of science

Finally, the *language* of science is often identified, both by teachers and students, as troublesome, but it almost certainly also creates a threshold. It may be argued that the use of technical terms specific to the discipline is fundamental to a rigorous understanding and to the effective communication of complex concepts and ideas – a key component of progress in research. The language of science is by its nature very specific, in part to maintain continuity in use of concepts, and in part to simplify the discussion of complexity. One word, often Greek or Latin in origin, can describe a process or object which may otherwise require a complex sentence or paragraph. Scientists therefore communicate in a short hand, and may be seen to be hiding behind the language, stereotypically to the exclusion of those not part of this community. 'Did you know that there are more new words in a first year university biology textbook than in a university first year French book?' (Interviewee 5).

Students are frequently introduced to biological concepts using this new language, which further compounds problems of understanding and making the necessary links within or between concepts. In order successfully to work and think within the discipline students must see the advantages in the use of such language and overcome their negative perceptions. Therefore students need to have the opportunity to appreciate the concept first, after which they, or the teacher, assign a word, or technical term, to it. Only then will they successfully cross the threshold and begin to function in their scientific environment.

> Biology is not generally where you think you'll walk out understanding differential equations, but you can introduce the concept so that when they read a formula they'll think in words about the biology. We slowly make the shift to symbols by talking about the process in words every time we see the symbols. This problem with language can really hold us back in educating people. You gradually force them into the scientific language funnel, which they do have to do to become scientists, rather than starting them down at the bottom of the funnel!
>
> (Interviewee 5)

Until the challenges of identifying true threshold concepts are overcome, we will struggle to create scenarios which can explore students' understandings of the concepts. Questions need to be couched at a sufficiently basic level to elicit a range of answers and conceptions, but also need to provide the stimulus which allows demonstration of a sophisticated level of thinking in science. The question of whether, and the extent to which, these concepts significantly *change* students' appreciation of the wider related fields of Biology has yet to be determined and presents a fascinating research opportunity. Perhaps an initial step requires further dissection of the concepts to identify the true threshold within? This process may be illustrated using an example inherent to most branches of Biology.

Case study: hypothesis creation as a threshold concept

Experimentation is a fundamental tool in scientific investigations and requires the creation of a hypothesis. From a teacher's perspective, the act of formulating the hypothesis is 'troublesome' and may constitute a *threshold experience*. The significance of this experience therefore lies in the crucial relationship between the ability to understand the arguments inherent in hypotheses and the ability to construct knowledge of the concept under investigation (Lawson, 2003). From the perspective of student understanding, however, it is the concept of the hypothesis itself which is the threshold conception. The conception, of the existence of a statement which integrates unequivocally all possible information and variables in a situation, must be grasped *before* an understanding of its use in transforming knowledge can be appreciated.

Students in a large first-year biology cohort (n=1000) were given two opportunities to demonstrate their understanding of hypotheses and their use. At the beginning of the course students were introduced to the concept of hypotheses and their place in scientific investigations and experiments, and were given a scenario based on an ecological observation. They were asked to work in groups to create a model to explain the observations and then to create a testable hypothesis based on the model. At the end of the course students were given a question in an exam in which another ecological scenario was presented and students again asked to create a hypothesis. Answers from 200 students were then analysed and categories of understanding of the concept of hypothesis creation and testing developed. Since this study constituted a pilot survey for a larger study in the future it was not possible to link pre- and post-answers for individual students. Rather, the exercise allowed a picture of general types of understanding and the extent of the threshold to be constructed.

Creating an integrative statement about the observations made in both scenarios proved difficult for all students, both at the beginning and at the end of the course. In general, the responses at the beginning showed that the abstract nature of the concept had not been grasped, and student responses remained grounded in explanations of the biology of the situation. There was no indication that they had constructed an understanding of the investigative nature of the exercise, and the vast majority of answers had no prediction which could be tested by, for example, counting the organisms discussed in the scenario. Students were working with biological facts they knew would form part of the scenario and would be involved in the interactions under investigation. It could of course be argued that their biological knowledge at this point overwhelmingly constituted the facts given by their teachers in lectures relevant to the topic. Thus, there had been little opportunity to work with the abstract and more holistic elements of biology which would inform an understanding of the nature of prediction and hypothesis creation.

The answers to the post-question posed in the final exam showed a progression in thinking to a more structured approach to hypothesis creation. This may, in part, have been due to the nature of the question and its context. Students were more focused on the concepts having revised for the exam and the question was more closed than that postulated earlier in the course. The reasons for the questioning are different in that the pre-question attempted to elicit discussion and 'thinking around the topic' whereas the post-question required a clear demonstration of competence from the students. The majority of answers to the post-question showed an understanding of the integrative nature of the system described in the scenario and recognized links between the key variables under investigation. However, the ability of students to articulate the relationship and provide a hypothesis which could be tested showed more variation. Overall, there was a significant, positive correlation between the nature of the hypothesis and the testing which followed. In terms of dissecting out the development of an understanding of the concept, this feature of their answer is certainly more indicative of any problems since it has less direction from the scenario provided. Thus, students who phrased their answer in terms of an alternate and null hypothesis could provide clear details of the tests they would carry out and data collected.

> I think not too many people get the alternate hypotheses. I would hope that after honours you would expect students to be setting limits to the change they expected to take place. That they would be saying this much change would represent a biological effect in the context of background variation.
>
> (Interviewee 1)

These students could also move towards explaining their appreciation of the limitations in the process of testing and interpretation, as described above, by discussing the roles of replication and impact of other variables. Some also discussed the possible need for further cycles of hypothesis creation and testing. The group, in this case the vast majority, who presented a hypothesis describing the relationship between appropriate variables, often became confused when describing their testing methodology. Some could collect data but could not explain what these data may indicate, and did not refer back to their hypothesis in terms of acceptance or rejection. A significant number collected data for only one variable and subsequently had no conclusions to make. Relatively few students in the whole cohort took inappropriate paths for testing. These included answers setting up inappropriate and unnecessary manipulations, and students who had no hypothesis and therefore had no testing.

The need to focus on a rigorous approach to scientific investigations and hypothesis testing is highlighted in this preliminary study. As teachers, biologists acknowledge this and use a variety of approaches to tackle the concept. The idea of repetition, even when students may not fully understand, was encouraged, in that familiarity with the philosophy and methodology will eventually 'turn on the light' of understanding. Furthermore there is a general acknowledgement that more focused and appropriate hypothesis creating is more likely to occur as students take ownership of their investigations – hence students in intensive honours projects develop their understanding of the concept quickly and productively (White, 2004). The concept of hypotheses and their testing clearly demonstrates the complex nature of the threshold and challenges us to further investigate the ways in which students make the transition to new thinking about the natural world.

Conclusion

In conclusion, discussion of threshold concepts in Biology has provided interesting insights and stimulated reflection on a number of fronts. The examples discussed above have demonstrated a clear distinction between *process* concepts and *abstract* concepts in Biology, *often encompassed in the same threshold concept*. Analysis of these topics has allowed us to further dissect the troublesome nature of threshold experience inherent in the concepts, and reveal some of the possible reasons for the problems. Many of these appear to lie with the approaches to teaching adopted in early undergraduate Biology courses, in that a traditional approach to these concepts has relied on an exposition of the facts as a necessary grounding in the topic. However, it may be that the threshold can be more easily surmounted if a different approach to the concept is adopted. Using a more abstract manifestation allows a holistic view of the concept and its context in a larger picture of living systems. While acknowledging this possibility, many biologists also pointed out that 'it may do no harm' to keep revisiting the facts until they are seen by students in a new and more relevant context. At this point, with appropriately framed help from teachers, students will construct their own understanding as they transform their knowledge. This variation in approaches to teaching such concepts may be advantageous in that it provides better, and more diverse, opportunities for students to engage with the learning. Such reliance on repetition and inclusion of lateral views of the concept has been discussed in terms of its potential to enhance student learning (Marton and Trigwell, 2000; Booth and Ingerman, 2002) and may also reflect the individual nature of learning where each student progresses and crosses thresholds at different rates and times. If we are to accommodate such patterns of learning in Biology we will need to construct learning experiences which clearly identify the threshold experience before moulding a variety of learning experiences and opportunities around this core. Given the flexibility of such a system the challenge for teachers is now to identify, and acknowledge, points at which students have crossed the threshold and moved to a more sophisticated understanding of Biology.

Acknowledgements

I would like to thank my fellow biologists who gave up their valuable time to discuss this topic, sometimes at great length. The conversations were all incredibly stimulating and constructive. Thanks are also due to the first-year students in the School of Biological Sciences at the University of Sydney for enthusiastically volunteering to be part of this pilot project.

References

Ashley, L. (2004) 'The role of large-flowered Grevilleas in Noisy Miner ecology in urban areas', unpublished Honours Thesis, University of Sydney.

Booth, S. and Ingerman, A. (2002) 'Making sense of Physics in the first year of study' *Learning and Instruction* 12: 493–507.

Crawford, K., Gordon, S., Nicholas, J. and Prosser, M. (1998) 'University mathematics students' conceptions of mathematics' *Studies in Higher Education* 23: 87–94.

Hazel, E., Prosser, M. and Trigwell, K. (2002) 'Variation in learning orchestration in university biology courses' *International Journal of Science Education* 24(7): 737–751.

Hegarty-Hazel, E. (1985) 'A light on photosynthesis: students' understanding of an important biological science concept' *Research and Development in Higher Education* 8: 256–262.

Lawson, A.E. (2003) 'The nature and development of hypothetico-predictive argumentation with implications for science teaching' *International Journal of Science Education* 25(11): 1387–1408.

Lawson, A.E., Alkhoury, S., Benford, R., Clark, B.R. and Falconer, K.A. (2000) 'What kinds of scientific concept exist? Concept construction and intellectual development in college biology' *Journal of Research in Science Teaching* 37(9): 996–1018.

Marton, F. and Trigwell, K. (2000) 'Variatio est mater studiorum' *Higher Education Research and Development* 19(3): 381–395.

Meyer, J.H.F. and Land, R. (2003) 'Threshold concepts and troublesome knowledge: linkages to ways of thinking and practising within the disciplines.' In C. Rust (ed.), *Improving Student Learning. Improving Student Learning Theory and Practice – Ten Years On*, Oxford: OCSLD, 412–424.

White, B. (2004) 'Reasoning maps: a generally applicable method for characterizing hypothesis-testing behaviour' *International Journal of Science Education* 26(14): 1715–1731.

Chapter 7

The troublesome nature of a threshold concept in Economics

Martin Shanahan and Jan H. F. Meyer

Economics is fundamentally concerned with issues of choice and scarcity, and the concept of 'opportunity cost' – *the value placed on the best rejected alternative when an individual makes choices* – captures the fundamental idea that choice involves sacrifice. This concept, so simply stated, in fact represents a portal or gateway into the world of how economists think and 'see the world'. As Frank puts it:

> most students leave the introductory course never having fully grasped the essence of microeconomics ... the opportunity cost concept, *so utterly central to our understanding of what it means to think like an economist*, is but one among hundreds that go by in a blur.
>
> (1998, p. 14, emphasis added)

This chapter explores the acquisition of a threshold concept by first-year students taking an introductory course in economics. It illustrates how variation in students' initial understanding of a threshold concept can be externalised and examined, and in a manner that can inform university teaching practice. Perkins's (1999) framework of 'troublesome knowledge' is used to interpret the difficulties that students face in acquiring the threshold concept of 'opportunity cost'. Analyses are presented of the variation in students' 'understanding' of opportunity cost over the course of one semester. Issues of measurement, articulation and learner development are also identified. There appear to be important implications for the manner in which students are initially introduced to threshold concepts. It is speculated that in the acquisition of threshold concepts 'first impressions matter'. Efforts to make threshold concepts 'easier' by simplifying their initial expression and application may, in fact, set students onto a path of acquiring the concept as a form of 'ritualised' (routine and meaningless) knowledge that actually forms a barrier to the acquisition of the concept in a transformative sense. This conclusion impacts on what might otherwise be advocated as good pedagogic practice; namely, an introductory simplification of transformative concepts that some students experience difficulty in acquiring.

Introduction

In economics, the stated aim of many programmes is to produce people who 'think like economists'; meaning they perceive and interpret the world through that particular paradigm. A threshold concept, particularly in professional disciplines, is often more than just a 'core concept'; it is a 'transformative concept'. As such, a threshold concept may also be related to what Perkins (1999) has labelled 'troublesome knowledge' – knowledge that provides difficulty for the student because it is in some way alien, or counter-intuitive.

In earlier work, Shanahan and Meyer (2003) reported that student identification with statements that encapsulate troublesome knowledge (captured in a scale labelled economic 'misconceptions') is associated with a risk of failure in a first-year economics course. That approach began from a premise that asking students how they perceive economists 'think' can provide insights into student success. The argument here begins from the premise that asking students to express a concept that reveals whether or not they *can* 'think like an economist' may also provide important insights.

This chapter presents data from a pilot study conducted at the University of South Australia in 2003. It draws from a response pool of around one hundred first-year economics students who twice articulated their understanding of the concept of opportunity cost – a concept previously identified as a threshold concept (Meyer and Land, 2003).

The chapter begins with an introduction to the concept of opportunity cost. A number of conceptually discrete inhibitory dimensions of understanding, proposed here as underlying barriers to students' understanding of threshold concepts, are then discussed. The data collection methodology is then presented, together with individual student responses that appear representative of, or consistent with, the inhibitory dimensions. Some of the implications of the findings and resultant insights are then finally considered.

The troublesome nature of opportunity cost

Within the discipline of economics, opportunity cost is a threshold concept – a concept so fundamental to economics that it is found in both introductory micro and macroeconomics textbooks, and is taught in all introductory business economics courses. This concept is generally taught in week two or three of most introductory courses. The transformative effect of this concept, based on a personal communication by Shanahan, is encapsulated in Meyer and Land (2003, pp. 414–415):

'Opportunity cost is the evaluation placed on the most highly valued of the rejected alternatives or opportunities' (Eatwell *et al.*, 1998, Vol. 3, p. 719). Fundamental to the discipline of economics is the issue of choice: choosing between scarce resources or alternatives. Economists are interested in how individuals, groups, organisations, and societies make choices, particularly when faced with the reality that resources and alternatives are limited. No-one can have everything. . . . Fundamental to the economic way of approaching the issue of choice is how to compare choices. Thus 'The concept of opportunity cost (or alternative cost) expresses the basic relationship between scarcity and choice' (Eatwell *et al.*, *ibid.*); for this reason it is a fundamental (or threshold) concept in Economics.

Thus opportunity cost captures the idea that choices can be compared, and that every choice (including not choosing) means rejecting alternatives. A student who has a good grasp of this concept has moved a long way toward breaking out of a framework of thinking that sees choices as predetermined, or unchangeable. They have also moved toward seeing 'two sides' of every choice, and in looking beyond immediate consequences, and even just monetary 'costs' towards a more abstract way of thinking.

Thus to quote Eatwell *et al.* for a final time (*ibid.*), 'Opportunity cost, the value placed on the rejected option by the chooser, is the obstacle to choice; it is that which must be considered, evaluated and ultimately rejected before the preferred option is chosen. Opportunity cost in any particular choice is, of course, influenced by prior choices that have been made, but with respect to this choice itself, opportunity cost is *choice-influencing* rather than *choice-influenced*' (Emphasis in original). Thus, if 'accepted' by the individual student as a valid way of interpreting the world, *it fundamentally changes their way of thinking about their own choices, as well as serving as a tool to interpret the choices made by others.*

Exploring the question of how students *vary* in beginning to 'think like an economist' is therefore of immediate interest; such exploration may provide powerful insights into how the concept of opportunity cost is acquired, and how it might be taught. Such exploration is pursued here in terms of 'troublesomeness'.

Meyer and Land (2003, 2005) have argued that threshold concepts possess a number of attributes. For example, a threshold concept is likely to be: (i) integrative, in that it exposes the previously hidden interrelatedness of something; (ii) transformative so that once understood, it produces a significant shift in the perception of the subject; (iii) potentially irreversible, that is, once acquired it is likely to permanently alter the student's perspective to the extent of perhaps even transfiguring the identity of the student; (iv) potentially troublesome. Opportunity cost would appear to possess some of these characteristics.

Following Perkins (1999), troublesome knowledge – that which appears counter-intuitive or alien – may be so for a number of reasons. These reasons, outlined below, also provide an opportunity to examine and locate students' articulated understandings of a threshold concept. Indeed, Perkins's categorisations serve here as an *organising framework* for identifying students' articulation of the potentially troublesome nature of opportunity cost.

a   According to Perkins (1999), the first form of knowledge that may constitute troublesome knowledge is *ritual knowledge*; that which has 'a routine and rather meaningless character' – the 'routine' that is executed to get a particular result: 'Names and dates often are little more than ritual knowledge. So are routines in arithmetic . . . such as the notorious "invert and multiply" to divide fractions' (ibid., p. 7).

In economics, extensive use is made of *diagrams* in order to depict and simplify complex relationships, and such diagrams can represent a form of ritual knowledge in students' thinking. A classic signal that reveals this 'ritualised thinking' by students is when they use diagrams to discuss real-world phenomena (for example, an allocation problem), and assert that all that is required for the problem to be solved is to 'move along the line' or 'shift the curve'. Such students are able to 'plot' or 'explain' using a diagrammatic model, but are unable to articulate either the real-world relationships or the underlying conceptual or mathematical model. When engaging with the diagram, 'the picture' can serve to create the powerful illusion that something has been understood, when it has not.

b   A second category of troublesome knowledge is *inert knowledge*. This is knowledge that 'sits in the mind's attic, unpacked only when specifically called for by a quiz or a direct prompt but otherwise gathering dust' (ibid., p. 8). Perkins cites passive vocabulary, words that are understood but not used actively, as a simple example.

> Unfortunately, considerable knowledge that we would like to see used actively proves to be inert. Students commonly learn ideas about society and self in history and social studies but make no connections to today's events or family life. Students learn concepts in science but make little connection to the world around them.
>
> (Perkins, 1999, p. 8)

In economics this issue of conceptual inertness is frequently tackled by requiring students to locate and interpret discussions of economic concepts in newspaper articles. Introductory textbooks routinely use such newspaper excerpts as 'attention capturing' devices. However, for many students, the separation between that which is formally learned in economics, and the world around them, is wide and unbridged.

c   Knowledge that is *conceptually difficult* certainly exists in economics, as it does in most other disciplines. This category of troublesomeness according to Perkins is likely constituted by a mixture of misimpressions from everyday experience (in economics, for example, peoples' choices are *only* limited by their budget), mistaken expectations (economics is the study of how to make money), and the strangeness and complexity of terms (such as economists' use of utility theory). The resulting 'knowledge' is a mixture of misunderstandings in varying degrees and ritual knowledge applied in critical 'gaps'. Students learn ritual responses, but their intuitive beliefs frequently remain hidden unless examined directly in economic quantitative modelling applications or out-of-classroom contexts.

While the definition of opportunity cost, at first-year level, would not appear to represent conceptually difficult knowledge, there remains potential for 'mixed' understandings of the concept to be articulated in its application. For some students the definition that can be so clearly stated in one sentence simply fails to formalise, in terms of their own learning, an inclination to 'think like an economist'. As students progress in economics programmes, particularly when they encounter the interface between economic theory and measurement (econometrics), the potential increases for this version of troublesome knowledge to dominate.

d   Perkins's fourth category is *alien knowledge*; that which 'comes from a perspective that conflicts with our own. Sometimes the learner does not even recognize the knowledge as foreign' (ibid., p. 9). It is not uncommon in introductory economics courses to encounter students who reveal their 'anger' and 'disbelief' in the approach taken by the discipline. They just don't 'believe', for example, that it is 'appropriate' to put prices on say, wildlife, or that 'some' pollution may be acceptable if the benefit from the activity causing the pollution exceeds the pollution costs. This may be despite students agreeing that such approaches can serve to achieve objectives consistent with their original beliefs (such as wildlife preservation). In the extreme, such resistance to an 'alien' approach can result in the student withdrawing from the course.

e   Perkins suggests that troublesome knowledge may also emanate from the *complexity* of the knowledge or its *paradoxical* nature – often the result of subtle distinctions not detected by the student. While beginning students frequently 'miss' or do not 'appreciate' subtle distinctions, one aim of the educative process is to reveal these more subtle nuances. Such nuances are likely to be more difficult for students studying in a second language. Applied to the concept of opportunity cost, a subtle but critical element is the realisation that 'Opportunity cost is the evaluation placed *on the most highly valued* of the rejected alternatives' (Eatwell *et al.*, 1998, our emphasis). First-time learners tend to overlook this element for an understanding that views opportunity cost simply as the evaluation placed on the rejected alternatives.

f   Meyer and Land (2003, p. 419), in developing this sub theme, propose a further category of troublesomeness; that of *tacit knowledge*. In this case 'tacit knowledge' is 'that which remains mainly personal and implicit . . .

at a level of "practical consciousness" … though its emergent but unexamined understandings are often shared within a specific community of practice' (Giddens, 1984, p. 9). For western economists, such tacit knowledge is frequently linked to their shared understandings of the role of the market and government and the cultural mores behind accepted behaviour, institutional structures, laws, and incentives. When students *without* these understandings are taught economics, there is the potential for these assumptions to become barriers to their understanding of threshold concepts. A lack of tacit knowledge may apply more widely than first impressions would suggest. Many first-year university students (say under 20 years of age) appear to have relatively unsophisticated impressions of a number of phenomena in contrast to their lecturers. For example, many students have little experience with contracts or insurance, have not bought or sold houses, have only a fairly superficial impression of the role of government, and have not deeply considered the role of markets as a man-made device for allocating resources. Threshold concepts that can be applied to these phenomena and *help students to see them differently*, may prove troublesome precisely because students do not have the tacit understating of the context in which they are most applicable.

Language too may prove troublesome. Many first-year economics students report that they find 'economic jargon' the most difficult barrier to their understanding. For economists, 'learning the language' is one of the necessary elements in learning to 'think like an economist'. As Wenger (2000), points out, such discourses distinguish individual communities of practice and are necessarily less familiar to new entrants to such discursive communities or those peripheral to them. Thus troublesome knowledge may impact on 'ways of thinking and practising' within particular disciplines (Meyer and Land, 2003). This issue is not discussed further because in introductory courses teaching the concept of opportunity cost is initially aimed at getting students to think about and properly apply the concept in a circumscribed way, rather than requiring them to immediately and explicitly 'think like an economist'. This focus, however, does not lessen the impact that opportunity cost, and other threshold concepts, have in characterising 'how economists think'. Nor does it prevent an inclination by some first-year students to convincingly exhibit such thinking.

Conceptually distinct forms of troublesome knowledge, including troublesome language, can thus be viewed from a student learning perspective as representing dimensions of variation through which students (not all) may transit (or get stuck in) in *approaching and attempting to acquire* threshold concepts.

Data collection

The University of South Australia is a public university whose main campuses are located in Adelaide, South Australia, with approximately 29,000 students and 2,000 staff. The Division of Business represents approximately one-third of the university.

Within the Division of Business, all students undertake a core of business-related courses in their first year before continuing on to more specialised programmes. One course (of eight) taught to full-time students in their first-year is named 'Economic Environment'. This course is taken by most students in their first semester. It is a first-year macroeconomics course whose principle text is an Australian adaptation of the introductory American textbook by McConnell.

The course is a fairly standard first-year macroeconomics course, but with an introductory three weeks of 'microeconomic' concepts. Delivery of the course to local students consists of two hours of lectures and a weekly (one-hour) tutorial. Overall class numbers are around 800, and the average number of students per tutorial is 20–25. There are four components of continuous assessment and a final closed-book examination.

An important element of the course includes explicit efforts to raise students' metalearning capacity (see Meyer and Shanahan, 2004, for a full description). Part of this process involves students providing written answers to questions that focus on 'learning'. Their answers are completed prior to attending their weekly tutorial and handed to their tutor on arrival. In 2003, in weeks four and eleven of the thirteen-week course, students were asked to respond to the invitation to *Write an explanation in your own words, of what the term 'opportunity cost' means.* Responses, gathered in week four, were solicited one week after the concept was introduced in lectures and after discussion in tutorials. The concept, though applied extensively as an underlying concept through the course, was not directly defined or addressed again in lectures before the week eleven responses were gathered.

While over 800 students were originally enrolled in the course, it was only possible to collect 234 written responses from tutors after week four. Some tutors were not aware of the need to inform students that their responses were to be used anonymously for further research, while in other cases tutors handed papers back after review. In week eleven 118 responses were gathered and it was possible to match 109 responses gathered in weeks four and eleven. There is no obvious reason to suspect that the final matched sample is a biased subset of the students who finished the course. The verbatim examples presented below come from students' responses in week four.

Locating troublesomeness

The initial textbook definition of opportunity cost given to students was 'the amount of other products that must be foregone or sacrificed to obtain a unit of any product' (Jackson and McIver, 2001, p. 42). Critical to this definition (and frequently overlooked by students) is that it is provided in a 'two goods' context. That is, such a definition is absolutely correct only in the context of there being only *one* alternative. In this case the textbook uses the example of chocolate bars and tractors (to represent present consumption and investment in productive capacity), and illustrates the 'trade-off' between having more of one and less of the other. So, the 'opportunity cost' of producing one more tractor was 1,000 chocolate bars foregone. Subsequent discussion in tutorials focused on having students apply the concept in a broader context (more alternatives) and attempting to apply it in their own lives (for example, the opportunity cost of attending university). Thus the teaching method employed first introduces students to an extremely simple example (two goods with no complicating alternatives), and seeks to deepen their appreciation of the concept via subsequent discussion and application. (Other textbooks adopt different approaches. For example, the initial definition of opportunity cost in one adaptation of Parkin is that it is 'the best alternative foregone' (McTaggart *et al.*, 2001, p. 48).)

To examine whether there is observable variation in the quality of students' articulation of the concept of opportunity cost, the week four responses were examined in relation to the previous descriptions of troublesome knowledge. While examination of the responses revealed that *some* students found the concept troublesome, it also revealed that distinguishing the underlying types of knowledge associated with troublesome knowledge could be difficult. For example, while several responses were suggestive of 'ritualised' knowledge, it was difficult to detect whether this was because students also found the language troublesome or because their knowledge was more 'inert'. Nonetheless, the following verbatim examples are put forward as illustrations of expressions of a threshold concept whose articulation has been affected by one or more of the troublesome forms of knowledge.

(a) Ritual knowledge

A response that provides a clear example of 'ritual knowledge' is given by one student in week four:

> Opportunity cost is a term used in economics to describe the amount of product that must be sacrificed to get some other product. There are a limited amount of resources available to make products. These resources can be used to make many items. Because these resources are limited, only a certain number of items can be made. If all the possible quantity of one particular item is made with all of the available resources, no other items can be made. The number of items that weren't made is the opportunity cost. Another example: using half the available resources to make some item, and the other half of the resources to make a different

item, the opportunity cost would be the amount of items that were not made because the other item was made instead. The opportunity cost between two items can be shown on a diagram.

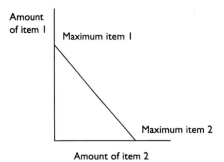

The diagram shows the amount of each item on the axis. The maximum amount of items that can be made from the available resources is shown by the curve. The two items can be produced at anywhere along or inside the line. A point on or inside the line shows the amount of each item being made. The opportunity cost is displayed as one item increases in quantity, the other item will be decreased.

(Response A12)

This response replicates not only the wording of the concept, but the context (2 goods), and even the style of presentation in the text (brief outline and diagrammatic representation). Almost the only element contributed by the student is the 'removal' of the references to tractors and chocolates. The wording also suggests a very mechanistic replication of the concept – almost to the point of confusion (that is, where the student varies the quantities traded off and gets 'tangled').

(b) Inert knowledge

The impact of inert knowledge can be difficult to separate from ritual knowledge, as it is expressed in a similar 'wooden' and 'unconnected' way. In the example, the student attempts to make the connection to everyday life, but 'falls back' to an example he considers 'better'.

Opportunity cost is a term used to describe a cost that is measured in terms of loss in opportunity. For example, when you decide to spend the afternoon watching 'Jerry Springer' instead of doing your economics homework, the opportunity cost there to you, is that you'd have lost that opportunity of maybe learning something in economics. Whereas lets say you decide to do your economics homework instead of watching 'Jerry Springer', the opportunity cost to you there then, would be that you'd have lost the opportunity to watch a perhaps interesting and entertaining episode of the 'Jerry Springer' show. A better example for an economic student would be something like having the decision to either produce more food or more weapons for a nation, since in economics opportunity cost is more likely to include decisions concerning tangible objects. Lets say you choose to make more weapons. The decision would involve sacrificing the production of food which is the opportunity cost involved in making that decision.

(Response A21)

This response again uses examples from the 'two good' case – but the student appears to be uncomfortable with the implications of the 'real-life' example and returns to the 'better' example – 'for an economic student' – of food and weapons.

(c) Conceptually difficult knowledge

The concept of opportunity cost is, perhaps, conceptually less difficult than other threshold concepts in economics. Nevertheless it may be difficult for novices to apply in the correct context. Consider the following example:

Opportunity cost is a complex notion of substituting something for something else. In everyday terms, opportunity cost can be used to explain many of the decisions we make and how we make them. If we wish to purchase a product, we exchange it for either cash or credit, which is ultimately what we have earned in one form or another. For example, if we purchase a television, we are exchanging our personal income for the television. Opportunity cost on the other hand refers to what must be substituted in order to purchase that television. This decision is the result of many determining factors, such as our wants, needs, desires, income (can we afford it), cost and so on. . . .

The cost of purchasing something (in this case a television) will result in the amount of other goods that must be used instead, an alternative. Buying a television may substitute the going out to dinner for a few months. In this case, the opportunity cost of the television is how many dinner outings must be forgone.

In economic terms it refers to the amount of one product that must be relinquished in order to obtain a unit of another product. Through economic markets, the laws of supply and demand determine what and how much of each product is supplied and at what price and cost. When the demand for a particular product decreases, producers decrease the production of that product and in its place, manufacture another product that is in higher demand. This can create economic problems. For example, decreasing the amount of school teachers to increase the number of army soldiers is not equal. Does a school teacher have the skills, knowledge and training to face combat and army exercises? This is another example of opportunity cost.

The cost of substituting one product for another is known as the product's opportunity cost.

(Response A193)

This student appears to be making a genuine effort to engage with the concept, but is struggling to apply it in a meaningful way. Here the implications of the student's example of how exactly one 'measures' the trade-off between soldiers and teachers appears to 'block' the student's development and articulation of the concept – and hence there is a quick return to a 'text-like' definition.

(d) Alien knowledge

While admittedly a question of interpretation, it is possible to view a student's response written from the perspective of an 'outsider' as reflecting 'alien knowledge'. One indicator used to categorise this explanation as 'alien' is the student's use of the phrase 'An economist'.

An economist sees the resources (Land, Capital and Labour) used to produce goods and services as scarce i.e. they are limited. Because resources are limited, sacrifices have to be made to produce goods and services. For example, if the government wants to give X amount of dollars to the Defence Force, some other area, eg education, has to get less amount of dollars (see model A). To produce more of one good or service, you have to produce less of another good or service. This is what 'opportunity cost' means.

(Response A150)

What appears to be signalled here is an inclination to state 'how economists think', rather than 'this is how I think in economic terms'.

(e) Paradoxical knowledge

This expression of troublesome knowledge is generally related to the student 'missing' some of the important nuances in the original concept. In the example the student has missed the important idea that opportunity cost reflects the value of the next best foregone alternative, and expresses opportunity cost simply as 'all foregone alternatives'.

Opportunity cost is a concept used in economics, but it can be applied to everyday situations. For example, if you sleep in on a Saturday morning, the 'opportunity cost' of your decision to sleep in, is *everything* else that you could be doing instead. It is, in other words, what you sacrifice in order to sleep in. Maybe you sacrifice breakfast, sport or watching television. Another example is if you have $2 to spend in a shop and the shop only sells 2 products, cans of coke and lollypops. If you purchase the can of coke (price $2) you have effectively given up 4 lollypops (price 50 cents each). The opportunity cost of your decision is 4 lollypops. It is important to remember that opportunity cost is not measured in monetary terms but in quantity (amount of something).

(Response A25, emphasis added)

Given the introductory text's definition, this lack of nuance is understandable; however, the student has clearly moved from the two good case to the 'multiple good' case without realising its implications. The subsequent example, based explicitly on two goods, highlights the student's lack of recognition of the difference between the two situations and the more precise definition of opportunity cost.

(f) Tacit knowledge

Detecting a lack of 'tacit knowledge' is difficult in these short explanations if, as before, students resort to ritualised responses to 'cover' their lack of understanding. Nevertheless, some responses suggest that the student lacks some crucial tacit knowledge.

An opportunity cost is for example the amount of something, or a product/object even, that one must surrender in order to gain another. To put it simply it is the means of sacrificing something for something else! Opportunity costing is often a very important part of decision making to balance out all of one's prospects, ideas, costs, and resources etc. This often means that alternatives must be made, and one in turn may not always be happy with the short term outcome. A reason as to why this method is important is so one can benefit by gaining from one source if sequentially it was not as needed. If there is an insufficiency or shortage (more often times than not, certain resources are scare and frequently hard to find) of something/product this is a great method to use. Opportunity costing is also used to keep demand and competition strong.

(Response A135)

This response, which could be characterised as being at 'arm's length', may be a function of the student feeling 'alienated' by the concept of opportunity cost. This form of response, however, is also frequently given by younger students who are 'ill at ease' in describing commercial settings or providing 'market-based' examples. The example appears to reflect a lack of the tacit knowledge assumed in economics courses – an ignorance of what Perkins (Chapter 3) refers to as the 'underlying game' that, in this case, the concept of opportunity cost essentially formalises.

(g) Troublesome language

Students frequently experience difficulty with the 'precision' of thought and language demanded of them in applying economic concepts. Others simply find the use of apparently similar terms in different contexts confusing. The following example suggests a student who has mixed up 'opportunity cost' with the term 'cost'.

> I think, the term 'opportunity cost' means that in the producer or supplier whose products cannot sell out, at some time or long time, and some inferior goods. So that they decided to use opportunity cost, forgone and or sacrificed to attract the people to wants their unit of product.
>   For example, a clothing shop of the boss who want to sell their summer clothing out, but at that time might be coming in winter, therefore the boss do not want any summer product accumulation before the winter season come. So that boss may consider to use sacrificed or forgone any product. However, if the boss has never studied economics, so the boss may be accumulate many product or give up to sell out.
>
> (Response A220)

Although it may prove difficult to isolate a particular category of troublesome knowledge, as this example shows the approach does allow insights into the 'gaps' or confusions expressed by students when they attempt to articulate their understanding of a threshold concept.

Concluding discussion

It appears arguable that students' articulation of a threshold concept can be located within a framework of troublesome knowledge for interpretive purposes. Two implications flow from this conjecture.

First, if it is possible to thus locate students' responses, then teachers have available to them an important insight into the possible *source* of any associated learning difficulties that students may have in acquiring the concept. This insight provides, in effect, an initial purchase on reducing the dimensionality of what Meyer and Land (Chapters 1 and 2) refer to as *pre-liminal variation*. Such purchase allows the teacher to locate more precisely, and respond more insightfully, to students' difficulties. For example, if a student is finding opportunity cost troublesome because the 'barrier' is a lack of tacit knowledge, then the focus of response may be on the 'underlying game' rather than the concept itself.

Second, if it is possible to locate students' articulation of a threshold concept within a troublesome framework, it may be possible to track the progression of their understanding of the concept over time. If, for example, a student presents a response that suggests they have a 'ritualised' view of a threshold concept in week four, and presents a similarly located response toward the end of the course, there is a reasonable inference that they have not advanced their understanding of the concept. There are implications here too for how opportunity cost and other threshold concepts may be assessed.

To illustrate further: the previous extracts were taken from students' responses in week four of the course. A subset of 109 matched responses was available in week eleven, and these were located within the same troublesome framework. In week four, 75 per cent of the matched responses were located as representing exhibited ritual knowledge. In week eleven only 45 per cent of the matched responses were thus similarly located. In week four approximately 5 per cent of matched responses could be interpreted as being accurate and self-expressed, while by week eleven about 25 per cent could be thus interpreted. Troublesome language accounted for between 5 and 10 per cent of responses on both occasions. The subjective and response bias of this exploration are fully acknowledged. However, what remains is the disturbing proportion of students who *persisted* in exhibiting ritualised responses. This finding suggests that, for these students, initial (mis)understandings of the concept remained relatively unaltered.

Refining the linkages between forms of troublesome knowledge and the acquisition of threshold concepts requires a clear and thorough understanding of how threshold concepts themselves 'come into view' for the learner, and an empirically based understanding of the troublesome dimensions of variation in learner engagement that may result. There is an immediate challenge here for teachers who may be required to identify subtle differences in students' articulations of 'understanding'.

Finally, there appear to be important implications for the manner in which students are introduced to threshold concepts. The conjecture here is that, seen from the student perspective, 'first impressions matter' when a threshold concept 'comes into view'. Efforts to make threshold concepts 'easier' by simplifying their initial expression and application may, in fact, set students onto a path of acquiring 'ritualised' knowledge that may actually prevent them from crossing the threshold.

References

Eatwell, J., Milgate, M. and Newman, P. (eds) (1998) *The New Palgrave. A Dictionary of Economics*, London: Macmillan.

Frank, R.H. (1998) 'Some thoughts on the micro principles course', in W.B. Walstad and P. Saunders (eds), *Teaching Undergraduate Economics: A Handbook for Instructors*, Boston, MA: Irwin/McGraw-Hill, pp. 13–20.

Giddens, A. (1984) *The Constitution of Society*, Cambridge: Polity Press.

Jackson, J. and McIver, R. (2001) *Macroeconomics*, sixth edition, Sydney: Irwin/McGraw-Hill.

McTaggart, D., Findlay, C. and Parkin, M. (2001) *Economics*, Sydney: Addison Wesley.

Meyer, J.H.F. and Land, R. (2003) 'Threshold concepts and troublesome knowledge: linkages to thinking and practising within the disciplines', in C. Rust (ed.), *Improving Student Learning – Ten Years On*, Oxford: OCSLD, pp. 412–424.

Meyer, J.H.F. and Land, R. (2005) 'Threshold concepts and troublesome knowledge (2): epistemological considerations and a conceptual framework for teaching and learning', *Higher Education*, 49, 373–388.

Meyer, J.H.F. and Shanahan, M.P. (2004) 'Developing metalearning capacity in students: actionable theory and practical lessons learned in first-year economics', *Innovations in Education and Teaching International*, 41, 443–458.

Perkins, D. (1999) 'The many faces of constructivism', *Educational Leadership*, 57(3), 6–11.

Shanahan, M. and Meyer, J.H.F. (2003) 'Measuring and responding to variation in aspects of students' economic conceptions and learning engagement in economics', *International Review of Economics Education*, 1, 9–35.

Wenger, E. (2000) *Communities of Practice*, Cambridge: Cambridge University Press.

Chapter 8

Threshold concepts in Economics

A case study

Nicola Reimann and Ian Jackson

Introduction

This chapter documents a collaborative investigation of students' developing understanding of two threshold concepts in Economics which was carried out in the context of the Enhancing Teaching–Learning Environments in Undergraduate Courses (ETL) project. ETL was a large-scale research project funded by the UK Economic and Social Research Council (ESRC) as part of their Teaching and Learning Research Programme (TLRP). The notion of a threshold concept is part of the larger conceptual framework developed by the ETL project. The main issues here are whether it provides practitioners with a novel and useful pedagogic tool and whether thinking about teaching–learning environments in terms of threshold concepts has the potential to enhance them. Many of the economists who were interviewed identified concepts which they regarded as thresholds for their discipline and some of them suggested that threshold concepts may be particularly important at the beginning of an Economics degree course.

The context of the case study

The setting for this chapter was a first-year introductory microeconomics module in a post-1992 UK university with a diverse student intake, which included a large proportion of students from non-traditional backgrounds. One member of staff was responsible both for the design and the delivery of the module. It was a compulsory component on three Economics degrees, taught in one hour of lectures and one hour of tutorials per week, with the first semester focusing on the introduction of fundamental microeconomic principles, while these principles were applied to empirical observation and analysis in the second semester. At the time of the investigation, recruitment to degrees in Economics was low.

The collaboration with the ETL project started during the academic year 2001/2. When the first round of data collection took place, there were 17 students on the module and the data which were collected during that year generated the subsequent focus on threshold concepts which was pursued in the academic year 2002/3 during a second round of data collection. Initially, 13 students attended the module during the second year, but only 8 of them completed it. The group comprised students with and without previous knowledge of Economics, school leavers as well as mature students, international students and students from ethnic minorities. Approximately a quarter of the students were female, three-quarters were male.

Elasticity and opportunity cost as threshold concepts

In interviews conducted during different phases of the ETL project and in different institutional and modular settings, several university teachers of Economics, including the teacher responsible for the module discussed in this chapter, identified *opportunity cost* as an important threshold concept for their discipline. Opportunity cost is at the core of conventional economic principles and is a concept which specifically represents how economists think. Economic theory assumes that there are finite resources (supply) and infinite wants (demand). If resources are scarce, there will be competing alternative uses and any use of resources will by definition have an opportunity cost. 'The opportunity cost of any activity is the sacrifice made to do it. It is the best thing that could have been done as an alternative' (Sloman 2003: 7).

The cost of any activity measured in terms of 'the next best alternative forgone' is actually a *ratio* and thereby not a cost per se. Hence, opportunity cost is a *relative* cost of one economic activity set against an alternative or competing economic activity. Opportunity cost can be denoted in monetary values to allow direct comparisons. For example, the law of comparative advantage uses opportunity cost as a monetary ratio when assessing specialisation of production by a given country, which can produce goods *relatively* cheaply, even though it may not have an absolute advantage in terms of direct production costs. In contrast, the accounting definition of cost would not recognise a cost ratio in this manner. An accountant would tally expenditure (receipts received) against revenue (invoices sent), thus generating a profit and loss account. An Economics definition would note that investment, consumption or production had occurred, but would then question if this use of resources had the lowest opportunity cost given the issue of scarcity, as exemplified by the seminal 'guns versus butter' argument. To view costs as a ratio rather than as directly measurable is a fundamentally different way to view business decision-making. This radical departure from analysing direct costs to a cost ratio is what marks out Economics from the other business disciplines and therefore makes opportunity cost a threshold concept.

In addition to opportunity cost, the concept of *elasticity* was singled out as a threshold concept for the module:

T: If they can understand elasticity, they won't come across anything at level 1 and even at level 2 that would be more difficult [than elasticity].

   (. . .)

T: What you really need to be looking at is changes in supply and changes in demand. So if you understand the elasticity of a supply and demand curve, you can understand the changes and the elasticity of any curve. And curves are essential to the way in which economic ideas are represented.

I: So it almost has a transformative quality to it, if you understand THIS, it will be easier for you to access other things as well?

T: Yes.

(Sta2)

Price elasticity of demand (and supply) is the responsiveness of the quantity demanded (supplied) to a change in price. This calculation is useful in discussing pricing strategy and tax. Related to this are other types of elasticity, such as cross-price elasticity and income elasticity. Elasticity can be applied to all areas of the diagrammatical representation of ideas. In Economics an understanding of the algebraic treatment and manipulation of elasticity is essential. However, while opportunity cost is a fundamental starting point for all students of Economics, even where non-mainstream approaches are incorporated, the concept of elasticity is part of the toolkit of analysis in Economics. So although opportunity cost and elasticity are similar in the way in which they open up new ways of thinking about economic phenomena, there are also large differences between them. However, both opportunity cost and elasticity can act as threshold concepts for any microeconomics module, being two of the wider set of economic principles that underscore the discipline and make a would-be economist *think* like an economist. The importance of these two threshold concepts for the module investigated, and Economics more widely, therefore provided the rationale for this case study.

Research questions

Research about conceptual change has highlighted that everyday, common-sense conceptions often override scientific ones (Scheja 2002). One example with particular relevance for Economics is Dahlgren's seminal study of conceptions of price held by first-year undergraduate students of Economics (Dahlgren 1978), which showed that for a considerable proportion of the students, their everyday conception of price had not been replaced by an economic one. Thomas (1991) argues that in order to help students to review their existing conceptualisations, we must first determine students' current understanding of everyday phenomena. '(W)ithout this stage it is impossible to be precise about planning to change students' ways of understanding since there is no means of identifying the critical differences between the various ways of understanding' (Thomas 1991: 82).

According to Siegfried (1998), the overarching goal of Economics Education is to enable students to 'think like economists'. Thus, if threshold concepts lie at the core of what thinking like an economist entails, gaining access to variation in students' acquisition of threshold concepts would allow us to evaluate whether this goal has been achieved, or whether students are at least on the way to achieving it. However, how could students' understanding be accessed? We needed to find suitable *proxies* for the concepts concerned. The focus of this case study has therefore been to use situations related to students' everyday life in order to investigate whether their thinking in such situations has changed as a consequence of learning and being taught about threshold concepts. The assumption is that if students have 'crossed the threshold' and have started to think like economists, then their thinking about economic problems encountered in everyday situations should have changed as well.

The use of practical examples and real-world applications is common in teaching–learning environments in Economics, as exemplified by the questions used in tutorials and textbooks. Students of Economics who were interviewed for the ETL project repeatedly highlighted the role and importance of examples and applications to real life, both for their engagement with and their understanding of Economics. We need to ask, however, whether students can genuinely engage with the *kinds* of examples that are commonly used in Economics teaching and how close these are to the economic problems which students are confronted with in their everyday lives. We therefore needed to find a way of tapping into students' thinking about such problems. This involved the design of questions using authentic scenarios which (1) were as close as possible to students' own experiences, (2) would potentially lead them to apply their understanding of the threshold concepts in question, and (3) could possibly provide an alternative to the questions typically used in Economics Education. Through using such questions we wanted to find out whether the students had started looking at everyday economic problems through the eyes of economists as well as detecting both qualitative differences between their answers and qualitative change over time.

Another aim was to gain insight into the relationship between conceptual change and the teaching–learning environment, i.e. whether, and in what way, students' thinking had changed *as a result of learning and teaching*. We also wondered whether this case study would have any implications for the enhancement of teaching–learning environments more generally as the notion of 'threshold concepts' was an attempt to create good 'action poetry' (Perkins 2002), i.e. language which would help to make ideas about learning and teaching actionable. In addition, we wanted to find out whether the notion of threshold concepts transformed the way in which the *teacher* concerned thought about and conceptualised learning and teaching, and whether it changed the way in which he went about designing and teaching the module.

Data collection

Data collection followed a longitudinal design in an attempt to capture students' *developing* understanding of the two threshold concepts of opportunity cost and elasticity. The number of participants in the study was low, 11 students initially, 6 at the end of the module. This was due to a general lack of recruitment to the module as well as students attending infrequently, dropping out altogether or being unwilling to participate in the study.

The first set of data was collected in the second teaching week and before students were taught about the concepts in question (some students were expected to have some existing knowledge about the concepts from prior learning in Economics, e.g. A level). Students were asked to provide written answers to the McDonald's and mobile phone questions (see box).

Everyday questions using authentic settings

McDonald's® question
In McDonald's fast-food restaurant the breakfast meals are served until 10.30 a.m.

1   Explain why McDonald's does NOT offer an all-day breakfast menu.
2   Do you think the breakfast meal is more or less expensive than the other meals?

Please explain your answers.

Mobile phone question
Assume you have a mobile telephone, which was broken. You have had it repaired without any guarantee for a cost of £50. The telephone has just broken once more and you have had an estimate for fixing it again, this time with a guarantee, for £25.

1   Would you pay to have the telephone fixed at the cost of £25? Please explain your answer.
2   Would you pay to have a new telephone if the price is £75? Please explain your answer.

We expected that eating at fast-food restaurants and using mobile phones were part of student life. The rationale for the McDonald's question was to generate a direct analysis of production decisions (supply) and an indirect analysis of consumption patterns (demand). This analysis would include references to the responsive rate of supply and demand to changes in price, i.e. price elasticity. The mobile phone question was introduced into the case study by Jan Meyer, drawing on an idea by Pong Wing Yan. The rationale behind this question was to create a very practical dilemma that would require students to make a decision. This dilemma would include an assessment of opportunity cost using the notion of sunk costs, i.e. that the decision to have had the phone repaired is irreversible and should be treated as historic data.

Interviews with individual students were conducted seven weeks later, during which students were presented with their own original answers to the questions. In another interview, the module leader reflected on students' answers (anonymised), the questions, the teaching–learning environment and the way in which the threshold concepts featured in it. This interview formed the basis of a questionnaire focusing on the conceptual content and the sophistication of student answers, which was completed by the module leader. At the end of the module, both the students and the module leader were interviewed once more and those students who were still on the module answered the two questions again. Table 8.1 outlines the data and the different stages of the data collection process.

Table 8.1 Data

Baseline data collected prior to case study
May 2002

1   One interview with module leader
2   One interview with group of students about teaching–learning environment

Data collected during case study
October 2002: start of module, before being taught about threshold concepts

1   Eleven written answers to everyday economic questions

November 2002: after being taught about threshold concepts

2   Nine one-to-one interviews about each student's written answers to everyday questions, the questions and the teaching–learning environment
3   One interview with module leader about written answers to questions and teaching–learning environment

May 2003: end of module

4   One questionnaire about conceptual content of written answers to questions
5   Six written answers to everyday economic questions (= step 1 repeated)
6   One interview with group of students about experiences on the module and threshold concepts
7   One interview with module leader about teaching–learning environment and threshold concepts.

Findings and discussion: the questions and the answers

First answers

When the teacher was asked to evaluate students' first answers (steps 3 and 4 in Table 8.1), interesting differences between the two questions emerged. While almost all answers to the McDonald's question were deemed to contain some elements of economic reasoning (albeit limited), the mobile phone question produced much more variation. From a research perspective, the mobile phone question was therefore judged to be more suitable as a tool to identify differences between the way in which students think about economic phenomena. The teacher, however, preferred the McDonald's question. This might be due to the relatively common occurrence of questions of this kind in Economics teaching. One might even hypothesise that not only despite, but *because* the McDonald's question produced answers which were more economic in nature, the teacher favoured this question.

When interviewing the teacher about the answers to the McDonald's question, it also became clear that this question had produced answers which made implicit reference to a much wider range of economic concepts and perspectives than the mobile phone question. Only one answer, however, was judged as referring to elasticity of demand and the term 'elastic' was explicitly used in the text. No answer explicitly mentioned opportunity cost. The almost entire absence of explicit references to both opportunity cost and elasticity was surprising as 4 of the 11 respondents had an A level in Economics and others had been taught Economics within HND, access or business courses. Several answers to the McDonald's question, however, contained economic terminology: three answers, for instance, referred to 'demand', one to 'supply'. Most answers to the mobile phone question were equally judged by the teacher to contain some economic language.

First answers versus interview statements

When the written answers to the question (step 1) were compared to the answers given in the interviews (step 2), very few differences emerged. Most interviewees had not changed their minds about their answers to the two questions *after they had been taught about elasticity and opportunity cost* within the context of the microeconomics module. No differences between the answers to the two questions emerged. Some examples:

Mobile phone question
a   first answer
1   It depends on my financial situation at the time. Also I'd take into account the benefits and costs of having the phone fixed again @ the cost of £25. As there is a guarantee, I'd probably have the telephone fixed but a strong option would be to buy a new phone.
2   I would pay £75 to have a new telephone, as it is I have spent £75 on fixing the old telephone. A new phone would come with a guarantee that is fixed for a period of time, so I'll not have to pay if the phone is broken or damaged.

(StuH)

b   answer in interview
I: What about the mobile phone? (. . .)
S: It depends on my financial situation at the time. And as well take into account the benefits and costs of having the phone fixed again. Because paying 50 pounds to (?) guarantee plus and it's just broken again, that means it's another 25 pounds with a guarantee and altogether it's about 75 pounds whereas (. . .) for the same 75 pounds I could buy another phone with a fixed guarantee for a period of time, meaning I don't have to pay for the problems when it's broken or damaged. And as well with number one probably have the phone feature but I'll be more inclined to get a new phone.
I: (. . .) In terms of what you've written, you would still answer the question very much the same way you answered it.
S: Yeah.

(StuH)

First answers versus second answers

Only 5 of the students who had answered the first set of questions answered the second set (step 5). In the second answer to the McDonald's question, students repeated some of the arguments they had used before, but they also introduced new ones. The answers tended to contain limited evidence of improved economic understanding and thinking by the students. In the example below, Student A showed little economic understanding on the McDonald's question in the first set of answers and only briefly mentioned choice and demand. The second set of answers for student A showed evidence of maximising choices subject to a constraint. The student also introduced the cyclical nature of demand and how demand can peak, although price elasticity is only mentioned implicitly.

McDonald's question

a   first answer

    1   I don't know. Maybe because people would prefer it than other meals. Or because all the people that would buy breakfast meals gather up in the first few hours, so there are more customers.

    2   It depends on what you get. If you get a full-breakfast meal it must be expensive. If you take just a cup of coffee it would be cheap. I think the food is different in each meal. Anyway, I wouldn't know because I don't eat at McDonald's.

b   second answer

    1   People are going to their jobs, students to their schools until 10.30. This is the time of the day that breakfast meal consumption is maximum. They are trying to sell as much as they can. They cut the expenses of breakfast meals by 10.30 am.

        If offering an all day breakfast menu people would not mind going there before 10.30. Thus McDonald's is trying to gather all the breakfast meals consumers before 10.30 am. since people are not used to go to restaurants at this early time of the day they are trying to increase morning sales.

    2   The breakfast meal is changeable. You can pick from a variety of goods each increasing the price of the meal. Since there is a time frame until 10.30 am this is a high peak time so breakfast might be a little more expensive than the other meals sold all day.

(StuA)

A largely similar pattern emerged from the second answers to the mobile phone question. Of the 5 students who answered each question twice, two changed their minds from wanting to buy a new phone to having the old one repaired. The recognition of sunk cost evident in those answers can be interpreted as a qualitative conceptual change towards a more economic answer. Only two students vastly improved the economic quality of the answer and correctly answered the question in terms of sunk costs (without explicitly using the term). Their first answers had been much weaker in terms of economic principles and had focused on general and vague matters of consumerism.

Mobile phone question

a   first answer

    1   If it was the same fault then first of all I would return back to the place I first got it fixed and try my hardest to get some money back. If I have no chance getting my money back, then I would consider repairing the phone for £25 with the guarantee, if would work out cheaper then buying the same phone again.

2   I would buy a new phone for £75 if it was a newer model to what I had before. If it wasn't then I wouldn't because I would have already spent £50 on repairing the old phone, then plus £75 would of made it £125 for the same which I would have paid only an extra £25 on the £50 which would got in repaired and also with a 12 months guarantee.

b   second answer
1   I would pay for the phone to be fixed for £25 with the guarantee, because first of all it is cheaper than before and this time with a guarantee and now knowing that it could break again having the guarantee will be reassuring, knowing if it did break I wouldn't be paying £50 of £25 again.
2   It depends, if the old phone's only problem is the one being fixed, with the guarantee, then no because that means me paying out £50 more than I need to. If not then, only if the new phone has a guarantee if it breaks down.

(StuB)

Overall, there was some evidence of (limited) improvement between the first and second attempts as some of the second answers reflected the two threshold concepts and showed modest positive changes in understanding. This seemed to suggest that students were generally *starting* to think like economists, without, however, explicitly referring to the economic principles under investigation. Opportunity cost did not feature explicitly in any of the answers to the mobile phone question, although nearly all of the answers referred to it implicitly. Only one first and one second answer to the McDonald's question contained the term 'elastic'. However, there seemed to be a tendency for some individuals to use more economic terminology in the second answer to the McDonald's question. (Some students also used some economic terminology in their first answers, but these were not necessarily the same individuals who answered the question again at the end of the module.) This development was most pronounced in Student A who used the term 'customers' in his/her first answer, whereas in the second answer s/he talked about 'consumers' and 'consumption' as well as 'goods', 'expenses', 'increase sales', 'increasing price' and 'high peak time'. There was much less evidence of obvious economic terminology in both answers to the mobile phone question. The increase in the use of discipline-specific terminology in the McDonald's question is in line with Dahlgren's (1978) study where the same phenomenon was observed. It must be noted, however, that evidence of economic terminology does not necessarily imply that an answer is also economically sophisticated.

Students' perceptions of the questions

Some students highlighted the importance of having had relevant personal experience in order to answer the questions adequately. Several of them perceived the McDonald's question as an *economic* question, whereas the mobile phone question was described as less economic and more *personal* since it depended on individual, subjective judgements.

> s: Yes, it [the McDonald's question] brings up some good economic theory, don't it? I mean the second one [the mobile phone question] is debatable, don't it, because it is more our personal preference (than?) actual economic theory. And if you get it fixed it depends on your income or anything, while. It's economic to a degree, but not as much as the first one is, the McDonald's question.
>
> (StuJ)

When the questions were designed the intention had been to access students' personal, everyday conceptions of the threshold concepts under investigation. Did students' comments imply that this aim was achieved with the mobile phone question? Mainstream economic thinking assumes rational decision-making and choice. Describing the mobile phone question as 'more personal' might imply that their decision contained an element of *irrationality*. The mobile phone question was asked and answered from a *consumer's* perspective and this may also be why several students stated that they would buy a new phone if it offered more and newer features. The McDonald's question, on the other hand, cast them into the role of the *supplier* which is per se removed from their own personal experience. When we first asked the questions, the students demanded additional information, such as the original price of the new phone and whether the new phone came with a guarantee. Their personal experience with mobile phones made them consider various 'buts' and 'ifs', while this did not arise in the less familiar situation of the McDonald's question.

The situated nature of the questions

Halldén (1999) argues that contextualisation might be the key to understanding what appears to be students' difficulties in acquiring new conceptions.

> If we ask students direct questions pertaining to theoretical principles, we risk getting responses that mirror verbatim learning only. If, on the other hand, we ask real-world questions, we are in fact testing much more than the students' knowledge of theoretical principles. We are also testing their ability to contextualize problems in the realm of the appropriate

scientific field as well as their ability to identify a problem as a case in which a scientific principle is to be applied.

(Halldén 1999: 56)

We must therefore take into consideration that the students' answers to the two questions might have been influenced by their perceptions of what the questions were trying to elicit, rather than by a lack of understanding of the two threshold concepts per se. The students may have interpreted the McDonald's and mobile phone questions asked by an educational researcher as requiring very different answers to, for instance, the same questions being put to them in the context of an Economics *examination*. The fact that the mobile phone question cast students in the familiar role of consumers has already been mentioned above. This can perhaps be approximated to what Halldén refers to as students contextualising the question within a more familiar, popular 'speech genre'. We do not know the reasons for students' decisions to answer the questions in the way they chose or whether students whose answers did not bring up opportunity cost and elasticity might have deliberately decided on another non-economic method of answering the questions. Halldén also points out that there might be other situational reasons for omitted responses, such as a respondent's reluctance to participate.

The impact of the teaching–learning environment on students' understanding of threshold concepts

The concept of elasticity was taught as a discrete 'topic', which was allocated a block of two weeks on the module timetable. The teaching broadly followed a *theory first* approach, 'in which students are schooled into an understanding of various theoretical models and then invited to apply such models to contemporary problems' (Vidler 1993: 179). For the initial introduction of elasticity, a set sequence was used: first, the concept was derived, defined and discussed, then the students were shown the relevant graphs and, after that, the formula for the calculation of elasticities was given. This was followed by a variety of examples. Finally, the students applied elasticity to the analysis of authentic, up-to-date market data from a Mintel Report in an assessed essay.

T: What I was hoping to do was build up layers of learning so they get an intuition about what elasticity is and how useful it can be. They then get an idea of diagrammatically representing the ideas and then using algebra to represent the ideas and then in the tutorials that are going on at a similar time draw through the ideas by using examples and making it relevant. (. . .) I try to put into context why elasticity is used in hopefully a non-linear way so that they are getting a wider picture. Not that: 'this is elasticity and we'll move on to the next topic of costs.'

(Sta2)

When the students were asked about their perceptions of the way in which they had been taught about elasticity, they also mentioned the definition, graphs, calculations and examples. The role of graphs for understanding was highlighted in particular.

S: It's taught like in demand and supply curves, so it was drawings really, start with just graphs.
I: So would he go to the board and –
S: Yeah, put it, just draw it up, so it's like inelastic could be a steep slope and elastic could be a shallow slope and then go from there, explain how it works. So you just like draw two points on and show how much quantity'd change if price didn't change and.
I: So graphs in that respect are the most important means of –
S: They help you understand a lot really, yeah. I think that's true in a lot of Economics.

(StuJ)

Other aspects of the teaching–learning environment also helped the students to understand elasticity. One student grasped the concept when the metaphorical nature of the term had been pointed out. Several interviewees stressed that attending lectures alone was not sufficient and reading in particular was identified as the best way of achieving understanding. The fact that another module dealt with the mathematical representation of elasticity also aided understanding as it reinforced the material.

Most interviewees said that the basic idea behind the concept of elasticity was relatively easy to understand, in particular if they had prior knowledge of Economics. There were, however, aspects of elasticity which were described as difficult. Those related either (1) to the more specific, additional types of elasticity, i.e. cross-elasticity, income elasticity, point elasticity, (2) to applying elasticity to complex, real-world examples and (3) to the mathematics behind elasticity.

S: It's not so difficult to understand what elasticity is, from the beginning, if you see just as elasticity. (. . .)
    (. . .) But if you try to use it in a market, like when you say if demand is elastic or inelastic, (. . .) it's like a little bit difficult to understand (. . .).
I: (. . .) So you are saying the basic idea is quite straightforward?
S: You can understand what it means. When you say elasticity, when you first try to learn elasticity you'll probably understand it. It's not so difficult, the meaning. But it's difficult to understand what kind of elasticity it is, like when elasticity starts to divide into –
I: – in different types of elasticity.
S: In different types of elasticity.

(StuE)

Six weeks into the module, the students were asked which concepts had been particularly important on the module so far. Without being prompted, only one student mentioned elasticity but then went on to say that really all concepts were of equal importance. Only two students talked about the relative importance of elasticity but only once the interviewer had asked them about it.

S: That's quite important with everything really because if a company knows that their product is inelastic, then they can put the price up by a massive amount and they won't lose much demand. (. . .) It's useful when making decisions about how much they charge for a product because they can make massive profits. It was also introduced with taxes because if the government will tax a product (. . .), say cigarettes are inelastic because people won't give them up, so they can tax them by a massive amount, and (. . .) make massive revenues on them.

(StuJ)

In the group interview at the end of the module, the students were asked once again which concepts had been important. This time elasticity was brought up without prompting:

I: OK, anything else in addition to supply and demand you thought was particularly important?
S3: Elasticity (laughs).
I: Why are you laughing?
S3: (. . .) If in doubt, use elasticity, something like that.
I: (. . .) What made it so important? Was it just because he [the teacher] kept going on about it?
S5: It is a part of microeconomics that you need to know as well.
I: Why is it so important?
S1: We (will) find out next year.
     (Laughs)
I: You don't know. You think it's important, but you're not sure why it's important?
S5: It's important because it's prices and things. It's when you buy products and why certain products can be taxed highly and why certain products can't and things like that.

(Stu2)

I: Can you see any development in your understanding of elasticity?
     (. . .)
S3: Well, from not knowing what it is to knowing what it is, that is the big step one. So that can be knowing how to apply (the?) concepts that we

use. We had to use it in an essay, say, or in an exam. That's a big step as well.

(...)

I: Do you think elasticity is important for Economics as such, as a discipline, as a subject? – Yes. Why?

S5: It's just a massive part of it.

I: Do you think it's quite fundamental for the subject, to understand?

S5: Yes, supply and demand is the biggest part of anything, isn't it, and if you understand that you basically understand Economics. And elasticity is just a part of that.

I: (...) There are some things, when you learn, you suddenly think, wow, suddenly everything seems different, (...) you now see the world quite differently. (...). Has elasticity had that effect? (...)

S3: I don't think it's just elasticities, I think it's a lot of things that we've learnt through the year. Watching the budget a few weeks ago, you understand what the things (are) that they're talking about. You think, oh yeah. It's not just elasticity, it's the whole thing.

(Stu2)

The extracts quoted above show that the students acknowledged the importance of the concept of elasticity, but the evidence does not allow us to conclude that elasticity is definitely perceived as a threshold concept *by the students*. The last participant's comment indicates, for instance, that crossing the threshold might be a question of several concepts working *in conjunction* with each other, rather than understanding elasticity on its own having a transformative effect.

Very different insights were generated in relation to opportunity cost. According to the teacher, opportunity cost was taught in a less discrete, much more continuous and less tightly structured way.

T: I have talked about it as one of the defining concepts within Economics. (...) Every time it has cropped up (...) I have spotlighted opportunity cost within a pricing decision or within an allocation of cost decision. So for example today (...) we were looking at the labour market and we were looking at the way in which students make an opportunity cost decision to come to university. So I spotlighted opportunity cost there and I have done that (...) virtually every week. I have used the word opportunity cost or encouraged them in their answers to think about opportunity cost. So it's gone sort of through the course.

(Sta2)

In the interviews which were conducted six weeks into the course, however, hardly anybody could remember opportunity cost featuring prominently. Students stated that their understanding of the concept was based on previous knowledge obtained elsewhere or derived from independent background reading. None of the students seemed to think that opportunity cost was important in any way, or had been highlighted by the teacher as being important. During the end-of-module group interview the students had much less to say about opportunity cost than about elasticity. The following excerpt suggests that it is unlikely that opportunity cost had served as a threshold for the students.

I: What about opportunity cost (. . .)? Is that important for the module, do you think?
S5: Not as important as elasticity.
      (. . .)
I: (. . .) Again opportunity cost, is there anything you found difficult about opportunity cost?
S5: No, just basic, just a definition.
I: In terms of the assessment, did opportunity cost come into the assessment?
      (. . .)
S5: I don't think it was, no.
      (pause)
I: Again, is opportunity cost, do you think that is important for Economics in general?
      (pause)
S3: It builds the foundations. It comes into it, but it's not a major part of it. You wouldn't sit there and, say, write six pages on opportunity cost. You'd have a paragraph on it or you'd include it into your thing. It's not a major part of it.
I: What would you say?
S2: Same.
      (. . .)
S3: Opportunity was really easy to grasp, it wasn't too hard to grasp.
      (. . .)
S5: It's a natural concept.
      (. . .)
S5: It's a natural, it's an idea, isn't it? Opportunity cost. It's just a sentence, like, really.

(Stu2)

There are additional factors discussed elsewhere (Reimann 2004), which cannot be discussed within the limitations of this chapter, that may have had an impact on students' perceptions of the teaching–learning environment and their developing understanding of the two threshold concepts. These include the role of some students' prior knowledge of Economics as well as the nature of the introductory Economics curriculum which tends to cover a large number of concepts of seemingly equal importance.

The teacher's conception of learning and teaching

Several interview statements as well as ongoing conversations with the module leader suggested that the case study may have stimulated him to focus more than previously on student learning, to move towards seeing teaching as helping students to change their conceptions (Prosser and Trigwell 1999) and perhaps to integrate students' conception of everyday economic phenomena more into his approach to teaching. In an interview discussing students' first answers to the questions, the teacher highlighted the way in which the case study had allowed him to get closer to the student perspective.

T: It's reminded me how I struggled with Economics in my early years and something that I had actually, if I was to be honest with you, forgotten because it is a difficult subject to grapple with and it isn't an easy subject. You never have the penny dropping, the light never comes on, it's a very slow (inexorable?) process where it's year upon year upon year of studying Economics, that you only then start to think like an economist.

(Sta1)

The case study also seemed to have made the teacher aware of a possible gap between the experiences of students and the types of questions, problems and real-world examples which are commonly used in Economics Education, including those normally used in the context of the module investigated. For instance, being involved in the case study cast some doubt on whether asking the students to read the economics pages of the *Financial Times* and the *Guardian* really helps them to 'live out economic problems' (sta2) and is likely to change their everyday conceptions of economic phenomena.

The teacher said that the focus on opportunity cost and elasticity had allowed him to drive two central themes through the entire module rather than conveying them as separate and discrete blocks of knowledge. It seemed as if one outcome of this case study was the development of 'throughlines' (Wiske 1998), i.e. a focus on the overarching understanding goals of the module or, in this case, the overarching threshold concepts, which the teacher and his students revisited throughout the course of the academic year. According to the teacher, one of the disadvantages of the focus on two threshold concepts, however, was the potential to encourage the student to be obsessive with these two ideas, at the exclusion of other concepts and approaches. This links in with Meyer and Land's (2003) observation that threshold concepts can lead to a privileged or dominant view of a discipline.

Conclusion

The case study discussed in this chapter has been exploratory and therefore included conjectures and raised additional questions. It has illustrated that the notion of a threshold concept can be a useful lens through which to view a specific teaching–learning environment as well as students' emerging conceptualisations within a particular modular and disciplinary context. The emphasis on two threshold concepts provided the teacher with a clear focus for his teaching and helped him to connect it more explicitly to the student perspective. Everyday questions as used in the case study seemed to have some potential as proxies as they allowed us, to a certain extent, to access students' developing understanding of the two threshold concepts as well as their progress made in 'thinking like economists'. However, the case study also pointed to the practical difficulty of operationalising threshold concepts by designing appropriate everyday scenarios which are rooted in the student experience. The investigation of elasticity and opportunity cost illustrated that there can be distinct differences between individual threshold concepts, both in terms of the way in which they are taught and the process of conceptualisation. The discussion also highlighted a number of issues specific to teaching and learning in Economics and to the module in question and it can therefore be expected that other disciplines and modular contexts may generate different discipline and context-specific insights in relation to threshold concepts.

The findings of this case study can only be tentative and point to the need for more research. Such research ought to comprise investigations of the various possibilities for accessing students' understanding of threshold concepts, including different threshold concepts in different disciplines. The data provided an indication of some of those features of the teaching–learning environment which may promote or hinder the acquisition of threshold concepts. More systematic research is needed to establish a clearer understanding of the exact nature of teaching–learning environments which enable students to grasp threshold concepts, and such research should include an element of classroom observation. In addition, further research into the way in which the notion of a threshold concept impacts on teachers' practice and their conceptions of teaching and learning is needed as well as research into students' experiences of 'crossing the threshold'.

Acknowledgements

This chapter was prepared as part of the work of the Enhancing Teaching–Learning Environments in Undergraduate Courses project, which was funded by the Teaching and Learning Research Programme of the UK Economic and Social Research Council (http://www.tlrp.org). The case study originated in collaboration with Jan H. F. Meyer and Ray Land. The authors are grateful for Jan Meyer's support and his insightful comments on earlier drafts of this chapter. The idea for the mobile phone question came from Pong Win Yan; the way it has been applied to this case study is entirely the responsibility of the authors.

References

Dahlgren, L. O. (1978) 'Effects of university education on the conception of reality'. Paper presented to the Fourth International Conference on Improving University Teaching, Aachen, Germany, July.

Halldén, O. (1999) 'Contextual change and contextualisation'. In Schnotz, W., Vosniadou, S. and Carretero, M. (eds) *New Perspectives on Conceptual Change.* Amsterdam: Pergamon/Elsevier Science, pp. 53–65.

Meyer, J. H. F. and Land, R. (2003) Threshold concepts and troublesome knowledge: linkages to ways of thinking and practising within the disciplines. In Rust, C. (ed.) *Improving Student Learning: Improving Student Learning Theory and Practice – Ten Years On.* Oxford: OCSLD.

Perkins, D. N. (2002) *King Arthur's Round Table: How Collaborative Conversations Create Smart Organizations.* Hoboken, NJ: John Wiley & Sons.

Prosser, M. and Trigwell, K. (1999) *Understanding Learning and Teaching. The Experience in Higher Education.* Buckingham: Society for Research into Higher Education and Open University Press.

Reimann, N. (2004) 'First year teaching–learning environments in economics'. *International Review of Economics Education* 3(1), 9–38.

Scheja, M. (2002) Contextualising studies in higher education. First-year experiences of studying and learning in engineering. PhD thesis, Department of Education, Stockholm University, Sweden.

Siegfried, J. J. (1998) 'The goals and objectives of the economics major'. In Walstad, W. B. and Saunders, P. (eds) *Teaching Undergraduate Economics. A Handbook for Instructors.* Boston, MA: McGraw-Hill, pp. 59–72.

Sloman, J. (2003) *Economics,* fifth edition. Harlow: FT-Prentice-Hall.

Thomas, L. (1991) 'A new perspective on learning economics'. *Economics* 27(2), 79–83.

Vidler, C. (1993) 'Start making sense'. *Economics and Business Education* 1(4), 178–181.

Wiske, M. S. (1998) 'What is teaching for understanding?' In Wiske, M. S. (ed.) *Teaching for Understanding. Linking Research with Practice.* San Francisco, CA: Jossey-Bass, pp. 61–86.

Chapter 9

Threshold concepts, troublesome knowledge and emotional capital

An exploration into learning about others

Glynis Cousin

In this chapter I explore the notions of a threshold concept (Meyer and Land, 2003) and troublesome knowledge (Perkins, 1999) in relation to the teaching and learning of Otherness in Cultural Studies. This exploration is stimulated by interviews, focus group discussion and observations conducted across nine universities by the Communication, Culture and Media Studies (CCM) strand of the UK nationally funded project 'Enhancing Teaching–Learning Environments' (see acknowledgements). This research was designed to support understandings of key concepts in the teaching and learning of CCM and I will draw on some of the responses we received to animate my exploration. I have indicated where teachers were from 'old' UK universities (research-led with traditional, fairly homogenous student populations) or 'new' ones (more diverse and expanding student populations). All the student interviews were conducted in new UK universities. Since I am using the comments we have gathered to vivify my exploration rather than to substantiate it empirically, I have limited details of respondents to sex and broad type of institution.

At first glance, CCM looks like a disciplinary area which is likely to resist the construction of a taxonomy of stable threshold concepts; the sweep of CCM is too broad, too internally disputed and theoretically unfriendly to anything that looks like essentialist classification. However, we did receive agreement from the university teachers with whom we shared our notion of a threshold concept that this might provide a basis for thinking about curriculum design, particularly in relation to issues of difference, representation and identity – all of which require a grasp of the concept of Otherness.

Otherness as a threshold concept

Theorists like Said (1991) offered a critique of a European Enlightenment image of the West which was built partly on a demotion of anything beyond its shores as inferior and savage. This superiority complex licensed colonial violence, symbolic and real, and denied the scientific and cultural advances of regions beyond Europe. Self-aggrandisement operated through a process of belittling others; this dynamic has come to be known as Otherising. The concept of the Other also derived from existential explorations of woman as the Other of man (De Beauvoir, 1992), black as the Other of white (Fanon, 1986) and Jew as the other of Gentile (Sartre, 1948). More contemporary literature has modified the dualities suggested by some of these early ways of viewing social differences in favour of a more negotiable, relational and culturally hybrid interpretation of identity formation (e.g. Bhabha, 1994; J. Butler, 1990). However, the core notion that our identities are formed dynamically with our perceptions of 'Others' whose differences we come to characterise as not like ours remains 'central to the cultural studies project' (D. Butler, 1999).

There is no settled view about the meanings of Otherness. The instability of the concept is part of its territory. Indeed it would undermine the teaching and learning of Otherness were it to be treated as a truth to be unpacked since mastery includes a grasp of the debate about its explanatory scope and limitations. The idea of Otherness, then, captures contemporary understandings of social difference and, as such, I will argue, it contains key features identified by Meyer and Land (2003) and Perkins (1999) as being associated with a threshold concept. I now turn to a brief description of these features before discussing variation in students' affective and conceptual engagement with the learning of Otherness.

Learner transformation

Mastery of a threshold concept, argue Meyer and Land (2003), produces an ontological shift in the learner. New understandings are assimilated into the learner's biography, becoming part of what he knows, who he is and how he feels. Encouraging this shift is an acknowledged part of Cultural Studies teaching (see particularly Aldred and Ryle, 1999; Canaan and Epstein, 1997; Goldberg, 1994). Giroux (in Jacobs and Hai, 2002: 188), for instance, writes that the purpose of multicultural education is 'to get students beyond a world they already know in order to challenge and to provoke their inquiry'. This proposition certainly resonates with some of the comments we received from teachers. This is hardly surprising given that issues like Otherness require levels of personal engagement. Also unsurprisingly, we found indications of variation in students' willingness or capacity to so engage, as one teacher put it:

> Some students take to it and it changes their lives and their way of thinking and they get incredibly engaged . . . that's a minority . . . there's a bunch in the middle that work away at it and eventually get it by the third year but are in a state of high anxiety in the first year. . . . Some acquire it on the way and this becomes an important transition in their whole sense of self but there are a whole bunch of students, middle of the

road, for whom they are going through the motions and are finding a utilitarian route through it . . . some students can get 2:1s without really caring about it at all.

(female, new university)

Arguably, these differences could apply to any subject but, as I hope to show later, there are some distinctive features to the transformative character of learning Otherness.

Irreversibility

A second characteristic of a threshold concept is that it is *irreversible* in that once understood, the learner is unlikely to forget it. For teachers this can produce a low ability to empathise with students who have yet to gain mastery. They cannot get back to 'innocence' so to speak. For the student, understanding Otherness invites a personal 'turn', of the following sort: 'Being of mixed race myself I never really paid much mind to it but coming here I've had to define where I belong. I always have to address that' (first-year female student).

This question of irreversibility does not mean that students will forever rest their understanding on a threshold concept mastered; indeed they may well modify or reject the concept later but this will proceed from an internalised understanding of it.

Integration

A third characteristic of a threshold concept concerns its *integrative nature*, 'in that it exposes the previously hidden interrelatedness of something' (Meyer and Land, 2003). The importance of grasping the complex interconnectivity of Otherness was echoed by a number of teachers who suggested that any theme associated with it (e.g. gendered or ethnic identity) is best understood, pedagogically and conceptually, as a 'generative topic'. As one teacher put it: 'It's also about whatever is being problematised so its not that certain identities are ok – whatever you are looking at you're exploding and so seeing the tensions and contradictions' (female, old university).

This is a very important feature of grasping Otherness. Failure to grapple with the interconnectivity of social identities can result in serious misunderstandings, including politically correct and superficial ones. As the above teacher stresses, through any case of Otherness, students need to address how it structures thinking about identity and difference. They have to engage with understandings of cultural hybridity and to problematise notions of irreducible social differences within debates about essentialism. They will need to understand the interdependence of binary categories like black and white and to know that apparently innocent signs like 'non-white' or 'disabled' signify who people are not, rather than who they are. They will need to comprehend the dangers of constructing identity around a single axis (gender, sexuality, etc.) on the one hand, and of avoiding runaway pluralism which neglects tenacious power relations that sustain subject positioning on the other hand. In short, the concept of Otherness embraces complex and fluid understandings of social differences, representation and identity formation. This complexity and fluidity require careful thought about pedagogic strategy, not least because comprehending the integrative nature of Otherness demands personal involvement.

Troublesome knowledge

However it is approached, learning Otherness is likely to entail degrees of learner discomfort or even 'trauma', as one teacher put it. Arguably this, and the intrinsic conceptual difficulty of the concept, qualifies Otherness for Perkins's (1999) category of 'troublesome knowledge'. Such knowledge, writes Perkins, can involve difficult, specialist language or be counter-intuitive and alien (from another culture or discourse). For Land and Meyer (2003), troublesomeness inheres in many threshold concepts, but there are some modifications to be made to this assertion in the case of learning Otherness. While nearly all of the students we spoke to agreed that the language of Cultural Studies was difficult, the extent to which Otherness is counter-intuitive and alien as a concept may relate to the learner's subject position. Brah (1992: 134) for instance, notes that the 'Racialisation of white subjectivity is often not manifestly apparent to white groups because "white" is a signifier of dominance'.

Similarly, some students may be accustomed to placing people within ethnic minorities but may be less inclined to locate their own identity formation in ethnic majorities. And some students have trouble understanding that masculinity and femininity are not synonyms for male and female, that relations between sex, sexuality and gender are more slippery than social appearances might suggest to them. My point is that subject positioning might have a bearing on how alien or counter-intuitive the learning is, and perhaps troubling knowledge is a more apt term to use for the learning of Otherness because everyone, teachers and learners, has an internal relation to it (Johnson, 1997). Take for instance, what this teacher says: 'Nobody's got it right ... its not like if someone is black in the class, they know all the questions ... its not straightforward ... everybody in the class, whatever they are, it can be uncomfortable' (female, old university). And Richard Johnson: 'Studying culture is so rewarding and dangerous. It engages our existing forms of living, may enhance but also threaten them' (Johnson, 1997: 56).

Arguably, grasping any threshold concept is never exclusively to do with its inherent complexity or with activities of the mind. Learners will always be emotionally and socially positioned vis-à-vis whatever they are learning (e.g.

Shaw, 1995). To add to Perkins's (1999) very useful idea of troublesome knowledge, I propose a metaphor of emotional capital to complement that of Bourdieu and Passeron's (1977) metaphor of cultural capital.

Emotional capital

The concept of cultural capital rests on the view that its distribution tends to be as class-based as is the distribution of economic capital. Briefly, middle-class children participate in a set of cultural practices (social outings, dinner parties, piano lessons, sitting still and quietly to read, play chess, etc.) that taken together form a naturalised *habitus* which gives them a covert edge on working-class children whose own *habitus* will be less friendly to scholastic achievement, particularly since it is likely to clash with that of the teachers. The simple but powerful idea that students bring skills and knowledge from their family and cultural milieu to bear upon their scholastic achievement has provided a persuasive alternative to notions of innate intelligence.

The idea of emotional capital overlaps with but is distinctive from that of emotional intelligence (Goleman, 1995). Like cultural capital, emotional capital describes a set of assets rather than a facility to process emotional issues (the meaning of emotional intelligence). To illustrate, when the teacher above remarked that 'some students can get 2:1s without really caring about it at all', there is a hint that the students have wilfully decided to dismiss the importance of the subject to them. In offering the idea of emotional capital, I am attempting to locate this kind of problem, following Bourdieu and Passeron (1977), in social circumstances rather than in learner pathologies.

In so far as learning Otherness unpicks its way through questions like those of gender, racism, ethnicity, sexuality and disablement, the students with greater experiential proximity to the subject *may* bring more emotional capital to their understandings of them. It would be dangerous to over-determine student populations because there are no easy laws of causation to explain the distribution of emotional experiences. I do not want to import into this discussion a simplistic reading of identity politics in which provenance is believed to guarantee a privileged viewpoint. Rather I would argue for a broad understanding of 'experiential proximity' to include family and school cultures, ethical sensibilities and political awareness as well as social positioning. Age might be another factor; as one teacher of Cultural Studies in an Adult Education Department put it: 'I feel that the older students have much more sense of their own opinions and their own positions and they do challenge us' (female, old university). These students are felt to have more emotional capital in relation to their learning because they have life experiences on which they can draw. In contrast, when the following teacher was asked if he drew on students' experiences in his teaching, he appears to be suggesting that the distribution of emotional capital is too low because his students are socially homogenous, privileged and straight out of school:

I think the 18–19 year olds are fairly homogenous if I am honest. They tend to be middle-class kids to be honest – there aren't that many differences – increasingly you start to spot a greater range of students from different parts of the country but it is not that pronounced as it is in a lot of other universities. This is an issue that hasn't come to the fore yet (harnessing the students' experiences to the learning) because of our student mix which is basically lets be honest about this, white and middle-class. I think those questions are going to become more highlighted and indeed richer once the student cohort changes.

(male, old university)

This teacher might simply mean that a more diverse population will create richer exchanges of experience but there are hints in this passage that white, middle-class students are always experientially positioned at the starting line with only their books and lecture notes to help them. This contrasts with another teacher who talked about getting his students to deconstruct their middle-classness as a starting point to understanding Otherness. In the first suggestion, emotional capital is perceived to be too low to harness; in the second, it is read as simply variable. The risk with the former perspective is that students get stuck in what Meyer and Land (2005) call a pre-liminal state.

Liminality and variation in student positioning

In addressing learner incapability to master a threshold concept, Meyer and Land (2003) write that this 'may leave the learner in a state of liminality (Latin limen – "threshold"), a suspended state in which understanding approximates to a kind of mimicry or lack of authenticity'. The following two teachers' remarks offer some illustration of this point:

> With theoretical stuff, there's more uncertainty. Students are very young. Mimicry is a refuge.
>
> (female, old university)

> Quasi-plagiarism . . . copying it out of books and shoving it in . . . that's the students default position.
>
> (female, new university)

Mimicry, of course, can be a first stage of understanding but it can also be a form of ritualised learning described by Meyer and Shanahan (2003) as functional naivety – functional because it gets the students through their exams and naive because it does not lead to mastery. Meyer and Land (2005) refer to this functional naivity as a form of pre-liminal variation because, in this case, students do not even enter the prospectively transitional state of liminality. Perhaps this describes the students who 'are going through the motions and are finding a utilitarian route through it' described by the teacher above. The following four ideal types comprise my attempt to build on this kind of observation in order to draw out variation in student positions with respect to the state of liminality and the connectedness of this with emotional capital.

Spectator or voyeur

The spectator or voyeur describes the student who gazes at the Other at a distance and without looking at himself/herself. In the case of the *voyeur* this distance will be invested with exotic/erotic content. Some teachers indicated to us that a superficial understanding of Otherness tends to derive from a disinterested, distant, particularised reading of those vulnerable to oppression. For instance, in a day-long set of student presentations I observed with another researcher, we thought that one group appeared to offer a dutiful recitation of the problems of homophobia and the press. We were given a rather formulaic understanding of Otherness in which 'the good press' was tolerant of people's sexuality and 'the bad' was not. The teachers facilitating the session agreed. As one put it 'sometimes I think they are just trying to work out what boxes you want them to tick' (female teacher of journalism, new university).

There were resonances with this instance and Williamson's (1992) observations of schoolboys exploring women's oppression as an assessed project. Williamson (1992) has argued that students can 'do sexism' just as they can 'do the Ancient Romans'. They can bypass an interrogation of their own gendered positioning by studying others as a remote and victimised group. They can even churn out assessment assignments that attract good marks, alerting us to the possibility that variation in understanding produced by a distancing from the subject of Otherness may not come into view in conventional testing regimes. Of relevance to this point are David Butler's thoughts on learning criticality:

> In part it remains unclear whether being critical should be seen as a state of mind or a social practice . . . becoming critical could be seen as a matter of learning to reproduce the terminology and discourse structures of particular kinds of conventional critical writing and thus, in Bourdieu's terms, of acquiring a kind of cultural capital.
>
> (Butler, 1999: 182)

This can also be interpreted as a problem of domestication wherein the radical, transformative capacity of a concept is tamed by traditional academic assessment requirements. My next type may not even achieve at this functionally naive, reproductive level in that it describes a more conscious refusal to engage with the concept.

The defended learner

Teachers reported that they were well aware that a minority of students were resistant, hostile even, to the study of issues like Otherness, identity and representation:

> I think this might be the course that works for some students because you are talking about things close to their hearts and this can be engaging for students who have not been engaged before . . . it makes a difference on our courses if students are politically engaged because if you don't think there's a problem there is nothing than can interest you in all of this.
>
> (female, new university)

And 'Some disaffected students have problems seeing why there is a problem, why it isn't a case of reproducing the status quo' (female, new university).

It is well known among CCM teachers that some students are more interested in the practical aspects of Media Studies rather than the Cultural Studies dimensions to their degree. As one teacher of Media Studies in a new university put it, the 'technohead boys just want to press buttons'. Similarly, we had a few students reporting that they did not like the Cultural Studies side of their degree. 'I don't like the politically correct obsession' said one; and another, 'they keep telling us that we are suppressing (*sic*) people'. Taken out of context, comments like these can fuel a moral panic about political correctness in the CCM curricula. However, it is important to acknowledge and debate the fact that there are likely to be students of CCM with defensive, even aggressive, views about Otherness, however sensitively the subject is taught, and pedagogic strategies need to address this. For example, if a teacher takes an autobiographical approach in which learners are encouraged to look at their own lives for an interrogation of Otherness, this is best done without privileging the marginal and marginalising the apparently privileged. Notwithstanding its embrace of cultural hybridity and negotiated identity performances, integral to the concept of Otherness is the attribution of power to some and of powerlessness to others. If students match the concept's formal definitions of where power lies, they may feel over-determined by the categories under discussion if this caution is not heeded.

If we keep in mind Gorz's (1989: 176) reminder that 'no one actually coincides with what the sociologists call their social "identity" ', perhaps we can avoid the creation of a league table of victimhood (Medhurst, 1999) either as a conceptual framework for understanding Otherness or as a set of implicit judgements made about students in the classroom. This avoidance attempts to reduce the number of defended learners in the classroom in allowing the view that everyone has some kind of experience of inclusion/ exclusion on which to draw. In taking this direction, teachers will also be addressing the safety needs of learners.

In the concluding chapter we discuss the importance of constructing a safe learning environment for any threshold concept; arguably, for some concepts, like that of Otherness, it is a particularly pressing imperative, as this teacher confirmed: 'Thinking about an introductory module in the first year is thinking about ways in which to get the classroom environment right . . . they all need to feel comfortable and safe' (female, old university).

Learning can, of course, come through discomfort; one teacher said of male students learning about feminism: 'why shouldn't they feel uncomfortable?' There is a path to be navigated here. On the one hand, the right measure of discomfort requires a sensitivity to the defences of a defended learner. On the other hand, equal sensitivity is required for learners who are apparently rich in emotional capital. We should not assume that the latter group are willing to be 'bold disclosers' (Lupton and Henkel, 1999: 145). Whereas cultural capital can be gladly worn on a student's sleeve, some may choose to keep their emotional capital to themselves. Indeed, as the following teacher points out, it is often wise to advise them to do so: 'They don't have to discuss their experiences; that's an option. We do advise them not to choose something that is too traumatic' (female, old university). This warning is pressing for my next ideal type, namely the victim-identified learner.

The victim-identified learner

The reverse of the defended learner is that of the victim-identified learner (possibly a variant of the voyeur). In this case there is a readiness to be transformed but more through conversion than through critical engagement. The victim-identified learner, sometimes through personal experience and biography, sometimes through over-identification with 'others', is drawn towards the 'glamour of oppression' (Rushdie, 1988) and the moral high ground that can come from the full-time occupation of an oppressed group. This position is clearly linked to a particular form of identity politics though it might characterise an initial phase of awakening which eventually gives way to a nuanced understanding of self and the other. A more stuck victim-identified learner will be 'wound-attached' (Brown, 1995), fatalistic and angry about the inevitability of oppression and domination. Whereas defended learners will underuse their emotional capital, victim-identified learners might make excessive appeals to a conception of emotional capital as a depository for narratives of personal injury; this can license the frequent enunciation of the phrase 'as a woman' (or gay, Hispanic, etc.) to signify the privileged standpoint of the victim. Another challenge this poses for teachers is to honour and give space to the stories of those who bear the brunt of Otherising while encouraging multidimensional readings of them.

In their research on the teaching and learning of 'race', Jacobs and Hai (2002) discuss difficulties arising from the teacher him or herself taking up a victim-identified position with students. In talking about this question to two women teachers from ethnic minority backgrounds, they remarked that they were in no doubt that their presence changed the way students responded to them, particularly first-year students. 'I just know' said one of them (a black female teacher), 'that if I teach with a white, male colleague, the students are different'. While these teachers exhibited no investment in a victim identity, they suspected that a number of the students attributed this stance to them; frustratingly, they felt that some students second-guessed what was required in assessed assignments according to this projected image.

Unwittingly, teachers can encourage victim-identified learners. In this relation, Medhurst (1999) has cautioned teachers against prompting teacher-pleasing mimicry through the production of 'cloned acolytes' of themselves. Similarly, Lather (in Orner, 1997: 96) cautions against pedagogies which require students to change too fast, inducing in them a state of 'psychological vertigo'. Teachers risk encouraging such a hasty ascent to understanding if they are (or are perceived to be) closely aligned to a 'line' on Otherness. These cautions are important reminders that learning and teaching are always relational, that teaching or learning strategies are never simply discrete, neutral techniques because lurking beneath them is always the question of addressivity. Drawing on Bakhtin, Cheyne and Tarulli (1999) offer an excellent exploration of this question, implicitly exposing the difficulties of typifying learner approaches or styles without reference to the disturbances created by the authority of powerful others such as the teacher, the institution, the subject or the parent.

Whether they manage to transmit this preference to students or not, clearly, from the teachers' point of view, the best students to work with are going to be the ones who enter the transitional state of liminality and who journey towards a transformed understanding of self through mastery of the concept of Otherness. These I have typified as 'self-reflexive learners'.

Self-reflexive learners

The concept of the self-reflexive learner is based on Giddens's (1992: 14) claim that 'each of us not only "has" but lives a biography reflexively organised in terms of flows of social and psychological information about possible ways of life'. In the case of learning Otherness, clearly this ability to enquire into one's own making in the light of personal and public information is crucial. However, given that all the students we spoke to were in their initial years of study, arguably the responses we received from them were less likely to be illustrative of this kind of learner. It would have enriched my discussion if we had spoken to final-year students, asking them to reflect back on their learner trajectory to throw light on possible journeys through liminal states. This line of enquiry seems to me to be an important one for a research direction that progresses the discussion I make in this chapter. Generally speaking, self-reflexivity might be a condition of late modernity, as Giddens has argued, but we know little about how this translates into undergraduate academic life, given, for instance, the problem of addressivity mentioned above. Nonetheless, some indications of a turn towards self-examination in the light of 'flows of social and psychological information' are contained in the quote already cited above: 'Being of mixed race myself I never really paid much mind to it but coming here I've had to define where I belong. I always have to address that' (first-year female student, new university). And the following two: 'When I'm like watching T.V. I start looking at people differently . . . just reading newspapers, I can understand better the whole process of it' (first-year female student, new university); 'I like theorising about myself' (second-year male student, new university). There is an acknowledgement from these students that their learning has effected a personal change ('I start looking at people differently') and increased self-reflexivity about their own identity position ('I've had to define where I belong; I like theorising about myself'). Teachers confirmed that many students like these are self-reflexive because they are personally touched in some way by the issues explored: 'I think this might be the course that works for some students because you are talking about things close to their hearts and this can be engaging for students who have not been engaged before' (female, old university). Indeed, the following teacher pointed out that the opportunity for personal exploration is one of the distinctive features of the subject:

> Because the subject is about representation issues . . . they are directly carried into the pedagogy. Reflexivity about diversity and citizenship is part of the learning . . . it is grounded in experience. The subject matter is not divorced from people's experience. Issues in the curriculum are mixed into the pedagogy; students own their learning.
>
> (female, new university)

This depiction of the subject as intrinsically producing 'reflexivity about diversity and citizenship' is in tension with a line from an earlier quote from another teacher, namely: 'some students take to it and it changes their lives and their way of thinking and they get incredibly engaged . . . *that's a minority*' (my emphasis). Arguably, the variation in student positioning I have outlined above creates a number of possible disturbances to the transformational potential of mastering Otherness and its related concepts. While the claim that the 'subject matter is not divorced from people's experience' seems tenable, how this experience is viewed and harnessed to the learning is clearly a pedagogic question. As we have seen, the extent to which learners are reflexive depends on a complexity of factors including the teachers' reading of students' intellectual and experiential entry points to the subject, students' understandings of audience (addressivity) and the pedagogic perspectives teachers deploy.

Conclusion

In exploring the case of the teaching and learning of Otherness within the conceptual framework of threshold concepts, I have sought to expose the centrality of affective factors for the mastery of such concepts. In offering four ideal typical affective learner positions, I am not suggesting that students conform to these types in any static or pure form, or indeed that these exhaust an understanding of learner positionality. Like all ideal typical representations, they are offered as heuristic devices, in this case to prompt thinking about student states of liminality, their connection to pedagogic strategy and to questions of emotional capital for the mastery of the threshold concept of Otherness. In sum, I have suggested that ideal typifying learners as 'defensive' supports an exploration into non-judgemental pedagogic directions. The challenge for teachers is to discern whether some of their students are defended learners because they feel that they are being 'left out' of the analysis, except perhaps as power-invested agents, or whether they feel exposed/affronted as an apparent victim. In relation to the victim-identified learner, I argue that there is, *inter alia*, a tricky curriculum path to be trod in order to give voice to those who endure injuries of oppression while discouraging over-identification with such injuries. In the case of spectators or voyeurs, I have signalled the importance of creating spaces for students to personally engage with Otherness to avoid the risks of forms of mimicry which can be concealed in curriculum designs that exclude such engagement.

Acknowledgements

This chapter was prepared as part of the work of the Enhancing Teaching–Learning Environments in Undergraduate Courses project, which was funded by the Teaching and Learning Research Programme of the UK Economic and Social Research Council (http://www,tlrp.org). The project was undertaken by a team drawn from the universities of Coventry, Durham and Edinburgh. Members of the project team were Charles Anderson, Liz Beaty, Adrian Bromage, Glynis Cousin, Kate Day, Noel Entwistle, Dai Hounsell, Jenny Hounsell, Ray Land, Judith Litjens, Velda McCune, Jan Meyer, Jennifer Nisbet, Nicola Reimann and Rui Xu. Further information about the project is available on the website http://www.ed.ac.uk/etl). I would like to thank Liz Beaty and Adrian Bromage for sharing their data and all the teachers and students in CCM who gave us their time and views for this research project. Finally, much thanks to Bob Bennett, an inspirational teacher and learner of otherness.

References

Aldred, N. and Ryle, M. (eds) (1999) *Teaching Culture: The Long Revolution in Cultural Studies*, Leicester: NIACE.

Alvarado, M. and Boyd-Barrett, O. (eds) (1992) *Media Education: An Introduction*, Milton Keynes: Open University.

Bhabha, H.K. (1994) *The Location of Culture*, London: Routledge.

Bourdieu, P. and Passeron, J.-C. (1997) *Reproduction*, London: Sage.

Brown, W. (1995) *States of Injury: Power and Freedom in Late Modernity*, Princeton, NJ: Princeton University Press.

Brah, A. (1992) 'Difference, diversity and differentiation' in Donald, J. and Rattansi, A. (eds) *'Race', Culture and Difference*, London: Sage.

Butler, D. (1999) 'The value of theory in defining culture in Northern Ireland', in Aldred, N. and Ryle, M. (eds) *Teaching Culture: The Long Revolution in Cultural Studies*, Leicester: NIACE.

Butler, J. (1990) *Gender Trouble: Feminism and the Subversion of Identity*, London: Routledge.

Canaan, J. and Epstein, D. (eds) (1997) *A Question of Discipline: Pedagogy, Power and the Teaching of Cultural Studies*, Oxford: Weaver Press.

Cheyne, J. A. and Tarulli, D. (1999) 'Dialogue, difference and the "third voice" in the zone of proximal development', *Theory and Psychology*, 9, 5–28.

De Beauvoir, S. (1992) *The Second Sex*, Harmondsworth: Penguin.

Fanon, F. (1986) *Black Skins, White Masks*, London: Pluto.

Freire, Paulo (1996) *Pedagogy of the Oppressed*, Harmondsworth: Penguin.

Giddens, A. (1992) *The Transformation of Intimacy: Sexuality, Love and Eroticism in Modern Societies*, Cambridge: Polity Press.

Goldberg, D. (ed.) (1994) *Multiculturalism: A Critical Reader*, Oxford: Blackwell.

Goleman, D. (1995) *Emotional Intelligence: Why It Can Matter More Than IQ*, New York: Bantam.

Gorz, A. (1989) *A Critique of Economic Reason*, London: Verso.

Jacobs, S. and Hai, N. (2002) 'Issues and dilemmas: "race" in higher education teaching practices', in Anthias, F. and Lloyd, C. (eds) *Rethinking Anti-Racism*, London: Routledge.

Johnson, J. (1997) 'Teaching without guarantees: cultural studies, pedagogy and identity', in Canaan, J. and Epstein, D. (eds) *A Question of Discipline: Pedagogy, Power and the Teaching of Cultural Studies*, Oxford: Weaver Press.

Lupton, C. and Henkel, H. (1999) 'A postcolonial pedagogy: questions of difference and the "ethical horizon" ', in Aldred, N. and Ryle, M. (eds) *Teaching Culture: The Long Revolution in Cultural Studies*, Leicester: NIACE.

Masterman, L. (1985) *Teaching the Media*, London: Comedia.

Medhurst, A. (1999) 'Teaching queerly: politics, pedagogy and identity in lesbian and gay studies', in Aldred, N. and Ryle, M. (eds) *Teaching Culture: The Long Revolution in Cultural Studies*, Leicester: NIACE.

Meyer, J. H. F. and Land, R. (2003) 'Threshold concepts and troublesome knowledge: linkages to ways of thinking and practising within the disciplines', in Rust, C. (ed.) *Improving Student Learning – Ten Years On*, Oxford: Oxford Centre for Staff and Learning Development.

Meyer, J. H. F. and Shanahan, M. (2003) 'The troublesome nature of a threshold concept in Economics', paper presented at the European Association for Research on Learning and Instruction, Padova.

Meyer, J. H. F. and Land, R. (2005) 'Threshold concepts and troublesome knowledge (2): epistemological considerations and a conceptual framework for teaching and learning', *Higher Education*, 49, 373–388.

Orner, M. (1997) 'Teaching feminist cultural studies', in Canaan, J. and Epstein, D. (eds) *A Question of Discipline: Pedagogy, Power and the Teaching of Cultural Studies*, Oxford: Weaver Press.

Perkins, D. (1999) 'The many faces of constructivism', *Educational Leadership*, 57 (3), November.

Rushdie, S. (1988) *The Satanic Verses*, London: Viking.

Said, E.W. (1991) *Orientalism: Western Conceptions of the Orient*, London: Penguin.

Sartre, J-P. (1948) *The Anti-Semite and the Jew*, New York: Schocken Books.

Sarup, M. (1992) *Jacques Lacan*, Hemel Hempstead: Harvester Wheatsheaf.

Shaw, J. (1995) *Education, Gender and Anxiety*, London: Taylor & Francis.

Williamson, J. (1992) 'How does girl number twenty understand ideology?' in Alvarado, M. and Boyd-Barrett, O. (eds) (1992) *Media Education: An Introduction*, Milton Keynes: Open University.

Chapter 10

Developing new 'world views'

Threshold concepts in introductory accounting

Ursula Lucas and Rosina Mladenovic

Introduction and background

A threshold concept has been described as something akin to a portal, opening up a transformed internal view of subject matter, subject landscape, or even 'world view' (Meyer and Land, 2003). The notion of developing a new world view may be particularly relevant within the subject area of introductory accounting, where there is a body of research that provides an overview of contrasting world views possessed by both lecturers and students. On the face of it this might seem surprising. The introductory accounting curriculum is well established and represents a substantial body of teaching within higher education throughout the world. It is included in general business and other vocational degree courses, as well as being taught to students who wish to specialise in accounting, finance and/or information systems. Consequently it is taught to very large numbers of students, usually on the first year of an undergraduate course. However, this fact alone creates a problem. For those students who are not ultimately going to specialise in accounting, it is usually a compulsory course. Many of these students possess negative preconceptions of accounting and do not willingly study the subject (Mladenovic, 2000).

A second problem arises from the origins of the introductory accounting curriculum. The teaching of introductory accounting has been criticised in recent years for its narrow focus and rules-based procedural approaches. In part this has been attributed to the dominance of professionally influenced textbooks (Zeff, 1989a) and the accreditation requirements of professional accounting bodies (Zeff, 1989b; Dewing and Russell, 1998). Lecturers tend to rely heavily on textbooks for the provision of worked exercises. There are indications that this may have the effect of obscuring any emphasis on conceptual underpinnings or controversial issues that can be explored through discussion and critical analysis (Leveson, 2004; Lucas, 2002). Given that educators from other subject areas may recognise these issues within their own curricula it is hoped that this discussion within accounting might inform a consideration of threshold concepts in other subject areas.

Our discussion of threshold concepts is presented in four parts. We shall first explore the nature of threshold concepts in introductory accounting from an 'educator' perspective, arguing that that there are unresolved issues concerning the role of concepts and a conceptual framework within the teaching of introductory accounting. We shall then consider threshold concepts from a 'student' perspective. We shall use this perspective to develop our ideas about what comprises significant threshold concepts in accounting and barriers to their achievement. We shall conclude by arguing that educators might benefit from the development of 'new world views' of the domain of the introductory accounting curriculum and the introduction of new pedagogic approaches to widen the focus of introductory accounting education.

Threshold concepts: a familiar idea for educators, but strangely challenging . . .

The notion of 'threshold concepts' is, in one sense, familiar to educators, i.e. they are familiar with terms such as 'key concepts', 'core concepts' and learning objectives such as 'be able to think like an accountant'. Yet in another sense, it is one that causes problems. Despite its well-established place within the higher education curriculum, the teaching of introductory accounting can still be regarded as problematic. Drawing on two published sources (Mladenovic, 2000; Lucas, 2002) and one unpublished source (Mladenovic, 2001) we show that these problematic areas include: some confusion over what comprises a key (or threshold) concept, the nature of the conceptual framework for the organisation of such concepts, and an inclination to avoid conceptual issues as a way of making accounting more acceptable to students.

A study by Mladenovic (2000) compared lecturers' perceptions of the nature of accounting with those of students. She found that not only were students' perceptions significantly different to their teachers' but that variations in *lecturers'* perceptions of the nature of accounting was evident. A similar disparity was also found within a phenomenographic study of lecturers' experiences of teaching introductory accounting (Lucas, 2002). Further, whilst lecturers stressed the importance of conceptual understanding, they identified relatively few key concepts that it is important for a student to grasp. In addition, there was a lack of an expressed clear structure into which such concepts might be fitted. Lecturers perceived accounting in two main ways: first, as a micro activity which involved the preparation of financial statements (preparer perspective) and second, as a macro activity which involved the role and use of accounting information in a wider context (user perspective). The latter can provide a potential organising framework for a conceptual structure. However, a small minority of lecturers reflected on the need to provide such a structure. Not only was there a scarcity of articulated concepts but some lecturers went out of their way to avoid references to concepts, which at times they referred to as 'jargon'. This arose particularly because they felt that they had to overcome student preconceptions of accounting as dull and boring and being unduly numbers-based. An unintended consequence of this was a preoccupation with the teaching of techniques.

A further investigation into lecturers' understandings of what comprises a threshold concept was carried out at a workshop as part of an International Symposium on Approaches to Learning in Accounting Education held in the Faculty of Economics and Business at the University of Sydney in 2003. Once again, there was no consensus on what might comprise a threshold concept in accounting. Moreover, it also became apparent that the *process* of identifying potential threshold concepts was not straightforward. Lecturers were asked to identify a threshold concept, identify why it is central to the accounting curriculum and to identify any common misconceptions. From their written accounts and the discussions that followed, it was evident that all three of these enquiries were necessary steps in the process. The threshold concept initially identified was usually replaced by a different, underlying concept(s) as the reasons for centrality and misconceptions were considered. For example, a lecturer might state that there is a need for a student to understand the difference between cash and profit (i.e. that profit is calculated using accrual accounting, a basis fundamentally different from the cash basis that underpins cash accounting). However, in considering why this is a central topic, additional concepts and considerations come into play. For example, accrual accounting is necessary because of the need to report performance at an arbitrary point in time (e.g. at the end of a period) in a manner meaningful to decision-makers. As misconceptions are considered then it becomes apparent that a student has to recognise the implications of this arbitrary cut-off point in the life of an enterprise in terms of deciding *when* and *how* to *recognise* relevant revenue and costs, all of which require an understanding of related principles and concepts.

A further significant finding from the lecturers' workshop was the identification, not of discipline-specific threshold concepts to be grasped by students, but of central generic attributes that lecturers thought should be developed by students. One desired attribute was the ability and willingness to question i.e. demonstrate a healthy scepticism. Linked with this was a second attribute, that of an ability and willingness to 'problematise' issues. A third attribute was that students should be willing to accept that certain terms, such as 'cost' or 'value', may have different meanings in different contexts. Underpinning all of these attributes is the need for a student to be able and willing to accept uncertainty or subjectivity within accounting.

It is clear from the above that the experience of *teaching* introductory accounting raises issues that are problematic within the curriculum. In part, some of these issues arise from a response by lecturers to a perceived problem, that of teaching accounting at an introductory level to students who are perceived as possessing negative preconceptions about the subject. In part, other issues arise from the different world views amongst lecturers of the subject matter being taught.

Exploring the nature of threshold concepts in accounting

In this section we shall review research into student understandings of accounting and the student experience of learning introductory accounting. In order to obtain a rounded view of those understandings and experience, we shall review findings from two contrasting modes of enquiry. The first mode of enquiry provides a specific focus on understandings of accounting within the context of classroom-based exercises. Here students provided written and verbal responses to a specific task. The second mode of enquiry provides a wider focus. Within a phenomenographic study students were provided with an extended opportunity to talk generally about their experiences of learning accounting. These two modes of enquiry produce complementary findings and a broader view of what might be taken into account when considering the nature of threshold concepts.

A review of student understandings derived from classroom-based exercises reveals the central importance of modes of reasoning or explanation, rather than the nature of the understanding of a specific concept. Lucas (2000) provided students with the opportunity to give a verbal response to an exercise designed to elicit their understandings of the nature of cash and profit. A key distinguishing factor within student responses was the mode of reasoning or explanation provided by the students. Students provided either 'disaggregated' explanations which focused on discrete components of the financial statements or 'global' explanations which focused on the totality of the financial statements. Several students provided a disaggregated explanation of why the change in cash does not equal the change in profit. They identified individual examples such as depreciation, inventory, the lease and fittings that would explain why cash is different from profit. For example (Lucas, 2001, p. 172):

> Well, the first thing you've got to explain is that cash and profit aren't the same thing. Well profit, you've got things like depreciation in there, you've got things like prepayments and accruals because that's matched with the period of the accounts, whereas cash is the cash in and out, it's actually gone in and out and so if you've got something accruing that would make it profit but you haven't paid it yet.

A global explanation of the difference between cash and retained profit would state that profit will result in an increase in net assets, of which cash is but one component. Whilst no student provided a comprehensive global explanation, two students came close to it. Whereas a disaggregated explanation would focus on disaggregated elements lacking an explanatory framework, a global explanation would focus on what is *represented* by those individual elements in a wider context. Disaggregated and global explanations are not mutually exclusive but Lucas (2001) found that there was a predominance of disaggregated explanations.

The importance of the mode of reasoning or explanation was supported by further classroom-based work carried out by Lucas and Mladenovic (2005). Here written explanations about, first, the relationship between profit and cash and, second, depreciation, were obtained from students. The level of responses were analysed using the Structure of Observed Learning Outcomes (SOLO) categories of prestructural, unistructural, multistructural, relational and extended abstract (Biggs and Collis, 1982). These five categories are hierarchically arrayed in terms of the cognitive effort deemed necessary and the level of conceptual complexity achieved. The levels of structural complexity are ordered in terms of characteristics that include: progression from concrete to abstract; increasing number of organising dimensions; increasing consistency; and the use of organising or relating principles, with hypothetical or self-generated principles being used at the most complex end (Biggs and Collis, 1982, p. 14). The SOLO categories provide educators with a way to establish whether accounting students' responses show reasoning at higher levels thus indicating whether students have grasped or understood a concept (Ramburuth and Mladenovic, 2004).

Each SOLO category, from prestructural to extended abstract, can be seen as a way to 'measure' or 'identify' when a student has moved through another threshold. For example, if a student's response is classified as prestructural, the student has exhibited one or more 'misconceptions' in relation to the threshold concept. If at a later stage the same student provides a response that is classified as multistructural then the student has passed through a threshold from completely misunderstanding the concept to being able to identify a number of relevant aspects in relation to the concept. Findings from SOLO analysis indicate that the *key qualitative differences* in student responses arise between the multistructural and relational/extended abstract levels of understanding. This transitional point in SOLO is similar to the distinction identified by Lucas (2001) between disaggregated and global explanations. For example, we can see in the following extended abstract response (Lucas and Mladenovic, 2005, p. 4) that the student uses a clear explanatory framework and relates it to the principle of the accrual basis of accounting:

> Lesley does not realise that over the life of a business cash flow statements and profit and loss statements will not always match. This is due to the accrual basis of accounting that records transactions when they occur as opposed to when cash changes hands. In most cases there will

be a time lag between when a transaction is made and recorded in the accounts and when the cash is received or paid for the transaction. This is due to the fact that most businesses perform transactions on a credit basis. Therefore it is reasonable that Lesley's profits do not match up to the extent that there is a profit of $15,000 and a reduction in cash of $25,000.

This is in contrast to a multistructural explanation where several relevant aspects are referred to but they lack an explanatory framework (ibid., p. 23):

Profit/loss is not determined by cash flows alone. In fact sales can either be cash sales or credit sales. A profit may occur because sales were credited. Similarly, expenses incurred may not be actually paid out in cash or maybe even not in this period.

We see this distinction between global and disaggregated explanations and between multistructural and relational responses as characterising a significant shift in the understanding of accounting. In other words a *threshold* in accounting is the recognition of the *interrelatedness* of aspects of the technique within *an organising or explanatory framework*. The recognition of this interrelatedness is demonstrated when the student engages in a mode of reasoning whereby techniques are explicitly seen as an attempt to put organising principles into practice.

A review of student responses where this recognition of interrelatedness is *not* achieved provides further insights into the nature of threshold concepts within introductory accounting. Many explanations provided by students were far from coherent and quite difficult to understand. They contained inconsistencies and misunderstandings. Sometimes one point correctly explained might be contradicted by a later explanation. The student could be viewed as being stuck within what Meyer and Land (2005) describe as an 'in-between' state in which students oscillate between earlier, less sophisticated understandings, and the fuller appreciation of a concept that their tutors require from them. Meyer and Land (2005) term this in-between state as a state of 'liminality', from the Latin meaning 'within the threshold' and one outcome is that students present a partial, limited or superficial understanding of the concept to be learned, characterised as a form of 'mimicry'. It was possible, within the SOLO framework, to identify transitional categories between each of the five main SOLO levels that indicate that a student has moved beyond one category but has not quite reached the higher category.

The above discussion has considered findings from classroom-based research and highlighted that it might be more appropriate to consider the nature of a threshold *conception* (or *episteme* as referred to by Perkins in Chapter 3) rather than a threshold *concept*. The threshold conception is that of a world view of accounting as comprising an *organising structure* or *framework* which provides the explanatory rationale for accounting techniques.

We shall now move on to consider further the nature of threshold concepts by looking at student understandings in a more everyday setting. This can be obtained by providing students with an *extended* opportunity to talk about their understandings of accounting and of learning accounting. We shall, first, review the findings that point to the significance of *everyday* understandings of accounting. We shall then discuss findings that consider the nature of students' *preconceptions of accounting* and the ways in which these affect students' learning.

A more leisurely enquiry into student understandings through the use of interview (Lucas, 2000) revealed that students' 'alternative' conceptions of accounting topics was as of much interest as what might be termed their 'authorised' conceptions. The latter are those conceptions that are endorsed and maintained by the disciplinary community and in textbooks. By way of contrast 'alternative' conceptions of events and transactions are independent of authorised conceptions. They arise from intuitive or everyday (common-sense) understandings of a concept such as profit or depreciation.

These alternative conceptions of accounting take two forms. In the first, students attach significance to aspects of the business which were *not* reflected in the financial statements or recognised by accounting. Yet students took this exclusion *for granted*. Dick found no contradiction in the fact that financial statements do not include all the costs of running a business (in Lucas, 2000, p. 495).

> if you put the hours in and you're a sole trader, I think it's one of those things. [. . .] It's one of those things I learnt about our business in [overseas country], and you get a set wage and that's it. My brother works 20 hours a week, and I work 75, you put the hours in, and that's just the way it goes. If you want your business to succeed and you do what you have to do. It's not a case of saying how does it show the hours I've actually put into it.

Here, Dick reflects on the realities of working in a small business. However, he does not question a set of financial statements that fail to recognise the hours 'put in' when indicating, in numerical terms, what resources have been consumed for the 'business to succeed'. Dick thinks in one set of terms in relation to his experience of working in a family business, and in another when compiling a set of financial statements.

In the second form, students describe conceptions of profit, cash and depreciation that are at variance with the authorised conceptions. These understandings appear to relate to an 'everyday' understanding of accounting phenomena. For example several students expressed a personal view of assets which led to a conception of depreciation at variance with the authorised conception. In accounting terms, depreciation is the allocation of part of the cost of a fixed asset to an accounting period. This is done for two main reasons. First, in recognition that an asset 'contributes' to the generation of profit over a period of time, costs are *matched* with revenues to calculate profits and, second, that the asset has a finite economic life. This view of depreciation focuses on the asset's 'value in use' to the firm in generating profits. However, some students related depreciation solely to loss of value by focusing on the asset's value if sold (that is its 'value in exchange') and did not refer to the asset's value in use in relation to the asset's potential to generate profits. In particular, depreciation was connected with a writing-down to a second-hand value. This was a notion with which students readily engaged as evidenced in the example below (Lucas, 2000, p. 497).

> Well she's obviously bought some equipment that she wouldn't be able to sell on, whether it be a phone or whatever, but once they're used and second-hand . . . they're not going to be, so to value them at what she bought them for would be unrealistic because she wouldn't ever be able to get that amount of money back for them.

What emerges from these interviews are *alternative* views of events and transactions which arise from students' everyday experiences of life and which *contrast* with the authorised academic view of accounting encountered in their course. Often, where students hold these alternative conceptions, they do not *recognise* that these conceptions are in opposition to the authorised conceptions promulgated within the course. Thus a particularly important threshold *conception* may be, again, to recognise the *difference* between authorised and alternative conceptions. As discussed above, the threshold conception is that of a world view of accounting as comprising an *organising structure* or *framework* which provides the explanatory rationale for accounting techniques. However, to this we can also add that the student needs to recognise that the existence of *one* organising structure can also imply that this may be *challenged* or *complemented* by another. In this sense, accounting may be viewed as a particular way of thinking, or of utilising a particular organising framework for viewing a situation.

We shall now consider students' preconceptions of accounting and the way in which they may be relevant to a discussion of the nature of threshold concepts. Anecdotally many lecturers will recount how students' negative preconceptions of accounting are a problem within the teaching of introductory accounting. There is now a body of work within introductory accounting that confirms the existence of such negative preconceptions (Lucas, 2000; Mladenovic, 2000). Further research also indicates that such negative preconceptions are related to a focus on learning the technique, rather than on the organising framework of accounting (Lucas, 2000, 2001; Lucas and Meyer, 2005). These preconceptions include perceptions of accounting as: boring and dull, a technical subject being primarily about numbers and as being objective and involving little judgement. They can thus be viewed as a threshold *barrier* to engagement with accounting as an organising structure or framework. Such a barrier has to be passed through before students can fruitfully engage with accounting. This focus on the technique might be regarded as a form of 'mimicry' (Meyer and Land, 2005) whereby students present a partial, limited or superficial understanding of what is to be learned.

The above review of the nature of student understandings of accounting and their experience of learning introductory accounting points, initially, to the importance of a central threshold conception within accounting rather than a series of threshold concepts. It also raises the issue of threshold barriers that arise from the particular nature of accounting. One barrier arises from students' negative preconceptions of the subject. A second barrier arises from students' everyday understandings of accounting. However, a potential further barrier arises from our earlier discussion of the educator perspective. There is a perception on the part of some lecturers that students may be reluctant to accept uncertainty or subjectivity within accounting. Such an acceptance may be regarded as an inevitable prerequisite for the recognition of the competing and alternative frameworks within which accounting might be viewed.

Towards new pedagogic approaches within accounting

We have argued that a central threshold conception in accounting is the recognition of the *interrelatedness* of aspects of the technique. The recognition of this interrelatedness is demonstrated when the student engages in a mode of reasoning whereby techniques are explicitly seen as an attempt to put organising principles into practice. However, this recognition involves, at the same time, an acknowledgement of the *subjectivity* of accounting processes. A recognition of organising principles (or an underlying conceptual framework) always involves the recognition that there might exist *other* frameworks. Lecturers recognise that this subjectivity may be challenging for students who are not willing to question frameworks or live with a form of uncertainty. A focus on technique through a process of ritualisation and mimicry provides a high level of certainty when compared with a discussion of the relevance of different conceptual frameworks. And yet, as we have discussed, students do possess alternative ways of viewing accounting and are often not aware that they contrast with the authorised view(s) that they are taught. Faced with this situation we would argue that new pedagogic approaches may be required to support students in passing through a threshold barrier and to engage with the learning of accounting, not solely as a technique, but as a social practice through which organising frameworks come to be *generally accepted*.

First, we propose that the barrier to engagement and learning should be addressed as a specific part of the introductory accounting curriculum. Mladenovic (2000) demonstrates how carefully designed teaching interventions can bring about significant changes in negative preconceptions of accounting. These interventions include an aligned teaching environment (where course objectives, curriculum and assessment were aligned), class discussions of students' preconceptions of accounting and comparisons with their lecturers' views. They also included discussion of the social context of accounting, its affinity with politics and literature, and critically evaluating accounting within the context of controversial issues. Subsequent feedback from students in focus groups (Mladenovic, 2000, pp. 148–149) indicated the changes that occurred in their conceptions of accounting following interventions and what this involved.

> I think I can see a bit more of the *theoretical* thing behind it . . . I was probably one of the persons who wrote – it's just writing down numbers. But now I see that there's probably a bit more to it.

> I didn't realise it was so central to the *business world* . . . I didn't realise it was such a big issue.

> More *interpretation and analysing*. There's more thought to it. There are different ways, it's not just . . . I'll copy that number here.

> Because I thought you had to be a mathematical genius to do accounting, and now I know it's different. You have to *understand* before you do any accounting.

> I didn't think that accounting was *controversial or subjective*, because all I knew about accounting was just putting numbers into different places. But now I understand it's all different.

These extracts from discussions with students provide rich and interesting data showing how students' initial preconceptions of accounting changed after intervention. Students were able to see well beyond their initial preconceptions and take on a new world view. They had learned that accounting had a theoretical base, involved complex applications and processes, was located in the real world, required judgement, interpretation and analysis, was controversial and involved understanding processes and terminology. It can be seen that this approach does not seek to make accounting look 'easier' by simplifying it and avoiding 'jargon'. The latter approach could encourage students to focus on the technique and learn accounting in a ritualistic way and to substitute mimicry for understanding.

Second, within accounting pedagogy, confusions and misunderstandings may arise because students fail to recognise that they hold everyday 'alternative' understandings of accounting that may be in contradiction to 'authorised' understandings. Linder (1993), in considering student learning, does not consider the everyday conceptions that students possess to be a problem. Nor is he concerned with students' resistance to changing their conceptions. He sees it as natural for a student to hold a variety of conceptions and places emphasis on the ability to recognise an organising framework and to evoke, within it, an appropriate conception. Thus lecturers and students might recognise that it is perfectly acceptable to possess two distinct understandings of depreciation. In a 'personal' context when buying a used car, a student might use one conception of depreciation (which reduces cost to net realisable value) and in a 'business' context use another (which reduces cost to net book value but not necessarily to net realisable value). However, both lecturer and student would need to consider the difference between understanding accounting in an everyday sense and understanding accounting in a disciplinary sense. Thus Linder proposes that learning be viewed as *contextual appreciation*. Students can be encouraged to recognise the way in which they, and others, use accounting terms in different ways in different contexts. The implications of the above two pedagogic approaches are that students have to recognise, and accept, that there are different ways of viewing both accounting and the concepts within it. In other words, there has to be an acceptance of diversity and, thus, uncertainty. This may be potentially 'troublesome' for the student.

Conclusions

The above discussion confirms that the five main characteristics of a threshold concept tentatively proposed by Meyer and Land (2003) may provide an effective way of viewing the curriculum within introductory accounting. A threshold concept is, first, transformative. In other words it represents a significant shift in the perception of a subject, or part thereof. Second, it is probably irreversible, in the sense that it cannot be unlearned and represents a new world view. Third, it is integrative in that it exposes the previously hidden interrelatedness of something. Fourth, it may potentially represent a boundary – a point at which the student would move into territory seemingly outside of the discipline. Finally, it may potentially be troublesome to the student, that is, counter-intuitive, alien (emanating from another culture or discourse) or incoherent (lacking an obvious organising principle).

This way of viewing the curriculum may be challenging for educators. We have argued that new pedagogic approaches may be required to support students in passing though threshold barriers, to engage with the learning of accounting and to develop new world views. It may be that the well-established curriculum within introductory accounting forms a threshold barrier in its own right. If educators wish to engage with the notion of threshold concepts they may need to come to a new way of thinking, or world view, about their own teaching.

References

Biggs, J. and Collis, K. (1982) *Evaluating the Quality of Learning: The SOLO Taxonomy (Structure of the Observed Learning Outcome)*, New York: Academic Press.

Dewing, I.P. and Russell, P.O. (1998) 'Accounting education and research: Zeff's warnings reconsidered', *British Accounting Review*, 20: 291–312.

Leveson, L. (2004) 'Encouraging better learning through better teaching: a study of approaches to teaching in accounting', *Accounting Education: An International Journal*, 13: 529–548.

Linder, C.J. (1993) 'A challenge to conceptual change', *Science Education*, 77: 293–300.

Lucas, U. (2000) 'Worlds apart: students' experiences of learning introductory accounting', *Critical Perspectives on Accounting*, 11: 479–504.

Lucas, U. (2001) 'Deep and surface approaches to learning within introductory accounting: a phenomenographic study', *Accounting Education: An International Journal*, 10: 161–184.

Lucas, U. (2002) 'Uncertainties and contradictions: lecturers' conceptions of teaching introductory accounting', *British Accounting Review*, 34: 183–204.

Lucas, U. and Meyer, J.H.F. (2005) 'Towards a mapping of the student world: the identification of variation in students' conceptions of, and motivations to learn, introductory accounting', *British Accounting Review*, 37(2): 177–204.

Lucas, U. and Mladenovic, R. (2005) 'What should students understand?: a review of threshold concepts within introductory accounting', paper presented at the British Accounting Association Annual Conference, 30 March–1 April, Edinburgh, Scotland.

Meyer, J.H.F. and Land, R. (2003) 'Threshold concepts and troublesome knowledge: linkages to ways of thinking and practising within the disciplines', in C. Rust (ed.) *Improving Student Learning: Improving Student Learning Theory and Practice – Ten Years On*, Oxford: OCLSD.

Meyer, J.H.F. and Land, R. (2005) 'Threshold concepts and troublesome knowledge (2): epistemological considerations and a conceptual framework for teaching and learning', *Higher Education*, 49: 373–388.

Mladenovic, R. (2000) 'An investigation into ways of challenging introductory accounting students' negative perceptions of accounting', *Accounting Education: An International Journal*, 9: 135–154.

Mladenovic, R. (2001) 'The effects of alignment in the learning context on students' perceptions and learning approaches in accounting', unpublished PhD thesis, University of New South Wales, Sydney.

Ramburuth, P. and Mladenovic, R. (2004) 'Exploring the relationship between students' orientations to learning, the structure of students' learning outcomes and subsequent academic performance', *Accounting Education: An International Journal*, 13: 507–527.

Zeff, S. (1989a) 'Does accounting belong in the university curriculum?' *Issues in Accounting Education*, 4: 203–210.

Zeff, S. (1989b) 'Recent trends in accounting education and research in the USA: some implications for UK academics', *British Accounting Review*, 21: 159–176.

Chapter 11

Disjunction as a form of troublesome knowledge in problem-based learning

Maggi Savin-Baden

Introduction

This chapter draws on research into problem-based learning undertaken across different disciplines but largely in the areas of health and social care. It will be argued through this chapter that problem-based learning is a threshold concept and that there is an interrelationship between disjunction and troublesome knowledge. In the final section of the chapter I will argue that problem-based learning is a *threshold philosophy*, or possibly an 'underlying game' or underlying episteme in Perkins's phrase (Chapter 3 this volume), that gives rise to disjunctions in the lives of staff and students when constructivist forms of problem-based learning are adopted. This is because issues of identity, knowledge and power become contested spaces in the kind of problem-based learning contexts that prompt personal and pedagogical shifts for students and staff.

Being a troubled facilitator

My interest in disjunction, the idea of staff or students becoming stuck in learning, first emerged as a result of being a facilitator of problem-based learning seminars in the mid-1980s. Although this active form of learning initially seemed to interest the students, and was an approach I thought would help them to become critical practitioners, they seemed to become frustrated and angry about the process of learning. To begin with I thought they disliked working in groups and that they believed that as a facilitator I was being lazy because I did not offer them 'facts' and 'right answers'. Instead I supported them in their own learning and encouraged them to take control of what counted as knowledge. After facilitating four groups for six months little seemed to have changed and I was experiencing disjunction too. What I failed to realise at the time was that disjunction can be both enabling and disabling in terms of its impact on staff and student learning. My fascination with these different forms of stuckness resulted in my subsequent years of exploration into staff and students' experiences of problem-based learning and the troublesomeness that this approach seems to bring.

Problem-based learning is not only troublesome because it challenges our notions of learning and knowledge but also because it is difficult to define, pin down and agree on ways in which it should be implemented. Compared with many pedagogical approaches, problem-based learning has emerged relatively recently, being popularised by Barrows and Tamblyn (1980) following their research into the reasoning abilities of medical students at McMaster Medical School in Canada. Barrows and Tamblyn's study and the approach adopted at McMaster marked a clear move away from problem-solving learning in which individual students answered a series of questions from information supplied by a lecturer. Rather, this new method they proposed involved learning in ways that used problem scenarios to encourage students to engage themselves in the learning process, a method to become known as *problem-based learning*.

Problem-based learning has expanded worldwide since the 1960s, and as it has spread the concepts associated with it have changed and become more flexible and fluid. In an attempt to move beyond narrow and prescriptive definitions Boud (1985) and Barrows (1986), two of the stronger proponents of the approach, have outlined broader characteristics of problem-based learning. However, for me problem-based learning is an approach to learning that is characterised by flexibility and diversity in the sense that it can be implemented in a variety of ways in and across different subjects and disciplines in diverse contexts. As such it can therefore look very different to different people at different moments in time depending on the staff and students involved in the programmes utilising it. However, what will be similar will be the focus of learning around problem scenarios rather than discrete subjects.

Problem-based learning as a threshold concept

Problem-based learning is contested ground and the research into this approach remains complex and difficult largely because of the different ways it is implemented and enacted in various institutions in different countries by assorted staff. Yet such diversity demonstrates the versatility of problem-based learning for both staff and students and also indicates that it is a challenging approach because it generates disjunction and 'stuckness' in people's lives. Although Meyer and Land (2003) argued in early work that threshold concepts were something distinct within a set of core material that university lecturers would teach, more recently (Meyer and Land, 2005) they have broadened this to include wider concepts such as staff experiences. An example of this might be that university staff who have used lecture-based methods experience disjunction when undertaking a diploma in learning and teaching that is taught using a problem-based approach. Therefore I suggest that problem-based learning is something that for many staff and students begins as such a threshold concept. Problem-based learning is often a difficult approach for staff and students to grasp because it challenges them to see learning and knowledge in new ways. Once staff have entered the portal they very quickly move away from the idea that it is necessarily foundation knowledge(s) and core concepts that students require, and tend to argue instead that learning and knowledge need to be guided by the students' needs. However, in order to exemplify disjunction and its relationship with problem-based learning I will draw on a number of studies. Staff and students' stories illustrate how encounters with problem-based learning prompt disjunction in a variety of ways.

The studies, the methods, the stories

The three studies drawn on in this chapter all used forms of collaborative enquiry. The first explored staff and students' experiences of problem-based learning in four different undergraduate programmes in the UK: mechanical engineering, nursing, automotive design engineering and social work. The second study was undertaken in a newly formed School of Nursing and Midwifery, within a faculty of medicine at a UK university. It explored staff experiences of moving from being a lecturer to a problem-based learning facilitator with a group of over 20 staff from diverse backgrounds in the field of nursing and midwifery. The third study is still in progress and is exploring staff conceptions of disjunction and troublesome knowledge in a diverse range of disciplines in South Africa and Singapore. Data in all the studies were collected through 1:1 in-depth interviews, informal discussions, email discussion and post-interview reflections.

The relationship between disjunction and troublesome knowledge

Many staff and students have described disjunction as being a little like hitting a brick wall in learning and they have used various strategies to try to deal with it. It has similarities with troublesome knowledge in that it often feels alien and counter-intuitive. This is because it invariably feels a negative place rather than one that is seen as a space for growth and development. It is also similar to troublesome knowledge because until disjunction is experienced in a learning environment it is difficult to explain, particularly in terms of students feeling fragmented, which for many students can feel both constructive and destructive at the same time.

It is noticeable that disjunction is an area addressed by few in the field of problem-based learning and in higher education in general. Yet disjunction is not something to be seen as unhelpful and damaging, but instead as dynamic in the sense that different forms of disjunction, enabling and disabling, can result in transitions in students' lives. As disjunction is not something readily understood it is therefore not easily managed, particularly as it does not tend to occur as a result of a simplistic cause and effect relationship. Instead it is multifaceted in nature and 'emerges out of mutually interacting influences' (Weil, 1989: 112). Staff who set up modes of learning such as group work or problem-based learning that may cause a distinct challenge to students' life-worlds, will need to treat disjunction, and its management, as a pedagogical concern. The concept of life-world is taken from Habermas (1989) and represents the idea that as human beings we have a culturally transmitted stock of taken-for-granted perspectives and interpretations that are organised in a communicative way.

Although disjunction occurs in many forms and in diverse ways in different disciplines it does seem to be particularly evident in curricula where problem-based learning has been implemented. This may be because problem-based learning programmes prompt students to critique and contest knowledge early on in the curriculum and thus they encounter knowledge as being troublesome earlier than students in more traditional programmes. However, it might also be that problem-based learning encourages students to shift away from linear and fact-finding problem solving. Instead they move towards forms of problem management that demand the use of procedural and personal knowledge as students are asked to engage with strategy or moral dilemma problems. Thus it might be that disjunction is not only a form of troublesome knowledge but also a 'space' or 'position' reached through the realisation that the knowledge is troublesome. Disjunction might therefore be seen as a 'troublesome learning space' that emerges when forms of active learning (such as problem-based learning) are used that prompt students to engage with procedural and personal knowledge. Alternatively disjunction can be seen as the kind of place that students might reach after they have encountered a threshold concept that they have failed to conquer.

Disjunction is thus a form of troublesome knowledge because it bridges Meyer and Land's (2005) notion of engagement with troublesome knowledge and the state of liminality. They suggest that when students find particular concepts difficult they are in a state of liminality. This state of liminality tends to be characterised by a stripping away of old identities, an oscillation between states and personal transformation. Although they argue for pre-liminal variation, I would suggest that what occurs for students is not just 'variation' but different ways of managing the disjunction being experienced. For example, Meyer and Land (2005) believe pre-liminal variation is a means of distinguishing between 'variation in students' "tacit" understanding (or lack thereof) of a threshold concept'. This, they argue, means that it may be possible to understand why some students approach and manage the threshold concepts while others cannot. Yet it might not just be about students' ability to manage the threshold concept but also their reaction to it. However, given the notion of pre-liminal variation, the questions remain: how do we decide what counts as a threshold concept and what does not, and who makes that decision? Perhaps we should also ask whether the use of problem-based learning reduces the instance of pre-liminal variations because of the shifts that are made away from a belief in core concepts and the idea that some knowledge is necessarily foundational to other knowledge. This may in turn result in students on problem-based programmes having fewer requirements for engaging with threshold concepts because problems are designed to engage students with issues connected with learning, life and the development of future (professional) identities.

Responses to disjunction

Students deal with disjunction in a number of different ways, which means that the conflict, ambiguity and incoherence experienced by individual students cannot be defined by distinctive characteristics, but there are some general trends. What seems to be apparent is that disjunction is dealt with by students in one of four ways, through forms of decision making that are conscious and/or unconscious. Thus, students may opt to *retreat* from disjunction, to *temporise* and thus choose not to make a decision about how to manage it, to find some means to *avoid* it and thus create greater disjunction in the long term, or to *engage* with it and move to a greater or lesser sense of integration.

Retreat

In this position students who experience disjunction choose not to engage with the process of managing it. Here they want to avoid engaging with the struggles connected with disjunction and often retreat behind some form of excuse that means that they do not engage with the personal or organisational catalyst to the disjunction. Students who retreat may also take up a particular position, entrench themselves within it and then reinforce the bunkers around that position.

Temporising

Students who do not directly retreat from disjunction may adopt an indecisive or time-serving policy. They acknowledge the existence of disjunction and also that they have to engage with it in order to enable an effective transition to take place, but they decide that it is preferable to postpone making any decision about how to manage it. Thus there is, in the area in which the disjunction is occurring, a postponement of any activity.

Avoidance

In this situation students do not just temporise but adopt mechanisms that will enable them to find some way of circumventing the disjunction. The result will be that although the student has found a means of bypassing the disjunction, this may have taken more effort than engaging with it. Furthermore, in the long term, because of the nature of the disjunction, they will still have to engage with it in order to avoid always becoming entrenched in this position.

Engagement

Engaging with disjunction requires that students acknowledge its existence and also attempt to deconstruct the causes of disjunction by examining the relationship with both their internal and external worlds. Through this reflexive examination process students can engage with what has given rise to the disjunction and they are then enabled to shift towards a greater sense of integration.

Managing disjunction

Students' stories demonstrate that there are particular issues that facilitate students' transitions in learning. The notion and experience of transition, emerging from disjunction, appears to prompt an interrogation of traditional perspectives of learner, learning, the learning context, professions, institutions, etc. Transition is used here to denote shifts in learner experience caused by a challenge to the life-world. Transitions occur in particular areas of students' lives, at different times and in distinct ways. The notion of transitions carries with it the idea of movement from one place to another and with it the necessity of taking up a new position in a different place. Leaving the position and entering the transitions may also be fraught with difficulties that may result in further disjunction for the student. Thus transitions can often be difficult and disturbing and yet simultaneously be areas where personal change takes place. For example, any transition may result in someone being able to make greater or lesser sense of their learning lives. In the context of problem-based learning, students' concepts of learning and knowledge are often challenged because they are expected to be researchers and creators of knowledge in ways that few have encountered in their prior learning experiences. Thus problem-based learning can be a significant challenge to students who expect learning to be discipline-based even if the knowledge being learned coalesces around a problem scenario. Students in higher education, particularly in lecture-based programmes, rarely receive opportunities to integrate knowledge across disciplines and rarely expect to be asked to do so. Furthermore it would seem from research into students' learning that students still construe learning tasks as predominantly assimilating and reproducing material supplied by academics, rather than engaging with what is meaningful for them and framing experience for themselves. The ability of students to manage disjunction and to move on from it is a complex activity with which they often have little help and support. For many staff and students problem-based learning becomes a threshold philosophy because of the way they experience challenges to their life-world – challenges that are at odds with or bear little relationships to their current meaning systems.

Problem-based learning as a threshold philosophy

Problem-based learning may begin as a threshold concept for many staff and students. However, I would argue that it becomes a *threshold philosophy* for many people because of the impact it has on their lives as learners and teachers, particularly in terms of changes in learner identity, perceptions about knowledge and their views about control and power in the learning context. This occurs in particular when constructivist forms of problem-based learning are adopted. In earlier work (Savin-Baden, 2000; Savin-Baden and Major, 2004), I delineated a range of models and models of problem-based learning that are in operation around the world. Examples of such constructivist approaches to problem-based learning include:

- *Model V: Problem-based learning for critical contestability* This form of problem-based learning is one that seeks to provide for the students a kind of higher education that offers, within the curriculum, multiple models of action, knowledge, reasoning and reflection, along with opportunities for the students to challenge, evaluate and interrogate them (Savin-Baden, 2000)
- *Mode 8: The complexity model* This mode is an approach to curriculum design that transcends subjects, disciplines and university curriculum impositions, and embraces knowledge, self, actions and curriculum organising principles (Savin-Baden and Major, 2004).

Challenges to identity, knowledge and power seem to prompt a shift towards life-world becoming. Life-world becoming (Barnett, 1994: 178–9) captures the idea that what is required is an education for the whole of human life. Such an education would include the development of reflective knowing, metalearning and metacritique along with an understanding of the value of dialogue, discourse and argument. Such capabilities can be developed through some forms of problem-based learning (see for example Savin-Baden, 2000, Chapter 9) but also through engaging with and managing challenges to identity, knowledge and power.

Troublesome identity

The notion of troublesome identity reflects the idea that staff or students reach a place where their beliefs about who they are and the way they operate in a learning environment is challenged. For many people this occurs when they realise that it is possible to learn and teach in different ways than they had formerly believed. Troublesome identities are evident when challenges to personal beliefs about learning have occurred and have then promoted some kind of personal shift. In the studies staff spoke of role transitions from lecturer to problem-based learning facilitator as challenges to their identity, suggesting that the discipline in which they taught affected the pedagogical options they believed they had about ways knowledge should be taught and learned. Issues of personal and institutional power and control in turn affected this. Staff in these studies re-examined their understanding of their role as a lecturer, of their students' roles as learners, of the structures of their disciplines and of their views of teaching.

Tutors all described initial transitions from lecturer to facilitator. To begin with, tutors saw themselves as novice facilitators whose role it was to control and direct the team, fill in the gaps in the students' knowledge base and ensure that the course content was covered. Many participants expressed similar concepts about the facilitator role, emphasising the student-centred nature of problem-based learning and the facilitator's role in 'encouraging' students to take responsibility for their own learning. Staff seemed to have an awakening as they gained more experience with the facilitator role. For example Simon, a facilitator at a UK university, was involved in multiple forms of teaching and learning. He had been given the overall remit of implementing curriculum change towards problem-based learning, and at the same time was also implementing technological learning. His background in mental health nursing led him to believe that working and learning through a variety of approaches was useful and he assumed that as a facilitator he would not be particularly directive:

> I didn't think for a minute that my normal teaching style was going to be okay as a problem-based learning facilitator, but I thought like many others do, that I do a lot of those things anyway. I ask a lot of questions, but it isn't until you actually think about being a facilitator, its not just about asking questions, it's about the type of questions that you ask. And are the questions that you ask sufficiently open and non-directive to allow your students to think about issues and to find direction for them-selves? So that I think I was just surprised about how much of a change was required of me.

Simon realised that he needed to change his approach in order to offer students more autonomy; he saw the shift he needed to make as the differ-ence between directing and guiding, and acknowledged that he was often directive.

Several changes in perception of tutor roles were evident with tutors from all the studies. Exposure to the problem-based process increased the realisation that facilitation required skills that were different from those used previously. The concept of tutors no longer being central to student learning raised many issues including threats to self-esteem and fear of job loss. Staff experience of problem-based learning led them to realise that the concept of teacher-centrality in student learning had to be redefined before different skills could be put into practice. Further, exposure to problem-based learning brought recognition over time that the variation in student personalities and abilities, linked to the range of material, required facilitators to be flexible, adaptive, responsive and inclusive.

For students, problem-based learning appeared to prompt a form of identity building through the group and a sense of being able to gain or construct a voice in the learning context. It was apparent that transitions which took place through dialogue often then became an arena for recognising and developing learner identity: students' reflections upon their own roles within groups, the roles of other group members and the relationship between group members seemed to force individual students to consider the ways in which they related, and wanted to relate, to others. It also prompted them to question the extent to which they did and did not belong to the group. For example, Ian's pedagogical stance (the way he saw himself as a learner, Savin-Baden, 2000) was linked to the values he saw as being implicit within both knowledge provided by academics, and experiences and knowledge with which he was supplied in practice, both before commencing his social work course and on practice placements. Ian argued that problem-based learning offered students opportunities, though somewhat limited, for exploring their perspectives and values in relation to the social work values that they were being encouraged to adopt:

> I think where the difficulty is, is that the problem-based learning course hasn't taken into account that there's a continual interaction between your own experiences and your particular Social Work philosophy or perspective. And that if you're actually going to talk about your experiences within the group work context or whatever it is, you have to take into account that there is a Social Work philosophy which develops out of that, which also affects the way you work.

For Ian, learning was the process of evaluating personal knowledge in the light of propositional knowledge. Encountering other students' views of the world had encouraged him to become increasingly reflexive and revisit his own assumptions and values. Yet he was concerned about the extent to which knowledge could be legitimately explored in the context of practice. Within social work practice there were dominant values that were seen to be unchallengeable, and for students to become increasingly reflexive within their pedagogical stance it was vital to understand that knowledge and learning were related to more than discipline-based values, learning facts and passing the course. Evaluating prior experiences of social work practice was vital to seeing learning and epistemology as flexible entities, and thus being able to evaluate concepts, ideas and assumptions.

Troublesome pedagogy

The notion of troublesome pedagogy captures the idea that a pedagogy that was deemed to be valid (such as discipline-based pedagogy, that is teacher knowledge and beliefs about what to do and how to do it in their subject area) is challenged and through the process of deconstruction then becomes troublesome. The reconstruction of what counts as pedagogy is often the most troublesome issue to manage, as Mark's story below indicates. Staff across the studies expressed new understandings of their disciplines. For staff, designing problem-based learning scenarios added to the depth of their knowledge in their content area, and frequently prompted changes in their ideas about how to teach the content of their discipline. For many staff discipline-based pedagogy became troublesome knowledge in problem-based learning. Changes in perspective, particularly the shift away from some knowledge necessarily being foundational to other, resulted in the breaking down of artificial boundaries within the discipline and in breaking down barriers across disciplinary areas. Staff also believed that the course redesign process towards problem-based learning made them reconsider their pedagogical stances and their views about the nature of knowledge. Challenges also emerged about the relationship between knowledge and skills. For example clinical skills, with a large psychomotor element, such as taking blood pressure or giving an injection, are often seen as being fairly straightforward to teach, if not to learn. Yet such capabilities require the understanding of supporting knowledge and theories. Capabilities that are perceived to be more psychomotor are often seen as being harder, such as individualised care planning. Yet problem-based learning pointed up the difficulties with dividing knowledge from skills and demonstrated that this division does not stand up to scrutiny. Staff realised that it was the questions they asked students and the way knowledges were managed that enabled or prevented the development of criticality in students. For example, Mark was a facilitator in a medical school and his own student experience of learning a body of knowledge at Cambridge had been challenged by being a problem-based learning facilitator in a different country and a different discipline from his own. He explained his belief that students encountered troublesome knowledge and related disjunction much earlier on in the programme than the lecture-based programmes he had both experienced and taught in the past:

> I think that students in a problem-based learning programme start to make the shift very much earlier, it took me probably two or three years after finishing university to begin to see the knowledge as being troublesome, whereas these students are running up against it very quickly and

that's another way in which I have a problem at times, that dynamic that we were talking about previously. I make people aware that I am not here to discipline them in the way that they might have had at school, I'm not here to give them answers in the way that they might have got at school, the way that I do that can vary from just not providing it, to an appropriate moment, raising it to the surface but its very much depending on what the group struggling to come up with concrete examples, at times I am quite machiavellian because I'll see something developing and I'll see where its going but I'll hold back . . . and I will try and mirror or reflect or you know draw that out in some way.

For Mark troublesome knowledge was also linked with issues of power and control in the learning process. He argued that he was not there to discipline students but to raise questions and mirror the students' struggles. As a facilitator he also found that the position of power assigned to him by both the faculty and the students was troublesome power.

Troublesome power

Troublesome power refers to the idea that not only is power in itself a troublesome concept but also that covert actions associated with particular practices (such as what is allowed and disallowed in a learning context) affect the power plays within the discipline, the learning context and in staff and students' lives. Troublesome power is also seen in the interaction between staff and students in active learning approaches when 'power to learn' for themselves is offered to the students but what this means in practice is not made explicit. Thus students who may, for example, construct their own curriculum through problem-based learning seminars often encounter troublesome power because of the assessment practices that disable their own curriculum construction. The issue of power is rarely openly acknowledged in problem-based contexts, and nor are issues of control and subjectification in general. Usher and Edwards argue, drawing on the work of Foucault (1979), that institutions of education are important sites of regulation in modern social formations. Lecturers therefore are not only agents of, but also subject to, the disciplinary process of the assessment and measurement of individuals. The whole notion of objective measurement is thus seen as a natural process, a normalising process that students (as subjects) have to accept. Thus they become classified objects who have been measured and also subjectified, because of becoming subjects who learn the truth about themselves (Usher and Edwards, 1994). Surveillance comes not necessarily through direct encounters with tutors, but instead through the performance criteria that appear to be empowering because they are available, and because students can see what they are expected to know. For example, it is expected that because students are given the learning outcomes of the problem-based learning scenario, they will understand what to do and how to do it and will thus be empowered. What occurs in fact are hegemonic practices, practices whereby ideas, structures and actions are constructed and promoted by the powerful to maintain the status quo, and these come to be seen by the majority as working for their own good. Brookfield (1995) has suggested that our paradigmatic assumptions are the structuring axioms that we use to order our world into categories. To question our paradigmatic assumptions is challenging and often occurs as a result of some form of disjunction, but if they are examined and changed then the impact on our teaching and perspectives can be considerable. For example, if we have always believed that sound adult educational practices are essentially democratic and that problem-based learning promotes such ideals, then it can be a shock to discover that this is merely based on an assumption we have held for years, together with idealistic postgraduate teaching that we have received. To discover instead a world beyond adult education, such as medical education, where 'learning by humiliation' (Majoor, 1999) is still relatively common, forces a reappraisal, not only of a view of the education of doctors, but also of how those who teach medical students conceptualise learning, and possibly even problem-based learning.

It was noticeable that students across the studies suggested that there was a credibility gap between the portrayed role of tutors within the theoretical model of problem-based learning, which was presented to the students in the initial stages of the course, and the realities of their practice as facilitators. They suggested that even though tutors spoke of wanting to devolve power to the students, in practice they were neither prepared to devolve it nor capable of doing so. Students who believed that they were being offered power to learn for themselves believed that 'really useful knowledge' (Johnson, 1988) could only be gained when staff exercise of power was diminished. Examining the practices of factors can offer us a way of understanding some of the coded practices that underpin our teaching processes, the way we manage power in learning contexts and the decision about what counts as knowledge, what does not and who decides this.

Conclusion

Problem-based learning is contested ground and research into it remains complex. Yet such diversity demonstrates the versatility of problem-based learning for both staff and students and also indicates that it is a troublesome approach because it generates disjunction and 'stuckness' in people's lives. Problem-based learning can be seen as a threshold philosophy that promotes not just transitions but transformation in the lives of learners. Pre-liminal variation is vital to the realisation that there may be different levels and issues where disjunction occurs for staff and students. Problem-based learning is thus an approach to learning where, whether teachers, learners or both, we continue to stand on the threshold of troublesome identities, pedagogies and power.

References

Barnett, R. (1994) *The Limits of Competence*. Buckingham: Open University Press/ SRHE.

Barrows, H.S. (1986) A taxonomy of problem-based learning methods. *Medical Education*, 20: 481–486.

Barrows, H.S. and Tamblyn, R.M. (1980) *Problem-based Learning, An Approach to Medical Education*. New York: Springer.

Boud, D. (ed.) (1985) *Problem-based Learning in Education for the Professions*. Sydney: Higher Education Research and Development Society of Australasia.

Brookfield, S.D. (1995) *Becoming a Critically Reflective Teacher*. San Francisco, CA: Jossey Bass.

Foucault, M. (1979) *Discipline and Punish: The Birth of the Prison*. Harmondsworth: Penguin Books.

Habermas, J. (1989) *The Theory of Communicative Action, Vol. 2*. Cambridge: Polity.

Johnson, R. (1988) 'Really useful knowledge: 1790–1850', in T. Lovett (ed.) *Radical Approaches to Adult Education: A Reader*. London: Routledge.

Majoor, J. (1999) The challenges of problem-based teaching: a reply to Maudsley, G., *British Medical Journal*, 318: 657–661.

Meyer, J.H.F. and Land, R. (2003) 'Threshold concepts and troublesome knowledge: linkages to ways of thinking and practising within the disciplines', in C. Rust (ed.) *Improving Students Learning: Improving Student Learning Theory and Practice – Ten Years On*. Oxford: Oxford Centre for Staff and Learning Development.

Meyer, J.H.F. and Land, R. (2005) Threshold concepts and troublesome knowledge (2): epistemological considerations and a conceptual framework for teaching and learning. *Higher Education*, 49: 373–388.

Savin-Baden, M. (2000) *Problem-based Learning in Higher Education: Untold Stories*. Buckingham: Open University Press/SRHE.

Savin-Baden, M. and Major, C.H. (2004) *Foundations of Problem-based Learning: Illuminating Perspectives*. Maidenhead: SRHE/Open University Press.

Usher, R. and Edwards, R. (1994) *Postmodernism and Education*. London: Routledge.

Weil, S. (1989) Access: towards education or miseducation? Adults imagine the future, in O. Fulton (ed.) *Access and Institutional Change*. Buckingham: Open University Press/SRHE.

Chapter 12

On the mastery of philosophical concepts

Socratic discourse and the unexpected 'affect'

Jennifer Booth

Introduction

My aim in this chapter is twofold. First, I wish to suggest that philosophy, as a doctrine, is rife with what Meyer and Land (2003a) have termed 'threshold concepts'. As a result, my second suggestion is that the question of how best to teach philosophy is intimately related to the question of how best to facilitate students' mastery of these concepts.

In establishing this dual aim, I turn first to a theoretical consideration of the role of threshold concepts in philosophy, in particular the role of the concept of 'representation' in the philosophy of perception. Second, I focus on the practical considerations of how one might go about enabling students to master such concepts in a learning context. Specifically, I delineate two hypothetical stages in the student's achievement of threshold concept mastery – deconstruction and reconstruction – and it is in the service of facilitating both that I advocate the use of a certain Socratic methodology. In conclusion I highlight what might be termed an ethical consideration of using the Socratic method which, if ignored, could inhibit students' learning and threshold concept mastery.

The naive philosopher

Philosophy is a difficult subject matter to introduce to university students for at least two reasons. First, the ideas or suggestions it involves and the skills it requires will more than likely be entirely new to the student. This is not necessarily the case with other academic subjects such as history, or mathematics, where the student can bring with them an understanding of the type of material and skills needed from their school-age education. It is often the case that the issues with which philosophy deals and the skills of analysis that it draws upon will have to be introduced to the student for the first time at the university level. This applies not only to new philosophy undergraduates but also to older students whose main area of study lies in another discipline.

Both approach the subject without any substantial previous experience of thinking philosophically.

The second, and perhaps more recalcitrant, reason that philosophy can be hard to introduce to students is that in order to understand and appreciate the philosophical material, the student must re-evaluate or distort parts of their common-sense understanding about the world. They may have to challenge and abandon intuitions and opinions they thought were infallible. In other words, philosophical knowledge is not the type of knowledge which can be stored neatly in its own cortical punch pocket, alongside one's common-sense beliefs about the world. Often previous beliefs or understandings will need to fall by the wayside while other, perhaps more radical, ideas take their place. This process, it seems, is something students find instantly problematic. As Elkins (2005: 1) notes: 'we resist, in every way possible, the idea that we know less than we think we know ... we oppose with great energy the thought that our lives might be plagued by self-deception.'

It is for both these reasons, the originality and conflict-inducing nature of the material, that philosophy may strike new students as being rather hard to grasp. It presents what we might call 'troublesome' knowledge. In fact, this can be quite true to the atmosphere of a seminar with inexperienced philosophers, where opinions and intuitions fly forth to defend themselves in the face of a new confusion or challenge. Prima facie it seems that the level of understanding the student needs in order to grasp certain philosophical issues comes only when the student crosses certain 'thinking thresholds'. Many a teaching colleague will recognise the experience of the student who 'magically grasps' an idea at one point in time, and from thereon in never struggles with it again.

Arguably, to be truly in touch with any student's level of ability one must first recognise which thinking thresholds that student has or has not crossed. Second, one must also know how to go about enabling that student to cross the thresholds that he or she has yet to cross. To be sure of achieving either of these aims, one must know exactly what these 'thinking thresholds' actually are.

Characterising the 'threshold concept'

Meyer and Land (2003a) provide a means of capturing the essence of what is meant by the notion of a thinking threshold. They propose that in order for a learner to cross a thinking threshold, they must grasp or master a threshold *concept*:

> A threshold concept can be considered as akin to a portal, opening up a *new* and previously inaccessible way of thinking about something. It represents a *transformed* way of understanding, or interpreting, or viewing something without which the learner cannot progress.
>
> (Meyer and Land 2003a: 412, my italics)

These concepts are not just pieces of information that one can 'add' to one's knowledge of a subject matter; they do not behave as simple epistemological building blocks. On the contrary, grasp of these concepts entails a 'qualitatively different view of subject matter' (2003a: 415) for the learner.

Meyer and Land (2003a) characterise a number of distinguishing features by which we can 'recognise' a threshold concept. At this point I wish to draw attention to three of these features: they are transformative, irreversible, and integrative. (I will discuss their 'troublesome' nature elsewhere.) They are transformative in so far as they transform the perspective of the learner; they are not something that can be selectively looked upon like a matter of fact. The student cannot, as it were, stand back from their mastery of a threshold concept; once they have mastered it, their viewpoint on the subject matter will be transformed.

It is owing to this transformative effect that mastery of a threshold concept is an irreversible process. The new understanding that a learner has 'interferes' with their earlier outlook, and will colour their opinions and understanding of both new and previously acquired material. Threshold concepts are, in a sense, epistemological floodgates; once opened they cannot simply be 'undone'. Moreover, not only does mastering a threshold concept provide the student with a 'new' perspective on material, it is supposed to provide them with a 'better' one. The material should appear cohesive in ways that it did not prior to the student's grasp of the concepts, affording the student more insightful and integrated understanding of that material. In Meyer and Land's terms, mastery of the threshold concepts should expose the 'previously hidden inter-relatedness' (2003a: 416) of material.

Philosophical threshold concepts

Now we have a better grasp of what these 'threshold concepts' actually are, let us move to the question of how they relate to philosophy. In order to do so I want to consider an example of what might be thought to qualify as a threshold concept in philosophy; in particular in the philosophy of perception.

A central issue in the philosophy of perception is the epistemological role that the contents of perception have in informing the perceiver about the world. In particular, the question of whether a subject can know from the content of what he experiences that he is being presented with an objective or mind-independent reality. Now in order to understand much of the dialectic surrounding this type of question, students need a firm grip on the concept of 'representation'. Specifically, they need to understand the proposal that the contents of the mind might be such that they can 'represent' the contents of the world. Although there are a variety of ways in which theorists respond to the possibility of representation in perception, the crucial point is that the majority of these theorists will still navigate their position around the issue of representation, be it their target or trophy. That is, they certainly take for granted a primordial understanding of what 'representation' itself amounts to.

Prior to grasping the concept of representation, a student is limited to a dichotomous conception of the contents of perception as being either objects of the world or mind-generated ideas or fancies. Once they grasp the notion of representation, a third position opens up, namely the idea that the contents of perception might be mental pictures which represent – truthfully or not – the objects of the world. The introduction of this new possibility transforms the student's view on what the contents of perception might provide, and with such a transformation comes new questions and clarifications that were previously unavailable to the student.

We might claim then that 'representation' is an example of a threshold concept. Mastering it irreversibly transforms the students view and allows them to integrate previously diverse positions in the philosophical literature.

From theory to practice

Noticing that a doctrine plays home to a variety of threshold concepts does not suffice to tell us, as teachers, how to enable students to master those concepts. It is to this practical concern that I now turn. We have located the enemy as it were, but we have now to overcome him.

First, we need to be clear on the reasons why philosophical threshold concepts are to be described as 'troublesome'. Perkins (1999), in discussing different kinds of troublesome knowledge, includes that which is alien and that which is counter-intuitive to the learner. Meyer and Land (2003b) use the example of 'physical acquaintance' as a threshold concept that can present 'alien' knowledge to the students. They cite a history lecturer as saying that present-day students find the past importance of physical acquaintance in communities hard to grasp. It is difficult for students as they feel 'alienated' from the past way of life and its concomitant values. This does not seem to be the case in philosophy. Although some of the positions taken in logical space are extreme, they are not alien in the sense that past lives or unfamiliar cultures might be.

Philosophical threshold concepts seem more akin to the second type of troublesome knowledge, that which is 'counter-intuitive' to the student. Considering that much of philosophy is engaged in the service of analysing and challenging our everyday intuitions, it is perhaps unsurprising that some of the suggestions it makes might appear counter-intuitive to the student. Consider the workings of philosophical idealism which proposes the idea that the world which we think of as being composed of mind-independent objects is in fact no more than mind-dependent ideas and spirits. To any new student who approaches the nature of perception with common-sense 'epistemological baggage' this idea will no doubt appear counter-intuitive. So how do we go about enabling students to master these 'counter-intuitive' philosophical threshold concepts? Well, a lot can be learned by first considering how not to do it. Specifically, I want to consider two possible pedagogical strategies that might serve to inhibit students' mastery of threshold concepts: dogmatic information transfer, and the simplification of material.

By dogmatically forcing new material on students at a fast pace, or with little or no explanation of the reasons behind the motivation for that material, one risks inhibiting students' mastery of the threshold concepts in question. In particular, by forcing the students to learn too quickly, one risks the possibility of putting them in a state of what Cousin, in Chapter 9 of this volume, refers to as 'psychological vertigo' (after Lather, cited in Orner 1997). Although the students might then have a cosmetic grasp of the concept they have by no means mastered it enough to suggest that they have crossed the required 'thinking threshold'. Such students remain in a 'suspended state' of learning; the answers they give to questions which test their grasp of the material betray a certain 'mimicry' and 'lack authenticity' (Meyer and Land 2003a). Meyer and Land (2005) suggest that when a student first tries to get to grips with a threshold concept they are placed into a 'liminal state', a conceptual space characterised by the students tendency to oscillate between full mastery of the concept and their state prior to the introduction of the concept. A moment's anecdotal reflection will bring to mind the occasional student essay which oscillates between moments of clarity and opaqueness in regards to the proper use of a particular concept.

At the other extreme, trying to slow down the pace of learning by introducing an easier or simplified version of a threshold concept to students is also to be avoided. According to Meyer and Land (2005), attempting to use a naive version of a threshold concept as a proxy for the actual concept itself can result in the students failing to grasp the full concept. They discuss a study by Meyer and Shanahan (2003) in which a naive version of a threshold concept was introduced as an unsuccessful proxy for the full-blown concept. The implication here is that there is no gentle route to presenting a threshold concept; the students must meet it head on. Bearing that in mind, let us move to the question of how best to steer students through the successful mastery of these counter-intuitive threshold concepts.

Socratic discourse as a weapon of deconstruction

I suggested earlier that the learning process can be roughly broken down into two processes: deconstruction and reconstruction. Owing to the counter-intuitive nature of the philosophical material to be communicated, one needs to concentrate on first breaking down or perforating any pre-philosophical common-sense convictions that the students hold. This first stage of deconstruction of the students' knowledge clears the way for the introduction of new philosophical concepts and critiques. The post-deconstruction student will hopefully display certain receptivity to new ideas, avoiding the risk of a recalcitrant stalemate attitude that their pre-philosophical intuitions might have fuelled. The second stage of the learning process is the introduction and mastery of the new philosophical threshold concepts. It is by no means a given that these two stages are rigidly demarcated either by content or chronology; they can happen together and perhaps even be largely indistinguishable in practice. The only point that I do wish to press is that when intending to present students with counter-intuitive material it is wise to soften up their intuitions before doing so.

Let us start by characterising what we shall mean here by the phrase 'Socratic method', and then go on to show how it applies to these two learning phases. In Elkins's (2005: 1) words: 'The struggle at the heart of philosophy animated by Socrates' teaching is submitting ourselves to questioning about the lives we choose and let others choose for us.' According to this view, the Socratic method is to question and question again every issue that one encounters. As MacDonald Ross (1993: 12) puts it 'the Socratic position is that to think philosophically is to think questioningly and reflectively'. One does not simply impart information to students. Instead, one provokes their understanding by asking them a series of questions. The practice traditionally involves a learned fellow, namely the 'teacher', guiding the flow of questioning whilst engaging the student in an interactive search for defensible positions in logical space. It aims to encourage the student to be self-reflective and critical of their long-held assumptions. As a result, the student can be faced with a new scenario, where they have come to doubt things which they once thought indubitable. In such a state, the student is arguably ripe for the receipt of new perspectives on material, in the form of transformative threshold concepts. One can use Socratic, exigent questioning as a tool to effectively clear and yet fertilise the soil of past assumption. After all: 'The [only] resistance to questioning . . . lies in what we think we already know' (Elkins 2005: 1; the word in square brackets is my own).

This methodology embodies a student-oriented approach to learning, as it encourages the student to question their own views without being simply told the possible flaws within those views. Ideally, one guides the student with questions into seeing the weakness of their own position. Interactive dialogue is the tool by which the teacher can bring about a change in the student's perspective. In a Vygotskian sense the discursive partners use the praxis of debate to construct developing trains of thought and argument that they might not have generated alone. Just because the aim of the dialogue is to deconstruct pre-philosophical assumptions, it does not mean the method between the student and the teacher is not one of co-ordinated *con*struction of a logical train of thought.

Initiating reconstruction

So what of the process of epistemological 'reconstruction'? It is clear that the Socratic method can be of use in clearing away pre-philosophical assumptions, but can it be of similar use in introducing new ideas? On the one hand, to say that it could would be to reject the very ethos of the Socratic methodology, which is to encourage an enduring reliance on irrevocable doubt and permanent questioning. However, on the other hand, it seems quite plausible that we might adopt a general framework of discursive dialogue in the service of introducing the student to new ideas. As a resolution, one might say that we extract elements of the Socratic method – notably its interactive format and student-oriented focus – in guiding the students into a position where they can actively seek out the threshold concepts themselves. According to Curzon (1990: 249), Socratic questioning can naturally be divided into a negative stage where questioning is used to expose weaknesses in the student's position, and a positive phase where the newly curious student responds to further questioning in the search for new answers. Furthermore, not only will students be actively seeking out these conceptual 'tools', they will be in the perfect arena for testing their mastery of them. Full mastery of a threshold concept should only be granted to students if, in the face of spontaneous questioning, their 'clear communication directly reflects clarity of thought as opposed to mere regurgitation' (Cowley 2001: 44).

The unexpected dimension

I wish to end by drawing attention to a noteworthy consequence that could result from implementation of the Socratic method in the service of students' threshold concept mastery. Whilst the Socratic method might prove a useful pedagogical and diagnostic tool in the learning environment, the intense focus it brings on the students and their role in the learning process means one must remain explicitly aware of those students' emotional states. By endorsing a process that emphasises attention on the subjective state of the learner as being the target of attack, we run the risk of invoking strong affective states in that learner. When material is simply presented to students they can remain at a distance from it; the material is easily conveyed in an affectively neutral manner. This is often not the case when it comes to Socratic-style debate over philosophical issues. Philosophical material in itself is often inherently personal, in so far as it questions the nature of one's own body, mind and personal experience. When coupled with a learning methodology that focuses attention on the learner and the 'weakness' of their beliefs, the situation certainly becomes one where the affective state of the learner should be taken into account. To add to the argument, mastering any kind of threshold concept can itself be an emotional experience, a factor of the profundity of thought that they demand (see Cousin, Chapter 9 this volume).

The upshot of these concerns is that consideration of the emotional state of learners needs to be a factor in deciding which pedagogical style one chooses to implement in teaching students the mastery of philosophical threshold concepts. The stage of the learning process where this concern is arguably most important is in the deconstruction phase of the Socratic discourse. As it stands, perhaps our brute metaphor of simply clearing the soil of past intuitions and convictions is a little out of touch, in so far as the cleared ground may be more raw than expected. What one needs to do is modify the aggressiveness of Socrates' original style and create a less confrontational tone, a manoeuvre that almost certainly would not have been advocated by Socrates himself. For in its original state: 'Socrates' method was far from non-confrontational, and the object was not compromise . . . the process could prove emotionally painful and humiliating' (MacDonald Ross 1993: 11).

So the alternative is to put the Socratic questioning style to use without creating avoidable discomfort in the learner. There is certainly a difference to be recognised between emotionally stressful material and an emotionally stressful teacher. Both can place the learner in an uncomfortable state, but the latter can certainly be avoided. As teachers we need to keep in mind the affective state of our pupils. Our priority it seems should not only be to help the students to cross thinking thresholds but also to ensure they do so without fear, intimidation or upset.

On a final note, if the humanistic motivation alone is not enough, a conscientious teacher should always be wary of the fact that negative emotional states in the learner may defeat the whole exercise of education. Learner emotional 'positionality', suggests Cousin in Chapter 9 of this volume, can produce variation in levels of understanding of a threshold concept. On consideration then, as affectivity is an influential variable in the success of students' threshold concept mastery, we would certainly do well to accommodate it.

References

Cowley, C. (2001) Cultivating transferable skills in philosophy undergraduates. *Philosophical and Religious Studies Learning and Teaching Support Network Journal (PRS-LTSN)*, 1: 39–51.

Curzon, L.B. (1990) *Teaching in Further Education. An Outline of Principles and Practice*, fourth edition. London: Cassell.

Elkins, J. (2005) *Professional Responsibility: Socrates and the Socratic Method*. Available online at http://www.wvu.edu/~lawfac/jelkins/pr-03/virtue/socrates.html

MacDonald Ross, G. (1993) Socrates versus Plato: the origins and development of Socratic thinking. *Aspects of Education*, 49: 9–22. Available online at http://www.prs-ltsn.leeds.ac.uk/philosophy/articles/socrates/socplat.pdf

Meyer, J.H.F. and Land, R. (2003a) Threshold concepts and troublesome knowledge: linkages to ways of thinking and practising within the disciplines, in C. Rust (ed.)

Improving Student Learning: Improving Student Learning Theory and Practice – Ten Years On. Oxford: OCSLD.

Meyer, J.H.F and Land, R. (2003b) Threshold concepts and troublesome knowledge: epistemological and ontological considerations and a conceptual framework for teaching and learning. Paper presented at the Tenth Conference of the European Association for Research on Learning and Instruction (EARLI), Padova, Italy.

Meyer, J.H.F. and Land, R. (2005) Threshold concepts and troublesome knowledge (2): epistemological considerations and a conceptual framework for teaching and learning. *Higher Education*, 49: 373–388.

Meyer, J.H.F. and Shanahan, M. (2003) The troublesome nature of a threshold concept in Economics. Paper presented at the Tenth European Association for Research on Learning and Instruction, Padova, Italy.

Orner, M. (1997) Teaching feminist cultural studies, in Canaan, J. and Epstein, D. (eds) *A Question of Discipline: Pedagogy, Power and the Teaching of Cultural Studies.* Oxford: Weaver Press.

Perkins, D. (1999) The many faces of constructivism. *Educational Leadership*, 57 (3): 6–11.

Chapter 13

Using analogy in science teaching as a bridge to students' understanding of complex issues

Simon Bishop

Introduction: the nature of analogy

Analogies are a commonly used tool for communicating ideas and information, both inside and outside the context of formal education. They are used to identify similarities in things that are otherwise dissimilar in order to make a link or build a bridge between seemingly unrelated concepts. Because of this they can be a valuable tool in helping people to connect with complex new subjects based on the knowledge or experience that they already possess and may well be one practical means of helping students deal with the often troublesome transformations identified by Meyer and Land (2003) when students encounter threshold concepts.

When discussing the value of the analogy it is important to begin with a clear definition of the term. Numerous definitions have been used within academic and popular circles but an agreed definition is notoriously difficult to find (Goswami, 1991). The confusion arises principally because the word 'analogy' means different things to different people (Russell, 1989). It is derived from the Greek word 'analogia' meaning mathematical proportion (Kedar-Cabelli, 1988), but it has now developed a broader meaning to most people. A psychology-based definition provided by Reber (1985) describes analogical reasoning as 'reasoning whereby decisions about objects, events or concepts depend upon perceived similarities in the relationships between pairs'. This reference to pairing is an important one and underlies the essence of the use of analogy as it will be discussed here.

Base domain and target domain

Within an educational context, analogy can be described as facilitating mapping between elements of a base domain (that which is known) and a target domain (that which is unknown) (Gentner, 1983). Each domain contains knowledge or information, and each piece of information is a description consisting of related elements. For example, when introducing students to the concept of photosynthesis for the first time, this new idea would represent the target domain. In order to then formulate an analogy to help students to understand the target, it would be necessary to identify a 'known' base domain with which the students are already likely to be familiar. In this example a commonly used base domain is the process of baking a cake. Once the target and base domains have been identified, the next step is to clarify those elements in each that could be mapped across from the one to the other.

The key elements within photosynthesis are the production of carbohydrates from carbon dioxide and water by using light as an energy source and generating oxygen as a by-product. The elements involved in baking a cake are flour, sugar, eggs and butter mechanically mixed and then heated. Elements shared between the base and target domains therefore include ingredients being combined and changed through the use of energy to produce an end-product very different from the original constituents. The unshared elements, such as the differences between the ingredients and energy inputs and the absence of a tangible by-product in cake making, are analogically irrelevant.

Analogies are, then, most effective in producing student comprehension when the learner is properly familiar with the base domain and can map some well-understood elements from this onto unfamiliar elements in the target domain. For this reason it is important to use a base domain appropriate to the learner from which they will be able to develop viable analogical mapping events. For example, the analogy that a cell works like a factory is often used when teaching biology. The analogy works because most students will already have a degree of knowledge regarding the base domain (i.e. what goes on in a factory) and are able to link some of these ideas to the less-familiar target domain of cellular processes. Using analogies based upon more specialised base domains, such as the workings of an internal combustion engine or a microchip, might be fine for some learners but inappropriate for others. Without a sufficiently well-understood base domain it can be more difficult for students to understand the target domain. In a sense, it is like being given a map and being told where you have to get to but without knowing exactly where you are when you start – the 'you are here' point on any map is significantly important. Once an appropriate base domain has been chosen it is then the role of the educator to properly identify clear links to the target domain and then to facilitate the students' journey along these towards comprehension of the new concept. This process of information delivery through the use of similarities between a base and a target domain is called *analogical transfer*.

Analogical learning

Associated with the principles of analogical transfer are two other terms that relate to the use of this process in education: analogical learning and analogical teaching (Speirs, 1996); they represent, in effect, both sides of the analogical transfer event. As an educator making use of analogies in the classroom, it is important to develop a clear understanding of how a learner deals with analogies and then apply this understanding to the process of teaching.

Analogical learning involves a student gaining an understanding of new material or a new subject through the utilisation of the analogical transfer process. This should ideally involve more than just a single mapping event (i.e. the analogical transfer of just one element from base to target) in order for it to be effective, especially for more complex analogies.

For example, an analogy about a security guard can be used to describe how the human immune system is capable of identifying self from non-self and dangerous molecules from benign. An armed security guard at a bank must let in unfamiliar customers without challenge as part of his job. Similarly, the immune system must not mount a vigorous attack on all foreign particles it meets (proteins that you may have consumed at an earlier meal, for instance). But when a robbery is taking place and the alarm sounds, the guard should be suspicious of anyone he does not know while at the same time being careful not to shoot the bank staff or legitimate customers. The immune system can similarly go on high alert when tissue damage indicates an infection, but it must ensure that it does not attack its own cells (unless they are serving as factories for the replication of viruses). Sometimes the immune system can be tricked by false alarms (such as invasion of the nose by inhaled pollen) in a similar way as the guard might be misled into action by the sound of an alarm bell from an adjacent school.

This analogy works well because it links several elements of the base and target domains by outlining a variety of similarities between the immune system and a bank security guard. The student learns that the immune system exists to protect the body from pathogens and is capable of selectively screening foreign material prior to responding. They also learn that the immune system is sometimes capable of reacting inappropriately in response to relatively benign material. With this gap bridged it would then be possible to continue the thread by discussing antigens and antibodies and the concept of autoantibodies in diseases like rheumatoid arthritis.

Schema induction

In 1980 Gick and Holyoak first introduced the idea of 'schema induction'. A schema is a pattern imposed on a complex reality or experience to assist in explaining it, utilising the shared elements only and discarding those that are unshared. Without a minimum of two shared elements, no schema is induced. For example, imagine that an intelligent alien lands on Earth for the first time with no prior knowledge of what to expect. If they met a human for the first time and learnt that it was called a 'human' then their initial understanding of the concept would be everything about that particular human – its height, hair colour, etc. If the first human was tall and blond, then the natural assumption would be that all humans are tall and blond. If a short, dark-haired human later appeared and the alien discovered that it was also called a 'human' then they would realise that height and hair colour are not constants but rather variables of humanity. It would instantly become apparent that the core of invariance must be at a more abstract level. However, even this second meeting might not be enough for the alien to be able to fully comprehend what defines a human. The more different types of human that the alien met and entered into the induction engine, the more efficient the schema would become at understanding what a human was.

The concept of schema induction shares many commonalities with the principles of analogical learning. Each should be composed of a number of parallel threads all leading to the same target domain and working together in concert to reinforce each other and develop understanding. One thread will provide some information about the target domain but its effectiveness at illuminating the 'big picture' is often limited. By utilising multiple threads a student may develop a more accurate picture of the target domain than if they were forced to rely on a single mapping event, in a similar way as dots on a television screen work together to build up an image – the more dots there are then the more intelligible the picture becomes.

Analogical teaching

Analogical teaching approaches the use of analogy more directly from the perspective of the educator and refers to two basic ideas. It refers first to the use of analogical transfer as the principal method for assisting student under-standing, rather than relying solely upon traditional formal instruction. Second it refers to students being taught how to form analogies for themselves and how to relate these to the target subject matter. Reasoning by analogy in this way is really a method of recycling old knowledge, identifying differences and modifying parameters to make it fit. More simply, analogical reasoning represents learning by experience. The difficulty arising from this form of cognitive processing is that most people's 'old knowledge' rarely fits exactly any new situation and the skill therefore lies in its adaptation and application.

Many researchers in the field have been convinced of the importance of analogical reasoning as an important aspect of knowledge gathering and understanding. Oppenheimer (1956) says that analogy is 'an indispensable and inevitable tool for scientific progress'. In addition, Holyoak (1984) states that analogical thinking is 'a pervasive component of human intelligence and manifests itself in many forms throughout most of our life'. Taking this idea one stage further, Goswami (1992) argues that much of human reasoning is basically analogical, and the use of analogical reasoning is very important in cognitive development. This is a powerful statement and if we accept it as being correct then the implications for teaching practice are far-reaching.

It does seem clear that the process of understanding new concepts through analogy is an inherent part of human cognition. Oppenheimer (1956) outlines that people cannot avoid relying on their memories of previous events because that is all they have. These memories are shaped by other aspects of cognition – such as judgement, reasoning, and imagination – but remain fundamental as the primal ingredient of understanding. Humans naturally apply their knowledge and experiences to new situations they encounter. As a result, existing knowledge has an effect on the way people solve problems and make connections. It is this natural process that the use of analogy in teaching is able to capitalise on.

Theorising analogy

Several studies have looked at how people notice and use analogies and whether or not they just identify surface similarities or deep structural similarities. Researchers have sought to create a 'unified theory' of analogical reasoning, but there is still no agreement that fully explains the phenomenon. Despite this, much interesting work has been published in the field that helps to guide the use of analogy in education. Amongst this work is research by Gentner (1983) that suggests that humans prefer 'systematic' (very connected) analogies that map higher order (causal) relations in a one-to-one manner from source to target. This is the approach that most educators tend to adopt in the classroom as these are often the most obvious and well defined.

Interestingly it appears that analogical learning is not just the preserve of older students. Work by Alexander et al. (1987) has shown that children as young as 4 and 5 years old are able to effectively solve problems analogically, based on even their limited understanding and experience of the world. The point is that everything that we do, see or experience links into our understanding of the world and provides a loose set of rules that can be applied to help solve future problems, albeit with some cognitive 'tweaking'.

Analogies can appear in various forms and it is this aspect of their nature that makes them both difficult to study and interesting to use. In an attempt to simplify things as much as possible, Goswami (1992) asserts that there are basically two main types of analogy: 'proportional analogies' and 'story analogies'.

Proportional analogies and story analogies

Proportional analogies are common in intelligence tests (Masterson, 1993) and take the form 'A is to B as C is to D'. Verbal examples of this might be 'hoof is to horse as paw is to cat' or 'up is to down as day is to night'. They are designed to be reasonably uncomplicated and rely on both the base and target domains being known to the subject. The objective is to be able to link the pairs together using simple analogical reasoning. Although benefiting from their simplicity, proportional analogies are also limited by it, which prevents them from being used to help students to understand complicated new subjects in any substantial way.

Story analogies tend to be more difficult to use and understand than proportional analogies as they are often composed of more than one analogical inference and are involved in the transfer of complex packages of information. Nonetheless, they can be much more effective as an educational tool because of this and may well offer a helpful way through the troublesomeness of the liminal state encountered by students that has been discussed by Meyer and Land (2005). A commonly used example of the use of a story analogy concerns Duncker's 'radiation problem' (Duncker, 1945). In Duncker's problem, doctors need to destroy a tumour with radiation without destroying the surrounding tissue. It is impossible to operate on the patient, but unless the tumour is destroyed the patient will die. If the radiation is of high enough intensity it will destroy the tumour, but at such intensity it will also destroy the healthy tissue that it passes through. If lower intensity radiation is used it will not destroy the healthy tissue, but will not destroy the tumour either. The problem is to understand how the radiation can be used so that the tumour is destroyed without damaging healthy tissue. The solution is to use a number of low intensity bursts of radiation, fired from different angles, which alone will not harm the healthy tissue but achieve appropriate strength by converging onto the tumour.

Analogical experimentation

Gick and Holyoak (1980) conducted analogical reasoning experiments during which subjects were given an analogy before being shown Duncker's problem. The analogy was about a General who needed to capture a castle. The castle was located at the centre of a country with roads leading up to it. The problem was that all the roads were mined. The General required all his army to capture the castle but the weight of all his army would cause the mines to go off. The General solved the problem by dividing the army into smaller groups, each too light to set off the mines. He then sent each group down a separate road at the same time so that they all reached the castle together and could successfully capture it. The crucial point of this and all other story analogies is that existing knowledge should be used to make unfamiliar material familiar. This existing knowledge could be from the distant past or it could be information that has only recently been received, for example in the classroom prior to the analogy being presented. In this way it may be possible to teach a student a new but simple concept and then use this as the base domain to link through to a more complex set of ideas.

An important feature of story analogies like the one above is that they often contain several relationships that are interconnected, as well as plenty of irrelevant detail added to make them easier to understand and relate to. They are like fables – the point of the story is the moral, but without the rest of the narrative in support, the meaning and weight of the lesson is lost. Essentially, story-based analogies conceal the solution to the problem in their detail and this can often be very difficult to isolate. As a result, this can generate confusion for some students who may lose their way along the route and fail to make a clear connection. It is therefore important to construct as simple a narrative as possible to reduce any distractive effect to a minimum.

Some experiments looking at the effectiveness of story analogies in problem solving, rather than as teaching tools, have cast doubt on the effectiveness of analogies as mechanisms of reasoning. In 1983, Gick and Holyoak published their results of work with university undergraduates. During their study, the researchers had been interested in assessing the efficiency with which the students were able to formulate analogical links for themselves rather than to understand analogies presented to them. However, both the base domain and the target problem were chosen to be new to the students who subsequently failed to identify analogical inferences.

This approach runs contrary to our current understanding of effective analogical teaching in which the base domain must be thoroughly understood in order for links to be made to the target domain. When presented with two different domains, without any hint of similarity between them, the students were unable to find an analogy and make a connection. To the researchers, the analogies that they had set were obvious, and much confusion was caused by the subjects' inability to understand them. However, what is obvious to one person is not always obvious to another and in this instance the subjects were given problems that were just too difficult for them to solve without a clearer, more familiar base domain or a hint of where to look for the analogy. This effect was further compounded by Gick and Holyoak not presenting their analogies in a way that was particularly conducive to learning. They did not use analogical reasoning as a method for teaching within a logical framework but instead were concerned purely with the process of transfer without, necessarily, evidence of understanding.

Halpern *et al.* (1990) are clear that whilst people are quite able to learn a new piece of information via analogical instruction, they are significantly less likely to discover analogies set by other people without some direction. By ignoring this aspect of analogical reasoning, Gick and Holyoak reduced the effectiveness of the very thing that they were trying to observe. This may help to explain the reasons for the poor performance of the students rather than it being due to the fundamental failure of the analogical reasoning process. However, it does suggest that story analogies may be rather better suited to teach with than to test with.

There is good evidence to suggest that analogical reasoning is a valid cognitive ability in the right circumstances. The idea of spontaneous analogical transfer is when data or information from one problem is used spontaneously to solve another problem without a clear hint to direct its application. This concept does, however, assume familiarity with the base domain and in this way differs from the studies of Gick and Holyoak in 1983 outlined above.

Inter-domain knowledge transfer

Researchers Needham and Begg (1991) have stated that subjects rarely transfer relevant information to complex new problems without a clear hint. However, Brown *et al.* (1989) argue that useful spontaneous inter-domain knowledge transfer is possible if the conditions are right. In many situations insight does naturally develop in a series of small spontaneous analogical transfer episodes over a long period. Mankind did not spontaneously understand how to build aeroplanes but instead developed an understanding of aeronautics through a long series of very small steps with each step built upon the one that came before it.

Within formal education there is rarely the time to rely on this natural process alone to drive learning. For example, if you wanted your students to attend an educational event at another campus you could provide them with the name of the institution and then allow them to work out exactly where and when the event was taking place and how to get there. Alternatively, you could provide a minibus to collect them and take them directly to the venue. Both systems would provide the students with some chance of getting to the event, although the latter would do so much more efficiently and with far greater certainty. It is much better (and much quicker) to help students to learn through the provision of active teaching rather than expecting too much from spontaneous analogical transfer.

Limitations of analogy

Analogies, however, do have their limitations and are not always useful in accelerating the learning process. In some instances they can even become a stumbling block to a student seeing an idea clearly and end up hampering the knowledge transfer process. By relying too much on what is already known about a subject within the base domain a student can easily jump to incorrect conclusions by adhering too closely to the link between this and the target, seeking and finding similarities beyond those that exist. As a cognitive process, analogies are successful some of the time, but can be misleading (Glynn *et al.*, 1989). Ultimately, analogies can have a positive or a negative effect on learning, and only if we become aware of their weaknesses can we become less vulnerable to them.

To put this in context, an opportunity for confusion might occur when providing a student with an analogy when they already have sufficient background knowledge of the target domain. This may well have the effect of distracting their attention away from the target learning material and towards those elements of the story that do not map (Zeitoun, 1984). For example, a student who already understands something about the nature of electricity could be in a class that is taught using the analogy that electricity behaves like running water. Although this is an analogy that is commonly used at an elementary level, it rapidly collapses under detailed scrutiny – electrons repel one another while particles in water do not, nor do electrons display anything analogous to viscosity, boundary layer drag or turbulence. Unless the student is clear about which elements map across from the base domain to the target domain and which do not then they could easily become misled. In this case, rather than making the learning process easier, the analogy could load it down and slow the student's overall progress. The work of Weller (1970) states that, when used with care, an analogy can be a fine time-saving device, but when used incorrectly or inappropriately it can serve to obstruct the learning process. Using an improper analogy, which ignores the differences between domains, may lead the student to jump to incorrect conclusions.

It is important when using analogies to ensure that the connections between the base and target domains are made absolutely explicit to the learners. It is insufficient to expect the learners to discover the similarities for themselves and hope that the connections made are both accurate and ample to enable successful knowledge transfer. Even if the students do understand the similarities between domains, there is no way of being sure that these will be the similarities that they were intended to notice. In many studies assessing the transfer of knowledge using analogy, the role of the researcher was not as a teacher, but instead as a problem setter. Typically, analogies are not used in this way but are used instead for teaching to guide learners towards an understanding of a complex subject.

Analogy and abstraction

One of the benefits of analogy is that it can often make abstract concepts more concrete by providing a mental image that can be more easily remembered. Many threshold concepts, of course, are likely to involve the student in processes of abstraction, and analogy may have a particularly useful role to play here. Analogies that use concrete objects function as a 'visual mnemonic aid' and can help students to remember new information. Some systems of foreign language teaching utilise this principle by linking hard-to-remember words to more easily remembered images. For example, the French word for hedgehog is 'herisson'. By imagining your hairy son looking like a hedgehog, 'herisson' becomes mnemonically linked to hedgehog. This then makes the French word much easier to recall in the future than it would have been without this link.

As valuable as they are, analogies should always be used with care and only in appropriate circumstances. The art lies in understanding which circumstances are appropriate and which are not. An analogy can be a useful method of explaining ideas but eventually every analogy breaks down (Glynn, 1991), and at this point misunderstandings can begin to occur. For example, the anatomy and function of the human eye is often taught through analogy with a camera; they both have an aperture and a lens and both produce an inverted image. However, the analogy between the camera and the human eye breaks down with respect to focusing. A camera is focused by changing the distance between the lens and the film, whereas the human eye is focused by the cornea and the ciliary muscle around the lens. Ultimately, an eye and a camera have a number of very significant differences despite their commonalities.

Despite these potential dangers, analogies remain a highly effective method of learning and teaching. Work conducted by MacDonald (1984) has shown that adult students taught using analogical situations can gain a better grasp of subject matter than those taught by the conventional 'teach–practice–test' method. MacDonald classed analogical reasoning as an 'adult skill', and so his experiments were only carried out on adults. This was because MacDonald was influenced by Piaget's theory (1972) that children were unable to do analogical reasoning if they were below the age of 11 or 12, although, as discussed earlier, this belief is now generally regarded to be untrue.

Although the limitations of an analogical model can produce an unfavourable effect on the subject's ability to learn additional concepts, there is always going to be a trade-off when using another representation to aid the learning of new ideas. Difficulties occur with different representations of the target domains, as there is rarely perfect one-to-one mapping for all elements between the understood base domain and the unknown target domain. If there did happen to be perfect one-to-one mapping, then this would imply that the base domain would be just as difficult (or as easy) to understand as the target domain, potentially making the base domain redundant. For example, if a camera was as difficult to explain as the human eye then it would be far more effective to describe the eye directly without reference to the camera analogy.

Conclusion: the pragmatics of using analogy

Analogies can provide real benefits for learners and teachers as long as their limitations are understood. In order for analogical reasoning to provide the greatest benefit, the base domain has to be familiar, relevant and directly mappable to the target domain and the analogy should be designed to terminate before it breaks down. In addition, the connections between the base and target domains have to be made clear in order that students are able to bridge the gap. One of the greatest strengths of using analogy in teaching is that it can significantly speed up the learning process. Combined with the diversity that the appropriate use of analogies can add to the learning experience, there is much evidence to support their use. However, care must be taken in designing and applying analogies as part of an educational strategy or there exists the risk that the analogy will only serve to obstruct the learning process.

Ambiguity and over-complication are the enemies of understanding, especially when using a tool such as analogy, which is seeking to connect the unconnected. Clarity and simplicity should be the hallmarks of analogical teaching. If a knowledge gap is too wide to cross in one simple step then two simple steps should be used rather than attempting one over-complicated leap and risking the loss of student understanding. If a river is too wide to bridge across in a single span then supports are used along the way to prevent the whole structure collapsing under its own weight. This may take more time and be more difficult but if you want a safe, reliable bridge then there is little choice.

If we think of a student's progress in learning as a journey along a path, there may be times when they are obstructed by a ditch or gully that they will need to cross in order to continue. A well thought-out and appropriate analogy can be compared to a wooden plank that could be used to help a student to cross over such an obstacle. The plank might be very useful in saving the time and effort required to climb down into the ditch and back up again, as long as it was of sufficient size to reach the other side. However, once the student had crossed over, the best thing to do would be to put the plank down and leave it. To carry it any further would be unnecessary and a burden for the rest of the journey, slowing future progress. The real strength of any analogy is as a one-off knowledge transfer event to bridge across large gaps of understanding. Once a foothold has been gained in the target domain then other methods of learning and teaching may be better employed to fill out the detail.

Bibliography

Alexander, P.A. and V.L. Willson. (1987). Analogical reasoning in young children. *Journal of Educational Psychology* 79 (4), 401–408.

Alexander, P.A., C.S. White, P.A. Haensly and M. Crimmins-Jeanes (1987) Training in analogical reasoning. *American Educational Research Journal* 24 (3), 387–404.

Blagg, N., M. Ballinger and R. Gardner (1990) *Somerset Thinking Skills Course. Module 5: Understanding Analogies.* Taunton, Somerset: Nigel Blagg.

Brown, A.L. (1989) Analogical learning and transfer: what develops? In S. Vosniadou and A. Ortony (eds) *Similarity and Analogical Reasoning.* Cambridge: Cambridge University Press, 369–412.

Brown, A.L., M.J. Kane and C. Long (1989) Analogical transfer in young children: analogies as tools for communication and exposition. *Applied Cognitive Psychology* 3, 275–293.

Chee, Y.S. (1993) Applying Gentner's theory of analogy to the teaching of computer programming. *International Journal of Man-Machine Studies* 38, 347–368.

Duncker, K. (1945) On problem solving. *Psychological Monographs* 58 (270).

Gentner, D. (1983) Structure-mapping: a theoretical framework for analogy. *Cognitive Science* 7, 155–170.

Gick, M.L. and K.J. Holyoak (1980) Analogical problem solving. *Cognitive Psychology* 12, 306–355.

Gick, M.L. and K.J. Holyoak (1983) Schema induction and analogical transfer. *Cognitive Psychology* 15, 1–38.

Glynn, S.M. (1991) Explaining science concepts: a teaching-with-analogies model. In S.M. Glynn, R.H. Yeany and B.K. Britton (eds) *The Psychology of Learning Science*. Hillsdale, NJ: Lawrence Erlbaum, 219–240.

Glynn, S.M., B.K. Britton, M. Semrud-Clikeman and K.D. Muth (1989) Analogical reasoning and problem solving in science textbooks. In J.A. Golver, R.R. Ronning and C.R. Reynolds (eds) *Handbook of Creativity*. New York: Plenum Press, 383–398.

Goswami, U. (1991) Analogical reasoning: what develops? A review of research and theory. *Child Development* 62, 1–22.

Goswami, U. (1992) *Analogical Reasoning in Children*. Hillsdale, NJ: Lawrence Erlbaum.

Halasz, F. and T.P. Moran (1982) Analogy considered harmful. *Human Factors in Computer Systems Conference '82*, 383–6.

Hall, R.P. (1989) Computation approaches to analogical reasoning: a comparative analysis. *Artificial Intelligence* 39, 39–120.

Halpern, D.F. (1987) Analogies as a critical thinking skill. In D.E. Berger, K. Pezdek and W.P. Banks (eds) *Applications of Cognitive Psychology: Problem Solving, Education, and Computing*. Hillsdale, NJ: Lawrence Erlbaum, 75–86.

Halpern, D.F., C. Hansen and D. Riefer (1990) Analogies as an aid to understanding and memory. *Journal of Educational Psychology* 82 (2), 298–305.

Holyoak, K.J. (1984) Analogical thinking and human intelligence. In R.J. Sternberg (ed.) *Advances in the Psychology of Human Intelligence*. Hillsdale, NJ: Lawrence Erlbaum, 199–230.

Indurkhya, B. (1989) Modes of analogy. In K.P. Jantke (ed.) *Analogical and Inductive Inference, International Workshop AII '89*. Berlin: Springer–Verlag, 217–30.

Kedar-Cabelli, S. (1988) Analogy – from a unified perspective. In D.H. Helman (ed.) *Analogical Reasoning: Perspectives of Artificial Intelligence, Cognitive Science and Philosophy*. Dordrecht, Netherlands: Reidel, 65–103.

MacDonald, T.H. (1984) Exploiting adult learning styles in teaching basic maths. *Australian Journal of Adult Education* 24 (2), 8–12.

Masterson, J.J., L.H. Evans and M. Aloia (1993) Verbal analogical reasoning in children with language-learning disabilities. *Journal of Speech and Hearing Research* 36, 76–82.

Meyer, J.H.F. and Land, R. (2003) Threshold concepts and troublesome knowledge: linkages to ways of thinking and practising within the disciplines. In C. Rust (ed.) *Improving Student Learning: Improving Student Learning Theory and Practice – Ten Years On*. Oxford: OCSLD.

Meyer, J.H.F. and Land, R. (2005) Threshold concepts and troublesome knowledge: epistemological considerations and a conceptual framework for teaching and learning. *Higher Education* 49, 373–388.

Needham, D.R. and I.M. Begg (1991) Problem-oriented training promotes spontaneous analogical transfer: memory-oriented training promotes memory for training. *Memory and Cognition* 19 (6), 543–557.

Oppenheimer, R. (1956) Analogy in science. *American Psychologist* 11, 127–135.

Piaget, J. (1972) *To Understand Is To Invent*. New York: Viking Press.

Reber, A.S. (1985) *Dictionary of Psychology*. London: Penguin Books.

Robertson, I. and H. Kahney (1996) The use of examples in expository texts – outline of an interpretation theory for text analysis. *Instructional Science* 24 (2), 93–123.

Russell, S.J. (1989) *The Use of Knowledge in Analogy and Induction*. London: Pitman.

Speirs, G. (1996) An analogical reasoning based mathematics tutoring system. Unpublished PhD thesis. Lancaster: Lancaster University. British Library reference: DXN010158.

Sternberg, R.J. (1977) Component processes in analogical reasoning. *Psychological Review* 84 (4), 353–378.

Weller, C.M. (1970) The role of analogy in teaching science. *Journal of Research in Science Teaching* 7, 113–119.

Zeitoun, H.H. (1984) Teaching scientific analogies: a proposed model. *Research in Science and Technological Education* 2 (2), 107–125.

Conclusion

Implications of threshold concepts for course design and evaluation

Ray Land, Glynis Cousin, Jan H. F. Meyer and Peter Davies

Introduction

It has long been a matter of concern to teachers in higher education why certain students 'get stuck' at particular points in the curriculum whilst others grasp concepts with comparative ease. What might account for this variation in student performance and, more importantly, what might teachers do in relation to the design and teaching of their courses that might help students overcome such barriers to their learning? As students from a much wider range of educational backgrounds now enter higher education these issues are becoming of increasing importance across all disciplines. A further and related concern is why certain concepts within disciplinary fields appear particularly troublesome to students. What makes particular areas of knowledge more troublesome than others, and how might we make such areas less so?

As we have seen in the opening chapters of this volume, when a student has internalised a threshold concept they are more able to integrate different aspects of a subject in their analysis of problems. Students who have not yet internalised a threshold concept have little option but to attempt to learn new ideas in a more fragmented fashion. On acquiring a threshold concept a student is able to transform their use of the ideas of a subject because they are now able to integrate them in their thinking. The integrative aspect of a threshold concept presents distinctive problems for learners who are studying a subject (such as Economics) as part of their degree. Students who do not think of themselves as 'learners of Economics' are likely to face particular difficulties in grasping concepts that bind together aspects of a subject that may seem quite disparate to a novice. This problem arises because the acquisition of such concepts (e.g. opportunity cost, price and value, equilibrium) is intrinsic to grasping the ways in which economists 'think' and practice. Such discourses distinguish individual communities of practice and are necessarily less familiar to new entrants to such discursive communities.

> Now if you think about the word 'cost', really all it means is, it is a value, an acquisition value. So instead of using the word 'cost' you could say

this acquisition value, and it would mean the same thing wouldn't it? But the words 'value' and 'cost' are quite troublesome, literally, in Accounting (and in Economics), because 'cost' can mean very different things depending on who the user is, and for what purpose you are calculating the 'cost'. So, you know, in accounting you might have three or four very different understandings of what 'cost' means.

(1st year Accountancy lecturer)

We have also seen from earlier chapters that such integration and subsequent transformation, though necessary for progress within the subject, may prove *troublesome* to certain learners for a variety of reasons, not the least of which is that such transformation entails a letting go of earlier, comfortable positions and encountering less familiar and sometimes disconcerting new territory. Threshold concepts are inherently problematic for learners because they demand an integration of ideas and this requires the student to accept a transformation of their own understanding. The same Accountancy lecturer discussed the problematic nature of the concept of depreciation both for her students, and for her own attempts to get them to engage with the concept:

And why I think depreciation is a threshold concept is that it draws in to an understanding of depreciation a particular way of viewing business events or transactions which demand students to see these within a very particular framework (i.e. an accounting framework) rather than a commonsense or intuitive framework. It isn't a particularly natural process and actually the more you look at it the more contrived it gets, because it isn't just a straightforward alternative framework. Actually, within the framework, there are lots of compromises.

The transformation can also entail a shift in the learner's identity. The result may be that students remain stuck in an 'in-between' state of liminality in which they oscillate between earlier, less sophisticated understandings, and the fuller appreciation of a concept that their tutors require from them. A serious outcome is that students become frustrated, lose confidence and give up that particular course. It is the hope of the authors of this chapter that within our various subject areas we can devise ways of helping students to overcome such 'epistemological obstacles' (Brousseau, 1983). We would seek to create supportive liminal environments to help students through such difficulty – what might be characterised as a kind of conceptual peristalsis – that they might move on and succeed.

The underlying game

To complicate matters further, in some instances students may grasp concepts but the barrier to their learning appears to lie at a deeper level of understanding, where the student finds difficulty in appreciating what Perkins (Chapter 3) has termed 'the underlying episteme'. Like the characters in Buñuel's (1962) film, *The Exterminating Angel*, who cannot leave the house in which they have attended a dinner, but are unable to account for their immobility, the students similarly are unaccountably unable to move on. An example would be where students of Electrical Engineering can cope with the required concepts from Physics but do not have a working understanding of the highly unpredictable and surprising ways in which complex circuits might behave. In computer programming, similarly, students may grasp the concepts of class, objects, tables, arrays and recursion, but they may not appreciate the deeper threshold conception, the underlying 'game' as it were, of the interaction of all these elements in a process of ever-increasing complexity. Such instances present teachers with particularly difficult challenges in class to assist their students in coming to understand these puzzling underlying epistemological phenomena.

Savin-Baden's work on the notion of 'disjunction' in problem-based learning (Chapter 11) would seem to point to something similar to this notion of an underlying game.

> 'Disjunction' refers to the idea of becoming 'stuck' in learning and I have suggested elsewhere (Savin-Baden, 2000) that disjunction can be both enabling and disabling in terms of its impact on learning. Disjunction, then, can be seen as the kind of place that students might reach after they have encountered a threshold concept that they have not managed to breach. Many staff and students have described disjunction as being a little like hitting a brick wall in learning and they have used various strategies to try to deal with it. These include retreating from the difficulty and opting out of any further learning, using strategies to avoid it, temporising and waiting for an event or stimulus that will help them to move on or engaging with it directly in an attempt to relieve their discomfort.

If the portal appears 'bricked up' then clearly the threshold of new transformative understanding is not visible to the student. Savin-Baden argues that, although disjunction occurs in many forms and in diverse ways in different disciplines, it seems to be particularly evident in curricula where problem-based learning has been implemented. She suggests that this may be because problem-based learning programmes prompt students to critique and contest knowledge early on in the curriculum and thus they encounter knowledge as being troublesome earlier than students in more traditional programmes. However, she goes on:

> it might also be that problem-based learning encourages students to shift away from linear and fact-finding problem solving. Instead they

move towards forms of problem management that demand the use of procedural and personal knowledge as students are asked to engage with strategy or moral dilemma problems. Thus it might be that disjunction is not only a form of troublesome knowledge but also a 'space' or 'position' reached through the realisation that the knowledge is troublesome. Disjunction might therefore be seen as a 'troublesome learning space' that emerges when forms of active learning (such as problem-based learning) are used that prompt students to engage with procedural and personal knowledge

Considerations for course design and evaluation

The idea of a threshold concept presents important challenges for curriculum design and for learning and teaching. At a general level we would argue that programmes should be designed and systematically reviewed according to:

a   the sequence of content;
b   the processes through which learners are made ready for, approach, recognise, and internalise threshold concepts. We would argue that this process of the student's learning, their encounter with threshold concepts in a given subject, might be considered as akin to a journey or excursion. Such an *excursive* account of the learning experience would see these processes as a framework of engagements, designed to assist students to cope with threshold concepts (see 6 below);
c   the ways in which learners and teachers recognise when threshold concepts have been internalised – in effect what would constitute appropriate assessment for the attainment of threshold concepts.

More specifically we would draw attention to nine considerations that we feel are important in the design and subsequent evaluation of curricula in higher education.

1   *The jewels in the curriculum*   Threshold concepts can be used to define potentially powerful transformative points in the student's learning experience. In this sense they may be viewed as the 'jewels in the curriculum' insomuch as they can serve to identify crucial points in the curriculum that provide opportunities for students to gain important conceptual understandings. A focus on these jewels allows for richer and more complex insights into aspects of the subjects students are studying; it plays a diagnostic role in alerting tutors to areas of the curriculum where students are likely to encounter troublesome knowledge and experience conceptual difficulty – the 'stuck places' to which Ellsworth refers (1997: 71). Finally, it discourages a stuffed or congested curriculum in favour of one that focuses on really useful mastery.

2   *The importance of engagement*   There is already a considerable existing literature in relation to how tutors might help students develop genuine understanding of a troublesome concept. Many of these studies point to the need for active student engagement with, and manipulation of, the conceptual material. For example it is recommended that tutors ask students to explain it, to represent it in new ways, to apply it in new situations and to connect it to their lives. The emphasis is equally strong that they should not simply recall the concept in the form in which it was presented (Colby *et al.*, 2003: 263). We would wish to appropriate these emphases and, with Wenger (1998), think about constructing a *framework of engagement* within the course that might enable students to experience and gain understandings of the ways of thinking and practising that are expected of practitioners within a given community of practice, be this the recognition of the importance of contestability amongst historians, or the appreciation of the fluidity of double curvature surfacing in automotive design. We will wish our students not only to understand 'how historians think', but to begin to 'think like a historian'. But within this framework, as a course design question, what will be the specific *forms of engagement* which will be most appropriate to bring about these particular *transformative* understandings at various points in the curriculum and which will assist students to acquire the threshold concepts that are necessary to ensure satisfactory progression through the course? Lather has spoken of the kinds of engagement or praxis 'where the effort is to [. . .] provoke something else into happening – something other than the return of the same' (1998: 492). As course designers what 'provocations' might we be seeking through these forms of engagement to bring about the transformations in understanding that we would wish?

3   *Listening for understanding*   However, teaching for understanding of threshold concepts needs to be preceded by listening for understanding. In terms of what we will refer to below as 'pre-liminal variation' in the ways in which students approach, or come to terms with, a threshold concept, we can't second guess where students are coming from or what their uncertainties are. It is difficult for teachers, experienced and expert within the discipline, who long since travelled similar ground in their own disciplinary excursions, to gaze backwards across thresholds and understand the conceptual difficulty or obstacles that a student is currently experiencing. This is well described by the following student of mathematics who was interviewed at a UK research-led university:

> Once they start heading off into the realms of genius, you get people who have been locked in their room studying one equation for fifteen years but cannot contemplate where you are on this learning curve and don't understand that what they're teaching you is utterly

foreign, utterly random, and they can't understand how you can't understand it.

Learning to understand what the students do not understand requires 'cultivating a third ear that listens not for what a student knows (discrete packages of knowledge) but for the terms that shape a student's know-ledge, her not knowing, her forgetting, her circles of stuck places and resistances' (Ellsworth, 1997: 71). The acquisition of a 'third ear' might also discourage teachers from making hasty judgments about students' abilities and foster appreciation of the tough conceptual and emotional journeys they have to make.

4   *Reconstitution of self*   Grasping a threshold concept is never just a cognitive shift; it might also involve a repositioning of self in relation to the subject. This means, from the viewpoint of curriculum design, that some attention has to be paid on the part of course designers to the discomforts of troublesome knowledge. Knowledge may be troublesome because it has become ritualised, or inert, because it is conceptually difficult or alien, because it is tacit and perhaps requires awareness of an 'underlying game' imperceptible to the student (see below), or because of the discourse that has to be acquired for the concept to become meaningful (Meyer and Land, 2005; Perkins, 1999).

> as students acquire threshold concepts, and extend their use of lan-guage in relation to these concepts, there occurs also a shift in the learner's subjectivity, a repositioning of the self. [. . .] What is being emphasised here is the interrelatedness of the learner's identity with thinking and language. Threshold concepts lead not only to trans-formed thought but to a transfiguration of identity and adoption of an extended discourse.
>
> (Meyer and Land, 2005: 374–5)

This transfiguration and extension of the subjectivity of the learner might be exhilarating but might incur a sense of disquietude or even loss on the part of the learner as they let go the security of a previously held conceptual stance to enter less certain terrain. Again we return to the notion of the appropriate forms of engagement within which such trans-formations might take place and the need for the teacher to provide what Winnicott (1971) used to term a 'holding environment' or nurturing space. We prefer to call this a supportive liminal environment, feeling that Winnicott's term suggests a somewhat static, even inhibitive space, rather than the peristaltic process discussed earlier. Given, too, that the process of acquiring new knowledge tends to involve what Bonamy *et al.* (2001) would call 'provisional stabilities', this means that over the course of an entire programme such periods of letting-go and reconstitution will be repeated and call for metacognitive skills on the part of the learner to cope with such transformation and to tolerate uncertainty.

5   *Tolerating uncertainty*   Learners tend to discover that what is not clear initially often becomes clear over time. One of our respondents, a first-year student in Chemistry, came close to abandoning her course and dropping out halfway through the first year because she found the programme too conceptually difficult. She commented, however, that had she known, at the time of her encountering this troublesomeness in her understanding, that eventually she would come to cope with the programme (and the threshold concepts it involved), the transition would have been easier. The next time she faced such troublesome knowledge, she asserted, she would 'hang in there' with greater confidence because now she knew she would eventually find a way of coming to understand. So, in such a situation, there is a metacognitive issue for the student of self-regulation within the liminal state. Efklides (Chapter 4, p. 48) has emphasised the indispensable role of metacognition in the learning process 'both directly by activating control processes and indirectly by influencing the self-regulation process that determines whether the student will get engaged in threshold concepts or not'. Elsewhere she points out:

> What distinguishes metacognitive feelings is their cognitive and affective nature. Metacognitive feelings take the form of feeling of knowing, of familiarity, of difficulty, of confidence, and of satisfaction, whereas metacognitive judgments or estimates can take the form of judgment of learning, of where, when, and how we acquire a piece of information, of time and effort spent on a task. Metacognitive experiences serve the *monitoring* and *control* of the learning process and at the same time provide an intrinsic context within which learning processes take place. This intrinsic context is to a large extent affective and determined by self processes, individual difference factors as well as task factors, including task difficulty, task instructions, and feedback used. The intrinsic context influences students' strategies in problem solving, but also their emotions, causal attributions, and self-concept. In this way, metacognitive experiences affect both online task processing and future motivation towards learning.
>
> (Efklides, 2003: 1, abstract)

There are a number of ways in which teachers can encourage metacognitive skills among students. In our view, forms of peer assessment are of particular importance because they allow students to discover common difficulties and anxieties. Another strategy is for teachers frequently to reassure students in whatever ways they can (informally, assignment feedback, etc.) that not knowing, or glimpsing and then losing, is part of coming to know.

6   *Recursiveness and excursiveness*   Given the often troublesome nature of threshold concepts it is likely that many learners will need to adopt a recursive approach to what has to be learned, attempting different 'takes' on the conceptual material until the necessary integration and connection discussed in earlier chapters begins to take place. The need for the learner to grasp threshold concepts in recursive movements means that they cannot be tackled in an over-simplistically linear 'learning outcomes' model where sentences like 'by the end of the course the learner will be able to' undermine, and perhaps do not even explicitly recognise, the complexities of the transformation a learner undergoes. It is likely that any course requiring student engagement with threshold concepts and troublesome knowledge will entail considerable variation in the conceptual stances and outcomes that are reached by members of the cohort – what we might term *post*-liminal variation. Consideration of threshold concepts to some extent 'rattles the cage' of a linear approach to curriculum design that assumes standard and homogenised outcomes. Lather (1998: 492) offers a counter-narrative rejecting 'the rhetorical position of "the one who knows"' in favour of 'a praxis of not being so sure'. A 'praxis of stuck places' might tolerate 'discrepancies, repetitions, hesitations, and uncertainties, always beginning again' (491). What it refuses is 'the privileging of containment over excess, thought over affect, structure over speed, linear causality over complexity, and intention over aggregate capacities' (497). We would argue, similarly, for the notion of learning as *excursive*, as a journey or excursion which will have intended direction and outcome but will also acknowledge (and indeed desire) that there will be deviation and unexpected outcome within the excursion; there will be digression and revisiting (recursion) and possible further points of departure and revised direction. The eventual destination may be reached, or it may be revised. It may be a surprise. It will certainly be the point of embarkation for further excursion.

The notion of recursive movements in learning is not new. Most notably, Vygotsky (1978) has shown that learning takes this course. Perhaps the connected design challenge for teachers is to opt for a more rhizomorphic than tree-like structure for their module or course (Deleuze and Guattari, 1988). Whereas the latter implies a hierarchical, incremental building-up of understanding, the former would construct points of entry into the learning from a number of places. In part this would address variation in states of liminality and in part it would subvert the conventional passage from the 'easy' to the 'difficult' in most curricular models which are predicated on linear or staged notions of intellectual development (e.g. Piaget or Perry).

7   *Pre-liminal variation*   An abiding question for educators, and for course

designers in particular, is why some students productively negotiate the liminal space of understanding we have discussed earlier and others find difficulty in doing so. Does such variation explain how the threshold will be, or can be, or can only be approached (or turned away from) as it 'comes into view'? And how does it 'come into view' for individual students? We need to know more about the pre-liminal variation in the constitution of any student cohort, given the obvious implications this would seem to have for subsequent student retention and progression (Meyer and Shanahan, 2003). To this end a three-year funded study on threshold concepts within a given discipline is currently getting under way (see Conclusion below) to investigate systematically, amongst other phenomena, the issue of pre-liminal variation and its implications for the sequencing, structure and forms of engagement that a course will contain.

8   *Unintended consequences of generic 'good pedagogy'*   There is emerging indicative evidence from research into threshold concepts (e.g. Meyer and Shanahan, 2003; Lucas, 2000) that what has traditionally been considered 'good pedagogy' may, on occasion, break down or prove dysfunctional in relation to the acquisition of threshold concepts. For example, the conventional practical wisdom of simplifying concepts in order to render them more accessible seemed to prove dysfunctional in the case of teaching the threshold concept of opportunity cost in Economics in a South Australian context.

> one implication of the argument presented thus far is that 'first impressions matter'. Efforts to make threshold concepts 'easier' by simplifying their initial expression and application may, in fact, set students onto a path of 'ritualised' knowledge that actually creates a barrier that results in some students being prevented from crossing the 'threshold' of a concept.
>
> (Meyer and Shanahan, 2003: 15)

The simplified interpretation of the concept, intended to some extent as a proxy for the fuller, more sophisticated understanding which it was intended to lead on to, was found to operate more frequently as a false proxy, leading students to settle for the naive version, and entering into a form of ritualised learning or mimicry. Such findings may prove useful as future keys to understanding the pre-liminal variation in student approach discussed earlier.

In a similar fashion the often-advocated form of engagement of relating concepts to everyday phenomena, or to the personal experience of students, was found to be ineffective in a first-year Introductory Accounting course which sought to help students grasp the threshold concept of 'depreciation'. In this case it was the absence of any significant budgetary or financial experience in the students' experience which rendered the approach ineffective. It would seem salutary, therefore, periodically to cast a cold reviewer's eye over tried and tested 'good pedagogy'.

9   *The underlying game*   Finally, in the light of our earlier discussion of the underlying game, it would seem advisable for course designers to query whether, in addition to the forms of engagement they may have designed to assist students to cope with identified threshold concepts in a programme, there might remain what Perkins calls the underlying episteme. This, if not recognised and understood by students, might still render their learning troublesome and lead to further frustration or confusion in their studies. Lucas (2000), for example, provides an example of such an underlying episteme that Accountancy students are not always aware of. She distinguishes between 'authorised' and 'alternative' understandings of threshold concepts. 'Authorised' understandings are those endorsed and maintained by the disciplinary community and within textbooks. 'Alternative' understandings of events and transactions are independent of authorised versions, and arise from intuitive or everyday (common-sense) understandings of a concept such as 'depreciation' or 'profit'. 'Alternative' understandings might on occasion be substituted for, or provide an alternative to, the authorised versions. Often, where students hold these alternative understandings, they do not recognise that these conceptions are in *opposition* to the authorised (and perhaps counter-intuitive or troublesome) versions promulgated within the course. Thus students may be required to play an important, more sophisticated epistemological game in order to recognise the difference between authorised and alternative understandings of threshold concepts. One interesting consideration is whether such recognitions might be best supported through engaging undergraduates in research activities which enable them to enter more closely into the culture of enquiry of their subject (Blackmore and Cousin, 2003).

Conclusion

The task for course developers and designers here is to identify, through formative feedback, the source of these epistemological and affective barriers, and subsequently to free up the blocked spaces by, for example, redesigning activities and sequences, through scaffolding, through provision of support materials and technologies or new conceptual tools, through mentoring or peer collaboration, to provide the necessary shift in perspective that might permit further personal development. The way in which chess players talk of 'developing' a piece involves the removal of other pieces (obstacles) so as to free up various (multiple) ways in which the piece might now be empowered to move (Land, 2004: 113–114). The significance of the framework provided by threshold concepts lies, we feel, in its explanatory potential to locate troublesome aspects of disciplinary knowledge within transitions across conceptual thresholds and hence to assist teachers in identifying appropriate ways of modifying or redesigning curricula to enable their students to negotiate such transitions more successfully.

As a way of testing and implementing these considerations, and furthering our understanding of the issues of student variation in their acquisition of threshold concepts, we have now embarked upon an empirical study of the experience of first-year students in a given disciplinary context. A three-year national project, funded by the UK HEFCE FDTL5 programme, is currently under way as a collaborative venture led by Staffordshire University and involving the universities of Coventry, Durham and the West of England. By focusing curriculum development on threshold concepts in first-year Economics in the four universities this project provides an opportunity to re-evaluate the key binding ideas of the subject that should be introduced in level one, and what it means for students to understand these ideas in a deep-level transformative way. We aim to develop methods of assessing variation in the acquisition of threshold concepts. These methods will, we hope, help students as well as lecturers to recognise levels of understanding. Students' acquisition of threshold concepts will depend on their prior experience and learning, and the way they are therefore likely initially to approach their studies. The project will aim to develop ways in which teaching can respond to the variation in which students engage and acquire these concepts. We anticipate that careful evaluation of the process and outcomes of the project will be useful for other colleagues wanting to pursue these issues both in Economics and in other subjects. The emphasis on teaching strategies that can respond to variation in the ways in which students engage with and acquire threshold concepts provides the rationale for self- and teacher assessment that seeks to identify whether students have understood these concepts. This in turn, we expect, will provide information that will identify 'at risk' students.

References

Blackmore, P. and Cousin, G. (2003) 'Linking teaching and research through research-based learning', *Educational Developments*, 4 (4): 24–27.

Bonamy, J., Charlier, B. and Saunders, M. (2001) ' "Bridging tools" for change: evaluating a collaborative learning network', *Journal of Computer Assisted Learning* 17 (3): 295–305.

Brousseau, G. (1983) 'Les obstacles epistemologiques et les problèmes en mathématiques', *Recherches en didactique des mathematiques*, 4 (2): 165–198.

Colby, A., Ehrlich, T., Beaumont, E. and Jason Stephens, J. (2003) *Educating Citizens: Preparing America's Undergraduates for Lives of Moral and Civic Responsibility.* San Francisco, CA: Jossey-Bass.

Deleuze, G. and Guattari, F. (1988) *A Thousand Plateaus: Capitalism and Schizo-phrenia*. London: Continuum.

Efklides, A. (2003) 'Metacognition and affect: what can metacognitive experiences tell us about the learning process?' Keynote address at the 10th EARLI Confer-ence, University of Padova, Italy, August. Available online at http://earli2003. psy.unipol.it/invited.html.

Ellsworth, E. (1997) *Teaching Positions: Difference Pedagogy and the Power of Address*, New York: Teachers College Press.

Land, R. (2004) *Educational Development: Discourse, Identity and Practice*. Maiden-head: SRHE and Open University Press.

Lather, P. (1998) 'Critical pedagogy and its complicities: a praxis of stuck places', *Educational Theory*, 48 (4): 487–498.

Lucas, U. (2000) 'Worlds apart: students' experiences of learning introductory accounting', *Critical Perspectives on Accounting*, 11: 479–504.

Meyer, J.H.F. and Land, R. (2005) 'Threshold concepts and troublesome knowledge (2): epistemological considerations and a conceptual framework for teaching and learning', *Higher Education*, 49: 373–388.

Meyer, J.H.F and Shanahan, M. (2003) 'The troublesome nature of a threshold con-cept in Economics', paper presented to the Tenth Conference of the European Association for Research on Learning and Instruction (EARLI), Padova, Italy, August.

Perkins, D. (1999) 'The many faces of constructivism', *Educational Leadership*, 57 (3), November.

Reimann, N. and Jackson, I. (2003) 'Threshold concepts in Economics: a case study', paper presented to the Tenth Conference of the European Association for Research on Learning and Instruction (EARLI), Padova, Italy, August.

Vygotsky, L.S. (1978) *Mind in Society. The Development of Higher Psychological Processes*. Cambridge, MA: Harvard University Press.

Wenger, E. (1998) *Communities of Practice: Learning, Meaning and Identity*. Cambridge: Cambridge University Press.

Winnicott, D.H. (1971) *Playing and Reality*. New York: Basic Books.

Index

eBooks

eBooks – at www.eBookstore.tandf.co.uk

A library at your fingertips!

eBooks are electronic versions of printed books. You can store them on your PC/laptop or browse them online.

They have advantages for anyone needing rapid access to a wide variety of published, copyright information.

eBooks can help your research by enabling you to bookmark chapters, annotate text and use instant searches to find specific words or phrases. Several eBook files would fit on even a small laptop or PDA.

NEW: Save money by eSubscribing: cheap, online access to any eBook for as long as you need it.

Annual subscription packages

We now offer special low-cost bulk subscriptions to packages of eBooks in certain subject areas. These are available to libraries or to individuals.

For more information please contact webmaster.ebooks@tandf.co.uk

We're continually developing the eBook concept, so keep up to date by visiting the website.

www.eBookstore.tandf.co.uk